HERODOTUS

FATHER OF HISTORY

HERODOTUS

FATHER OF HISTORY

BY

JOHN L. MYRES

HENRY REGNERY COMPANY · CHICAGO
A Gateway Edition

GATEWAY EDITION PUBLISHED BY HENRY REGNERY COMPANY
114 WEST ILLINOIS STREET, CHICAGO, ILLINOIS 60610
BY ARRANGEMENT WITH OXFORD UNIVERSITY PRESS

MANUFACTURED IN THE UNITED STATES OF AMERICA
LIBRARY OF CONGRESS CATALOG CARD NUMBER 79-126156

FIRST PUBLISHED 1953 IN GREAT BRITAIN
FIRST GATEWAY EDITION, 1971

PREFACE

MY object is to examine the claim of Herodotus to be the 'Father of History', the man who first formulated its aims and method, and implemented this conception in his own writings.

Much past criticism of Herodotus has resulted from failure to appreciate his originality, not only as an inquirer into the past, and interpreter of it, but as an artist and man of letters, faced with an immense range of uncoordinated facts, and with literary traditions and techniques which were inadequate to present them intelligibly. In his work, as we have it, there are traces of experiments in current modes of composition, the epic, the Ionian *logos*, the Attic drama, the rhetorical 'speeches' and 'dialogues' elaborated later by Thucydides and by Plato. But all these are incorporated in a fresh literary form, the counterpart of the balanced 'rhythm' of representative arts, which culminates in the pedimental compositions of temple sculpture, at Aegina, on the Athenian Acropolis, and at Olympia, and in the rather later 'Darius-Vase' of which the theme is that of Herodotus' own book.

Readers accustomed to the logical development of a 'plot', from causes to final effect, seem to have overlooked even the more obvious examples of this technique. It has therefore seemed necessary, secondly, to supplement a few diagrammatic instances with an analysis of the whole work. Only in this way can the thesis be maintained that the order of presentation in Herodotus is deliberate and habitual. It will help also to explain how Herodotus selects and marshals his information, and imparts to his story that vivid and convincing quality which has preserved him his place among literary artists, even for readers and critics unaware how this literary effect was produced. *Ars est celare artem.* Most important of all, it offers a new standpoint for estimating Herodotus as an historian, ever seeking information on the facts, but assessing each fact in relation to its place in the composition, as well as in the chain of causes and effects.

It will be necessary therefore, thirdly, to superimpose—so to speak—the historical narrative of Herodotus on the diagram of events as they appear to modern historians. Every historian is at the mercy of his sources, even if he takes 'history'—ἱστορίη—as seriously as Herodotus evidently did. But though he may not add to their contributions, he may—at his peril—select and omit. How much more, for example, did Herodotus *know* about Peisistratus or Themistocles than he has recorded? In the light of his deliberate and express statements of his practice, it is less his garrulity that should be regretted than his silences, sometimes eloquent, more often perplexing. Did he really not know what the Aeginetans at Salamis had done to deserve the prize for valour? One thinks of the American strategy in the Battle of the Philippines. Was the obstinacy of Amompharetus really the turning-point at Plataea? One thinks of the defence of Hougoumont at Waterloo.

But to link the *Histories* of Herodotus with his times, and with the little we know of his life, is inevitably to repeat much that is common knowledge, if only to put a few novelties into perspective. Only so can we rediscover the 'Father of History'. Beyond eye-witness and hearsay, Herodotus claimed the historian's privilege of 'judgement', the duty to reveal causes. If any reader finds my opening pages journalistic, he need not read farther. That is how I have thought of Herodotus for more than sixty years.

Among teachers, I most gratefully acknowledge my debt to Thomas Case, Fellow and later President of Corpus: among recent writers, to Amédée Hauvette and to Felix Jacoby, the latter happily still active. To pupils, over nearly fifty years, my obligations are innumerable; not least to one of the earliest, who asked 'Sir, if Herodotus was such a fool as they say, why do we read him for Greats?' To the Delegates of the Clarendon Press I owe eventual publication and much technical help; to Mr. Russell Meiggs, Fellow of Balliol, searching criticism and patient revision; to Miss Daphne Hereward, of Somerville College, the correction of the proofs, and many references; to Miss Mary Potter, of the Oxford School of Geography, skilful rendering of my maps and diagrams.

J. L. M.

CONTENTS

ILLUSTRATIONS

I

THE MAN: HIS LIFE AND TRAVELS

ON an autumn day in the year 480 B.C., watchmen on the peaks between Halicarnassus and Termera signalled the battle-fleet of Queen Artemisia returning from the west. As the ships rounded the point opposite Cos, and the Coan squadron veered southward, it was clear that there had been losses. When the flagship entered the bay south of the city it was seen that its prow was damaged; and when the fleet came to moorings the first call was for shore-boats to land the wounded. The face of the Queen-admiral was set and sad.

On the quay Rhoio, wife of Lyxes, her bright cheeks aglow with excitement—her name means 'Pomegranate'—held fast her five-year-old 'Gift from Hera', wide-eyed, alert, for ever asking questions and putting together answers. And as they turned towards home there was one more question, never fully answered for him: *Mother, what did they fight each other for?*

Later the grown lad could slip away through the grey, pine-strewn hills—passing Pedasus, 'where the priestess grew a beard' (i. 175)—to Caryanda, looking north beyond Miletus to Samos, with Leros dark in the sunset; and sit with old sea-dog Scylax (iv. 44), who had served Darius in the Indies and sailed down Crocodile River into Ocean, and so back to the Isthmus. Gold-digger ants, Callatian cannibals, and the shape of the world, as Scylax knew it—all was grist to the mill. Some day Herodotus, too, would see the Great East and the Far North. There he would meet, too, shipmates of Scylax, men who had trapped the Persian force that came by Labranda and did not return (v. 121)—Harpagus' men could have warned them of that snare (v. 175): perhaps even men who had rowed at Lade and gone on commando to Sardis. Then there was that skipper at Myndus—hardly farther than Caryanda, and easier going—whom Megabates made to 'keep ship' so shamefully (v. 33): he had seen Persians besiege Naxos and retreat to a seething Ionia. And up the gulf, eastwards, it was but a short day's sail to the Cnidian isthmus where you can still see, unfinished and splintery, the cut which, 'had Zeus willed', might have made the long promontory an island (i. 174). Cnidus itself is barely out of sight from home; lovely Cos, with its medicine-men, in full view.

These are bright points in the darkness of those early days.

Halicarnassus was a city with an equivocal history. Originally Dorian, like Cos, Cnidus, and Rhodes, it had been expelled from their 'Triopian' League for unsportsmanlike conduct at its festival (i. 144), and became assimilated in speech, manners, and interests to its Ionian neighbours northwards. It had always a Carian element, like Miletus. Its western suburb, Salmacis, may have been an older native settlement, like the Artemisium at Ephesus and Branchidae by Miletus. In Herodotus' own family there were Carian names—Lyxes and Panyassis—as well as Greek; and under Persian overlordship, Halicarnassus was governed by the Carian dynast of Mylasa, Artemisia, daughter of Lygdamis and a Cretan woman. Her husband and son were dead, but she retained their principality (vii. 99) and brought also to Salamis the ships of Cos, Calymnos, and Nisyros off-shore; she was in high favour with Xerxes (viii. 68–69, 87–88, 101–7).

Artemisia slept with her fathers, still a Persian vassal. But Persian prestige was shattered, and under her grandson Lygdamis old differences between Greek and Carian were aggravated by the quarrels of rich and poor, landowners and traders, and between 'Medizing' and 'Hellenizing' interests. Panyassis, a relative of Herodotus,[1] who had tried to 'revive the epic' with a poem on Heracles, was killed in the troubles; Herodotus had to take refuge in Samos. Later a compromise was arranged,[2] and by 454 B.C. Halicarnassus was paying tribute, like most of its neighbours, to the Delian League. Herodotus is said to have returned to his birthplace, but he did not remain. After a period of travel, and some residence in Athens, he joined the new Pan-Hellenic

[1] Suidas, s.v. 'Panyassis'.
[2] Tod, *G.H.I.* 25[27-33]: compare the arrangement at Cyrene, iv. 161–3.

foundation of Thurii in South Italy; and there his inscribed monument was shown.

All the early references to him describe him as 'of Thurii'—Aristotle, Duris of Samos, Avienus paraphrasing a fourth-century geographer, the Lindian Temple-chronicle in 99 B.C., Strabo, and Pliny.[1] But in the opening words of his book he is 'of Halicarnassus', and the text is certain, though Plutarch says that 'many change the name to Thurian' and Julian used one of these amended copies. A portrait-base in the library built at Pergamum for Eumenes II (197–159 B.C.) is inscribed 'Herodotus of Halicarnassus'. His learned countryman Dionysius not unnaturally claimed him for his own city; and in Roman times, under Hadrian and Gordian, named portraits of him appear on its bronze coins.

The literary age which glorified his birthplace put together a few details about Herodotus' life and fortunes. He was reputed born about 484 B.C.; 'came into notice', says Eusebius, in 468/467; 'flourished' for Apollodorus in 444/443; lectured at Olympia, and in Athens, where he was rewarded, also in 444/443.

This is but a slight framework, into which to fit all that really concerns us—his travels and inquiries and the writing of his history. For these we must study his book.

Herodotus had no need to learn Ionic in Samos, as Suidas supposed. He wrote, as he doubtless spoke, in a colloquial blend of local Ionic dialects, as we read them in contemporary inscriptions, in the longer fragments of Hecataeus, and in the earlier parts of the Hippocratic *corpus*, representing the medical school in Cos. For though originally Dorian, Halicarnassus used Ionic dialect officially in Herodotus' time. But he is influenced by Homeric diction, and has wide acquaintance with Greek writers. Besides oracles quoted in full, his summaries of others include metrical phrases (pp. 77–145). On the other hand, in highly wrought passages his rhythm becomes iambic, especially in the Lydian story (p. 77); and in the later narratives he rises into hexameters.

---

[1] References in Jacoby, 'Herodotus', *R.E.* Suppl. ii. 205 ff.

The text of the Histories is in good order. The two groups of manuscripts—(1) A. *Mediceus*, x cent.; B. *Romanus*, xi cent.; C. *Florentinus*, x cent.; (2) P. *Parisinus*, xiii cent.; R. *Vaticanus*, xiv cent., and their satellites—differ mainly in small details of idiom. There are a few lacunae, and before the book was copied from rolls to codices a careless scribe had transposed the sections on the Pyramid Kings (ii. 124–36), which should follow ii. 99 not ii. 123.[1] Identical catchwords μετὰ δὲ τοῦτον (ii. 100, 124, 137) and the comparable length of the sections made confusion easy; but when the historical order of the dynasties is restored, other anomalies in the 'received text' vanish. More disastrous is the disappearance of the *Assyrian Stories*, the Mesopotamian counterpart to the 'Description of Egypt' (p. 94).

Travels

Herodotus classifies his sources of information as 'eyewitness' and 'hearsay'. Both contribute details about his travels. In Ionia he knew Samos well (iii. 60); and probably Miletus and Ephesus, the latter an easy starting-point for Sardis. In northern Greece he had visited Athens (v. 77), Thebes (v. 59), Delphi (i. 51), the battlefields, and the Gorge of Tempe (vii. 129). In Peloponnesus topographical references are rare: a votive trireme at the Isthmus (viii. 121), a shrine at Sicyon (v. 67), the waterfall of the Styx (vi. 74), the 'manger of Mardonius' at Tegea (ix. 70, cf. i. 66), the dolphin-statue at Taenarum (i. 24), the statue at Thornax (i. 69), besides Sparta itself (iii. 55). Travel in Peloponnese was possible in the peaceful intervals of the First Peloponnesian War and after 445 B.C. as well as in Olympic truces. In the islands there are glimpses of Delos (ii. 170) and Paros (vi. 134); on the way to the west, only Zacynthus (iv. 195), the Achelous delta (ii. 10), and Dodona (ii. 52), and the geographical passage about the shape of Italy (iv. 99).

The extent, the object, and the relative dates of the wider travels have to be inferred from the book. Exiled early, Herodotus was free to wander, at a time when wandering, as well as

[1] Petrie, *J.H.S.* xxviii, 1908, 275.

oversea trade, had become exceptionally easy for Greeks under the aegis of the Delian League. It is easy to suppose that Herodotus travelled as a trader, or with traders. He is interested in boats, soundings, and navigable waters; in interpreters and 'silent trade'; in weights and measures, trade-goods, and the social standing of industry.[1] But there is no hint of trade or profession; his visits to Thasos and Tyre were to compare sanctuaries of Heracles, in whom his kinsman Panyassis was interested; to Heliopolis, Buto, and other places in Egypt he went deliberately, to see or inquire. Travel after the manner of the Near East, though uncomfortable, was not costly. A companion so full of good stories would not want for a meal or a bed; and the colloquial style and vivid narrative of the *Histories* support ancient belief that Herodotus lectured publicly and was paid for this. At Olympia, where all forms of skill had their chance, he left two memories—of lecturing overlong, in the proverb ἐς τὴν ʿHροδότου σκιάν[2]—and of the young Thucydides, moved to tears of emulation.[3] These, then, were voyages either of exploration or of discovery, except at Samos and Athens.

Plotted on a map, the visits of Herodotus group themselves into four principal 'journeys'.

1. Into Pontus he went as far as Olbia and up the Borysthenes, tasting the 'first-class fish' and the 'excellent water' of Exampaeus, the 'holy well'—or was its name *Hexenpfad*?: perhaps also to the Tauric Bosporus and beyond (iv. 55). His observations on Colchis, and on the size of Pontus, seem to be his own (ii. 104–5, iv. 56). Was his luck so good that he saw one of the royal funerals in Scythia (iv. 11, 71–72), the relics of which are recovered from *kurgan* mounds? He certainly saw the royal tumuli on the Tyras. Perhaps it was on this northern journey that he saw the Plain of Troy (ii. 10), the shield of Alcaeus at Sigeum (v. 94), and an inscription of Darius at Byzantium (iv. 87). The monuments on the Tearus river (iv. 90), the lake-dwellings in Paeonia—where

---

[1] i. 194; ii. 96, 5; iv. 53, 24, 196; ii. 168; iii. 110–11; ii. 105; iv. 53, 61, 74, 151; vii. 31, 186; ii. 167, 44. [2] *Paroemiographi Graeci*, s.v.
[3] Marcellinus, *Vita Thuc.* 54; Suidas, s.v. 'Thucydides'; Photius, *Bibliotheca* 60.

'the horses eat fish' (v. 16) and babies are 'tethered lest they roll
off'—and the 'short cut' from the Strymon valley into the Axius,
where, crossing the ridge, 'there you are, in Macedonia' (v. 17),
suggest excursions during a coast voyage; so, too, the hill-side
in Thasos 'turned upside down in the search' for gold (vi. 47),
and the 'King's Way', still trodden and bare, into Chalcidice
(vii. 115).

2. From Samos, which Herodotus describes with eager interest,
it is a short journey by Ephesus to Sardis, where the gold-workings and miners' shanties lay right through the town (v. 101); the
tomb of Alyattes was hard by (i. 93); and there were Persian
officials, Greek clerks, and Lydian veterans from the war. But on
the way, the 'Pseudo-Sesostris' monument is mis-measured and
mis-described, as if from a sketch or description (ii. 106). The
route of Xerxes is followed closely in the coast-districts of Mysia,
and vividly over Mount Ida; but the market-place of Celaenae,
and the monument at Cydrara 'defining in writing' the boundary
between Lydia and Phrygia, are the only points on it east of
Sardis. The rest of Asia Minor seems to have been inaccessible,
unless there is eyewitness in the description of Phrygia 'richest in
corn and richest in sheep', which rings in the ear as you see from
the train the long lines of bullock carts, with solid wheels still,
creaking as they come to the grain-sheds, while white flocks pour
off the downs into the stubble. The account of the 'Royal Road'
must come from a guide-book or list of posting-stations, if not
from a map like that of Aristagoras (v. 49). There is no detail for
the Hittite capital, or the Halys Bridge; even Lydia 'does not
offer many objects of interest' (i. 93). If Herodotus went to
Persia, it was not by the 'Royal Road'.

Throughout Ionia and other Hellenized coastlands there was
no need to parade eyewitness; but there is tavern-talk as sea-
dogs 'bandy reproaches' about this or that squadron at Lade
(vi. 14). There is local folk-lore as far south as Xanthus and
Lindus (i. 144; ii. 182; iii. 47); then nothing till Poseideium at the
mouth of the Orontes, on the frontier between Cilicia and Syria
(iii. 91). From Cyprus there is a gruesome memorial of the Ionian

Revolt, the skull of Onesilaus dripping with wild honey on the gate of Amathus (v. 114).

Graphic phrases discover Herodotus again at Tyre (ii. 44), at the Nahr-el-Kelb monuments (ii. 106), at Gaza (iii. 5), and Ascalon (i. 105); on the Euphrates, and at Babylon (i. 175, 185–94), where he notes the half-way seats up the Tower of Babel (i. 181), and the governor's stud-farm and kennels (i. 192). But his description of Ecbatana is a diagram (i. 98); the references to Bactria (iv. 204) and the Caspian (i. 202), and even to Media and Susa are hearsay (i. 110–11; vi. 119); and the comparison of Arabian custom with Babylonian does not prove a visit (i. 198): all other references to Arabs are in Egyptian contexts (ii. 8, 12, 75; iii. 5, 107). There is, however, need for caution here; for Herodotus certainly planned, and probably wrote, a more extensive account of the Ancient East than has been preserved (p. 94).

3. Though it was a main caravan-route from Palestine to Egypt—on which there is a glimpse of the water-storage prepared for Cambyses' invasion (iii. 6–9), not obvious to sea-borne visitors—there is a glimpse of approach from the sea—as to George Sandys in 1610—in the soundings in eleven fathoms 'a day's run from land' (ii. 5). This voyage, moreover, was compatible with a visit to Cyrene (iv. 169). But the detailed accounts of North African peoples and of the oases, Lake Chad, and the Niger (ii. 32, 33) are not more than might be collected there.

4. The detailed account of Egypt in Book II rests mainly, as he says, on his own observation and inquiries (ii. 29). There is no reason to suppose either that he had not read Hecataeus, or that he copied from him. The lack of detail about Thebes (ii. 23, 42, 54, 143) is explained by his own statement that his description is supplementary to published accounts. Of the places which he visited, Naucratis (ii. 178), Sais (ii. 28, 62, 169), Memphis (ii. 99, 121, 150, 153, 155, 176), and the Pyramids (ii. 124) were on beaten tracks; Heliopolis (ii. 3) and the Fayum 'Labyrinth' (ii. 148) needed special journeys; other landmarks are Buto (ii. 158), Bubastis (ii. 137), Papremis (ii. 63; iii. 12), Pelusium (iii. 12) and Necho's canal (ii. 158; iv. 42). His 'farthest south' was Elephan-

tine (Assuan: ii. 29), where he made further inquiries about the
Sudan and the Nile sources. For the value of his observations
see p. 152.

The date of this visit has been disputed. As a Mesopotamian
parallel is quoted (ii. 150), it was probably after the journey down
the Euphrates. As Egypt was entirely in Persian hands and pacified (ii. 30, 98, 149) it must have been either before or after the
revolt of 460–454 B.C. The earlier date is precluded by the account
of the skull-strewn battlefield of Papremis (459 B.C.: iii. 12) and
Amyrtaeus, who was still in revolt in 449 B.C., had been succeeded
by Pausiris (iii. 15). There was no inducement to record the
Athenian disasters of 454 B.C.; and Athenian aggression ceased
after Cimon's death in 450 B.C. It was not a long sojourn, but
included both high and low Nile. Powell[1] distinguishes two
Egyptian visits, before 460 B.C. and after 448 B.C.

For Babylonia—or, as he calls it, 'Assyria'—in general Herodotus certainly planned a description and history (i. 106, 184)
like that of Egypt in Book II. But these *Assyrian Stories* are not
preserved, and the only ancient allusion to them[2] may refer to
Hesiod. If this account was written, it may have stood within or
after Book I, as a counterpart to the *Egyptian Stories* of Book II,
which is an ungainly excrescence as it stands: compare the
balanced arrangement of Book III (Samian and Persian history)
and Book IV (Scythia and Libya), and pp. 100–2 below, where
other suggestions are discussed. In any case, allusions in the book
as we have it cannot be taken to record the extent or the duration of the travels east of the Isthmus.

Other indications of date, or of earlier and later journeys, are
rare. When Herodotus described the 'Pseudo-Sesostris' (ii. 106),
he can hardly have seen a hieroglyphic inscription. On the other
hand, he professes to translate an inscription of Darius in Thrace
(iv. 91): like that on the Bosporus (iv. 87) it may have been
bilingual. As to the size of the Hera-temple in Samos (iii. 60), he
corrects himself after visiting Egypt (ii. 148). For an Italian
public, he expands his comparison of Scythia with Attica written

for an Athenian audience (iv. 99). Other editorial phrases seem added for Athenians (p. 11). In ii. 168 is a comparison between the Egyptian and the Samian cubit.

But it is the reason for the journeys, not their date, that is important, if we can discover it. Two explanations have been proposed: (1) that Herodotus began as an observer and inquirer on the lines laid down by the 'physical' philosophers of Ionia, and only later conceived the project of a history of the national struggle, and incorporated in it the collections—and perhaps the writings—of earlier years; or (2) that the 'grand design' was always in his mind, and the materials were accumulated, through the years, to realize it. The latter, announced in the *Preface*, was accepted by earlier critics, and has been recently reformulated by Pohlenz (1937). The former accounts better for the numerous back-references, repetitions, and other marks of progressive composition; and has been carried into minute detail by Jacoby (1913) and by Powell (1939).

Oral Information: 'Hearsay'

Besides alluding to visits, Herodotus says that he has spoken with inhabitants of more than forty Greek cities and districts, from Cyprus to Syracuse, and of more than thirty other countries, from Arabia and the Oasis of Ammon to Colchis and Scythia, and from Persia to Carthage. Some of these, such as Persians and Carthaginians, he may have met abroad; the 'Carthaginian' tale of gold-gleaning in West Africa might be picked up anywhere (iv. 195), but when he uses the plural he is probably summarizing the gleanings of a visit (iv. 150; vi. 75). Thus, what he calls 'eyewitness', *opsis*, was extended by 'hearsay', *akoê*, and both were checked and supplemented by 'inquiry', *historiê* (ii. 19, 44, 75, 113, 118). This word, related to the judicial *histôr* or *istôr* of *Iliad* xviii. 501, means literally 'tracking down'. It has a long and comprehensive usage for 'stories' of all sorts, sinking to the modern Greek meanings of 'excuses' and of 'illustrations'. Herodotus uses it for the inquiries of himself (i. 1) and of others (ii. 118, 119) and for the collective results. Where the popular story goes

astray, he corrects it (iv. 192) or qualifies it ('yet so much I do
know': vii. 152; cf. i. 140); or in default of eyewitness comes to
a negative conclusion (iii. 115; cf. iv. 16), sometimes emphatic-
ally.[1] Where accounts differ, he leaves the matter open[2] or states
his own belief.[3] Only rarely does he name his informant—an
Egyptian clerk (ii. 28), Archias (iii. 55), Tymnes (iv. 76),
Thersandrus (ix. 16), or quote a single source, such as Dicaeus
(viii. 65) or Epizelus (vi. 117). He expressly reserves judgement
on hearsay, while asserting his duty to record it (vii. 152; cf. ii.
123); and the most plausible version may be the most misleading
(ii. 22). He reserves, too, his right to suppress a name (i. 51) or a
statement (ii. 46; vii. 96); and to propound a view of his own
(ii. 24; iv. 11–12; v. 3; vii. 220) even about the unknown.

A crucial passage, which has been often discussed, is the
description (v. 77) of the monument commemorating the Athenian victory over Boeotians and Chalcidians (p. 183). Herodotus
describes it in two parts. (a) On walls smoke-stained when the
Acropolis was sacked in 480 B.C. (viii. 53) hung 'still to my time'
the prisoners' fetters 'opposite the *megaron* which is turned to
the west'. In viii. 53 the same word *megaron* is applied to the
Temple, of which the *opisthodomus* opened westward. Herodotus
could have seen these walls at any time before he went to Thurii;
but they can hardly have been left standing when the Propylaea
of Mnesicles were begun (437 B.C.). (b) A bronze chariot was
made from the ransom of those prisoners, with a two-couplet
inscription which refers also to the fetters. Of this inscription
parts of two versions are extant; in the earlier, and original,[4] the
line about the fetters stands first, and so also in the collected
poems of Simonides.[5] The chariot, therefore, originally stood
close to the wall with the fetters. In the later, mid-fifth-century,
version the line about the fetters stands third, and emphasis is
given to the votive team.[6] The monument may have been remodelled after the similar victory at Oenophyta (458 or 457 B.C.),

---

[1] vi. 14, 77; vii. 35, 53, 55; viii. 87, 133; ix. 84, 95.
[2] ii. 123; iv. 195; v. 9; vi. 52, 75–84; vii. 152.
[3] vii. 185–7; ix. 32.   [4] Tod, *G.H.I.* 12.   [5] 100 (Diehl).
[6] A. Raubitschek, *Dedications from the Athenian Acropolis*, nos. 168, 173.

or the final defeat of Chalcis (446 B.C.). It is this later version which Herodotus has transcribed; and he places the chariot 'on the left, as you first enter the propylaea'; but whereas he only says of the fetters that they hung 'down to my time', he expressly says of the chariot that it 'stands' at the time of writing. Whether it stood within (or just inside) the Propylaea of Mnesicles (which were left incomplete in 431 B.C.), or some earlier entrance, is a further question: what is significant is the change of tense—first noted by Powell[1]—and the certainty that Herodotus described the remodelled monument as well as remembered the original.

It has been suggested that it was his residence in Athens that not only determined the admiration of Herodotus for the Athenian people, but turned his attention from travel and ethnology to the writing of history. Several allusions presume an Athenian public (p. 9): the comparison of Ecbatana with the ring-wall of Athens (i. 98); of a Persian measure with an Attic (i. 192); of the distance from Athens to Olympia with that from Heliopolis to the sea (ii. 7); of a lake at Sais with that in Delos (ii. 170); of the shapes of Attica and of Scythia (iv. 99); and of Pitane, a district of Sparta, with a *dêmos* (iii. 55). On the other hand, Solon is twice introduced in words superfluous for Athenians (i. 29; ii. 177); and the Athenians themselves are 'those people' in ii. 177. He knows the sanctuary of Aeacus in the Agora (v. 89), the tomb of Cimon and his horses (vi. 103) and that of Anchimolius in Alopece (v. 63), and the west end of the Acropolis scaled by the Persians (viii. 53). He knows how Cape Sunium looks detached (iv. 99) as you sail round it, but his account of the return march from Marathon (vi. 116) confirms his over-estimate of the 'squareness' of Attica. His topography of Marathon and Salamis is correct, so far as it goes.

The date of this visit to Athens cannot be precisely fixed, and he may have been in Athens more than once. Stories unfavourable to Aegina, Thebes, Corinth, and Sparta indicate the war period after 460 B.C.[2] Besides earlier events (470–464 B.C.) he refers to the battle of Tanagra (458 or 457 B.C.: ix. 35). The date of the mission of Callias to Susa is doubtful (?449 B.C.: vii. 151; p. 240)

[1] p. 69. [2] ix. 105; viii. 109; vii. 170; iv. 75; ix. 35, 64; vii. 7.

and, after that, there is nothing till the Theban attack on Plataea
in 431 B.C. (vii. 233). This silence is explained if Herodotus left
Athens for Thurii at, or soon after, its foundation in 443 B.C. and
returned thither (if at all) only in 431 B.C. The almost verbal
coincidence between iii. 118–19 and Sophocles' *Antigone* 904–20
on the comparative value of a husband and a brother, quoted
from memory by Aristotle,[1] proves little. The *Antigone* was produced shortly before 440 B.C., but Herodotus' anecdote seems to
be originally Persian. Other reminiscences in Sophocles[2] have no
value as date-marks. The two men were friends, and Sophocles
wrote verses to Herodotus[3] whose interest in the Alcmaeonidae,
and especially in Pericles,[4] illustrates his intimate knowledge of
Athenian ideals and policy and his devotion to the Athenian
cause. Repeated digressions on the growth of democratic freedom
are a sincere attempt to account for this new force in the Greek
world, and for its share in the national victory (v. 55, 62–73, 78).
It may even be asked whether Herodotus would not gladly have
become an Athenian, but was a victim of the new exclusive-
ness which found expression in the legislation of 451/450 B.C.
(p. 184).

Plutarch[5] quotes from Diyllus a story that Herodotus received
from the Athenians a gift of ten talents 'on the proposal of
Anytus', who can hardly be the accuser of Socrates, if Eusebius'
date for the gift is correct (*Ol.* 83. 4 = 445/444 B.C.). But
Eusebius adds that the occasion was 'when he read to them his
books', and though Herodotus was probably in Athens in 445 B.C.,
it is doubtful whether the 'books' were completed then. The
award, moreover, would be excessive: Pindar received 1,000
drachmas for his dithyramb,[6] and Cleidemus a gold crown of
1,000 (or 500) drachmas for his *Atthis*.[7] Aly[8] has conjectured
plausibly that the numeral X (= 1,000 drachmas) has been misread as Roman X. Plutarch adds[9] that Herodotus asked the

---

[1] *Rhetoric* iii. 16. 9. 1417ᵃ28 ff.
[2] *Oed. Col.* 337; *Electra* 62; *Oed. Tyr.* 981; *Phil.* 1207 (cf. iv. 75); fr. 646 Nauck.
[3] Plut. *Moralia* 785 B.   [4] i. 61, 64; v. 62, 66, 70, 90; vi. 115, 121, 131.
[5] *de Malignitate Hdti.* 26, cf. 31.   [6] Isocr. *Antid.* 166.
[7] Tertullian, *de Anima*, 52.3.   [8] *Rh.M.* lxiv. 637.   [9] *de Mal.* 31.

Thebans for a reward, without success, and thereafter maligned them, implying that he had earned the Athenian gift by his praise. But was it a reward for literary merit at all? There had been diplomatic dealings between Athens and Persia about 449 B.C.; a travelled Greek with Persian acquaintances may have advanced or been entrusted with funds. The best discussion of this affair is by Jacoby.[1]

Herodotus at Thurii. How long Herodotus remained in Athens we do not know. But it is as certain as anything in his career that he passed on thence to Thurii in South Italy, not earlier than 443 B.C. and was, if not an original colonist, at least an early settler. The foundation of Thurii was an important event. The Crathis river drains a wide and deep basin between the main mass of South Italy and the rugged and forested highland which forms the 'toe' of the peninsula, and supplies most of the rainfall of this farmers' paradise. Through softer, marly uplands the Crathis has cut back nearly to the northern coast, so that the portage from sea to sea was easy; and the Greek colony of Sybaris, founded or refounded by Peloponnesian Achaeans about the same time as Naxos, Syracuse, and its own neighbour and rival Croton, exploited this short-cut to Campania and Etruria, and became proverbial for wealth easily gotten and lightly enjoyed. It was overlord of four native tribes and their territories. Its oversea friendship with Miletus (vi. 21) defines its position in the world of commerce, and helps to account for Croton's relations with Samos and peculiarly bitter feud with the lords of the Crathis. In 510 B.C. Croton overpowered and obliterated Sybaris (v. 44); and Herodotus, recording this severe blow to Miletus, notes how completely the Sybarite outposts on the northern shore had outlived the old ties when Miletus fell in 494 B.C.

The first phase of rivalry between Athens and Corinth, after the Persian War, was closed in 445 B.C. by the 'Thirty Years Truce', a statesmanlike recognition of spheres of influence, and of the freedom of third parties. In effect Athens was to have a free

[1] *R.E.*, pp. 226–9.

hand in the Aegean and eastward, Corinth in the west. But hardly was the 'Truce' in force when a struggle between parties and policies in Athens ended in the ostracism of Thucydides son of Melesias; and Pericles' first oversea adventure was the re-settlement of the site of Sybaris on a magnificent scale. As Athens had become heir to the wide interests of Miletus and its associates, this foundation of Thurii had a general as well as a local significance; in 440 B.C. Samos, the old rival of Miletus and an old associate of Corinth in the west, revoked its allegiance to the Athenian naval league and appealed to Sparta; and it was only the diplomacy of Corinth that prevented a general war. Thurii itself had been meant to be Pan-Hellenic, open to all men of goodwill; but there was friction between 'Athenian' and other factions,[1] though the city did not change sides till after the Sicilian disaster.[2]

It is easy to guess that this notable enterprise attracted a travelled exile with so strong an admiration for Athens, but there is no evidence that Herodotus was one of the founders, or that he had any official position in Thurii. That he became a full citizen, however, seems certain from the preface to his book, as quoted by Aristotle and others (p. 3).

There is no evidence of systematic western travels, but occasional allusion to western cities and events. Though Herodotus never mentions Thurii, he refers both to Sybaris (v. 44–45; vi. 21, 127) and to the river Crathis (i. 145; v. 45). For Metapontum there is eyewitness as well as hearsay (iv. 15); for Croton the story of Democedes (iii. 129–38) and the adventure of Dorieus (v. 39–48); for Tarentum the story of Arion (i. 24) and the disaster in Iapygia (vii. 170) in which Rhegium also was involved. More extensive is the retrospect of Sicilian history in Gelo's time (vii. 153–67). Expressly added for a western public is the comparison of Scythia with South Italy (iv. 99): perhaps of western origin is the attribution of tributaries, Alpis and Carpis, to the Danube (iv. 49).

A few references to events between 432 and 429 have been

---

[1] Thuc. vii. 33.   [2] Thuc. viii. 35.

thought to show that Herodotus revisited Greece—and, if so, Athens—enemy states being closed to him by the war.

1. Referring to the Delian earthquake of 480 B.C. (vi. 98) he shows no knowledge of that of 432/431 B.C.; in recording which Thucydides[1] tacitly challenges the earlier shock. The omission proves nothing about Herodotus' movements; only that vi. 98 was already written in 432 B.C. It is Thucydides whose information is defective.

2. The reference to the Theban attack on Plataea (vii. 233: March 431 B.C.) is hearsay and not quite accurate; Eurymachus was the instigator, but not expressly the leader.[2]

3. The curse on the Aeginetans for sacrilege (vi. 91) was fulfilled by their expulsion in 431 B.C.;[3] this, however, was notorious, and the news may have travelled far.

4. The immunity of Deceleia from Spartan devastation[4] need not refer to anything later than the first inroad (431 B.C.); it was of primarily Athenian concern.

5. The murder of Spartan heralds by the Athenians in the winter of 430/429 B.C.[5] is compared with Xerxes' clemency to Sperthias and Bulis, and with the murder of Darius' heralds by Sparta and Athens. The story is given on Spartan authority, but there were probably Spartan prisoners at Athens.

6. On the other hand, Herodotus never distinguishes Darius Hystaspes from Darius Nothus, who succeeded Artaxerxes in 424 B.C.; and the retrospect of the 'three reigns', which takes account of the war of 431 as well as that of 460, implies that the forty-years reign of Artaxerxes was near its end.[6]

7. The flight of the younger Zopyrus from Persia (iii. 160) may have been at any time after the Egyptian campaign of Megabyzus.[7]

8. Though Cythera was not occupied by Athens till 424 B.C.,[8] it had long been an obvious danger to Sparta (vii. 235).

With these few allusions in view, a date for the publication of

[1] ii. 8. 3.   [2] Thuc. ii. 3 and 5.   [3] Thuc. ii. 27. 1.
[4] ix. 73; cf. Thuc. ii. 23.
[5] vii. 133-7; cf. Thuc. ii. 67; vii. 32.   [6] vi. 98.
[7] 455 B.C.; Thuc. i. 109. See p. 159.   [8] Thuc. iv. 53.

the *Histories* is given by the travesty in Aristophanes, *Acharnians* 525–34 (425 B.C.) of the *cherchez-la-femme* view of history discarded by Herodotus in his prologue (i. 4); and by the burlesque of Persian officialdom in the 'Great King's Eye' (65–125). On the ground of these references to later events, and of the vigorous defence of Athenian policy in the Persian struggle (vii. 139), it has been suggested[1] that Herodotus, finding Thurii lukewarm in Athenian interest and Greek opinion veering against Athens, returned to render a last service by completing and publishing this vindication. If so, he may have died of the plague, still at work.

[1] By Powell, *Hist. Hdt.* 81–82.

II

HERODOTUS AND HIS CRITICS

A BOOK of so varied contents, so many controversial issues, and so novel a standpoint in historical research could not escape criticism. It is, indeed, only within living memory that the greatness of Herodotus' design and achievement has been appreciated, and there is still dispute as to his purpose and method. It is not easy to separate the inquiry into his sources and the objective value of them, from the study of his use of them and his own qualifications as an historian and man of letters; and confusion of these distinct issues has complicated the problem. But the history of Herodotean criticism is an essential preliminary to further inquiry. Only the principal contributions can be noted here, and some of these mainly as closing certain by-ways of error. And it must be insisted throughout that the test of relevance is intimate acquaintance with the book itself.

Thucydides, criticizing his predecessors (i. 20), gives instances of their mistakes. On the seniority of Hippias (vi. 54), Herodotus is right (v. 55). On the voting privileges of the Spartan Kings, Herodotus describes the same procedure, but in greater detail (vi. 57: p. 189). On the 'battalion from Pitane', at Plataea (ix. 53), Herodotus had visited the place (iii. 55) early enough to converse with survivors. Thucydides' general reflections on 'poetical' exaggeration, and the 'logographer's' preference for fiction over accuracy, are not exemplified from Herodotus, and are expressly repudiated by him. The meaning of 'myth-like' (*mythôdes*) has been misunderstood, and needs reconsideration in reference to Aristotle's description of Herodotus as a 'myth-teller' (p. 18).

In another passage, where Thucydides (iii. 68) gives ninety-three years as the duration of the Plataean alliance (i.e. from 519 B.C.), the date presumed by Herodotus (vi. 108: 509 B.C.) is probably right: if Thucydides' text is correct, he has 'carried the wrong figure' and discovered a mare's nest (p. 186).

Minor differences of emphasis are of little significance: whether Cylon's conspiracy was suppressed by the 'nine archons' (Thuc. i. 126 is an anachronism, as the coalescence of the archon-college was Solonian) or by the 'headmen of the naucraries' (v. 71: probably the pre-Solonian title of the traditional Council of Elders); whether there was one Delian earthquake or two, and when (Hdt. vi. 98; Thuc. ii. 8: p. 15); whether Sestus was besieged by Athenians (Hdt. ix. 114) or by Athenians and Ionians (Thuc. i. 89); whether Themistocles' naval programme envisaged war with Aegina (Hdt. vii. 144) or with Persia (Thuc. i. 14), seeing that Aegina had medized; or the precise terms of Themistocles' letters to Xerxes (Hdt. viii. 75, 110; Thuc. i. 137). The real continuity of thought between the two historians is revealed in their estimates of the Athenian contribution to the salvation of Greece (Hdt. vii. 139; Thuc. i. 18, 73–74); and the adoption by Thucydides (i. 89) of the capture of Sestus as the opening of a new period, as it is the close of the old for Herodotus (ix. 114).

Ctesias, a physician of Cnidus, who was at the Persian Court from 415 to 398 B.C., wrote on his return to Greece a highly coloured account of Persia and the Wars, of the kind deplored by Thucydides, and attacked Herodotus as a 'story-teller' (*logopoios*) and a liar. He is himself classed with Herodotus and the Ionian *logographoi* by Theopompus fr. 381; Strabo 507–8; Lucian, *Philopseudes* 2, *Vera Historia* 2. 31; but his book was popular.

Isocrates, writing before 380 B.C. (*Paneg.* 158–9), disparages Herodotus; *Aristotle* quotes him on points of natural history and also on his book.[1]

Diodorus (ix. 22), probably relying on Ephorus, quotes Herodotus, but inaccurately, on Median history (i. 96–100). Dionysius, also of Halicarnassus, gives him his place among the 'principal

---

[1] *Hist. Anim.* viii. 18 (601^{b}4) with a reference to the lost siege of Nineveh (H. i. 106); ib. vi. 31 (579^{b}2) (H. ii. 108); ib. ii. 2 (736^{a}10) (H. iii. 101); *Eth. Eud.* vii. 2 (1236^{b}9) (H. ii. 68); *Gen. Anim.* iii. 5 (756^{a}6) (H. ii. 93); *Rhet.* iii. 16 (1417^{a}28) ref. to *Antigone*; ib. iii. 9 (1409^{a}28) (H. i. 1); ib. iii. 5 (1407^{a}39) (H. i. 53).

historians' on literary grounds (*ad Pompeium* 3–5), and Cicero (*de Legibus* i. 1. 5) confers on him the title 'Father of History'. Strabo notes his ingenuous 'simplicity' (507, 508), his love of stories, his observance of prodigies (43). The criticism that under the form of a history he was competing with 'confessed mythographers' misconceived his outlook and purpose, and reflected the fourth-century rationalism of Ephorus. Josephus (*c. Apion.* 1. 14 (73)) quotes Manetho as attributing his mistakes about Egypt to ignorance, and says (*c. Apion.* 1. 3) that 'everyone criticizes Herodotus'. But to depreciate predecessors was a commonplace of ancient literature since Hecataeus (fr. 1*a*): Herodotus did the same.

Plutarch's severely critical essay *de Malignitate Herodoti* has two main motives: (1) to defend against 'ill-natured' assignment of praise and blame the reputation of all persons and states involved in the struggle for freedom, making wide use of victory monuments and laudatory local histories; (2) to refute Herodotus' unfavourable accounts of the Corinthians and of Plutarch's own Boeotian countrymen. This 'malignity' he attributes to Herodotus' chagrin at his cool reception by these two peoples, contrasted with his welcome by the Athenians, and his flattery of them. Much of Plutarch's criticism is trivial and irrelevant; but he preserves a few historical facts which supplement or correct the narrative. The attribution of this essay to Plutarch has been disputed, without sufficient grounds.[1] It illustrates a distinct line of attack, on the character, rather than the skill, of Herodotus.

In the Revival of Learning the *Histories* of Herodotus reappear in the Latin translation of Laurentius Valla (Venice, 1479) and in the Greek text of Aldus (Venice, 1502). The division into 'Nine Muses' was printed by Aldus in 1511 from his manuscript; his own division into chapters not till Jungermann's edition of 1608. In the Latin version of Stephanus (1566) and in his Greek text (1570) the fragments of Ctesias were appended; and

---

[1] It is from the same pen as the *Lives* of Themistocles and Aristides (L. Holzapfel, *Philologus*, xlii (1884), 23 ff.).

Stephanus's *Apologia pro Herodoto* (1566) was reproduced by Thomas Gale (London, 1679), Gronovius (Leyden, 1715), and Wesseling (Amsterdam, 1763). Stephanus amplified his defence of Herodotus in an *Introduction au traité de la conformité des merveilles anciennes avec les modernes* (Geneva, 1566), and subsequent criticism dealt mainly with discrepancies between Herodotus and other writers on the Ancient East.

A vigorous English translation of Books I and II by 'B. R.' appeared in 1584, and Book II has been edited by Andrew Lang (1888) and by Leonard Whibley (1924). In 1709 Isaac Littlebury translated the whole; William Beloe in 1791; G. Lemprière in 1792; P. E. Laurent in 1827; Isaac Taylor in 1829; Henry Cary in 1847. The standard English version by George Rawlinson (1858–60) was accompanied by full introduction and commentary, with special reference to the current excavations on Babylonian and Assyrian sites, and the decipherment of cuneiform documents by Rawlinson's brother Sir Henry.[1] More recent translators are G. C. Macaulay (1890), A. D. Godley (1921–4), and J. E. Powell (1949).

Revived interest in exploration inspired *The Geography of Herodotus* of W. Rennell (1800; 2nd ed. 1830), and J. Kenrick, *The Egypt of Herodotus* (1841), followed later by E. H. Bunbury, *History of Ancient Geography* (2 vols., 1879), and the topographical studies of Grundy and Kromayer (p. 25).

Meanwhile in Germany, under the influence of Macpherson's *Ossian*, Grimm's studies of German folk-tales, and Wolf's analytical treatment of the Homeric poems, B. G. Niebuhr assumed among the Greeks, as in early Italy, a boundless repertory of anecdotes, without coherent context, from which he thought the first chroniclers selected and combined at will. He was completely sceptical of historical tradition, even about the Persian Wars, and did not rank Herodotus above his Ionian predecessors.[2] Here was, however, a first attempt to separate Herodotus from his sources,

---

[1] 4 vols. 1858–60; 3rd ed. 1875; edited with notes by A. W. Lawrence, 1935.
[2] *Hist. u. philol. Vorträge*, II. i (1847), *Vorträge ü. alte Geschichte* (posthumous).

to indicate their variety and popular origin, and to credit Herodotus with historical discernment of the part played by Athens in the national struggle. But Herodotus was much more nearly contemporary with the Persian Wars than Niebuhr supposed; and earlier than Choerilus, from whose metrical *Perseis* he was suspected of borrowing. The numerous coincidences of phrase with the *Persae* of Aeschylus were offset by the dramatic presentation of the subject; monumental epigrams contributed little as yet to Herodotus' narrative of events. At most, Niebuhr formulated the obvious ultimate dependence of historical narrative on oral tradition; he distinguished some of the main forms in which oral tradition is transmitted; and he emphasized the difficulties of historical research among such sources.

A. Kirchhoff[1] applied contemporary methods of literary criticism to the structure of Herodotus' work, assuming that composition was gradual, and that internal evidence was fundamental as to the relation of its parts. He thought that in general the *History* was composed in the traditional order: Books i, ii, iii. 1–118 in Athens; iii. 119–v. 77 in Italy (on the ground of iv. 15, 99, and other allusions); v. 77, vi. 98, vii. 162, with the remainder, in Athens again, after 431 B.C.; interrupted by death about 428 B.C. A break in Book III seemed to result from omission (i. 106, 170; I. 184); the correspondence with *Antigone* (iii. 119) was dated to 441 B.C.

Whereas Niebuhr was baffled by the formlessness and heterogeneity of popular tradition, K. W. Nitzsch[2] argued for formal written sources, of various kinds, and limited Herodotus (as in ii. 123, vii. 132) to the role of industrious but unintelligent compiler; the counterpart of the final 'redactor' in contemporary criticism of Homer. But Herodotus uses *logos* and *legetai* ('it is said') in various senses; he records formal anecdotes (*novelle*)—Alcmaeonid, Philaid, and the like—and family tradition, on which Nitzsch laid great stress, but also personal reminiscences and the collated results of wide inquiry, initiated by himself and inspired

[1] *Herodotus* (ed.) 1868, revised 1878.
[2] 'Über Herodots' Quellen', *Rh.M.* xxvii (1872), 226–68.

by independent reflection. A pioneer in this line was B. Erdmanns-dorfer;[1] it has been explored fruitfully by W. Aly.[2]

The method of Nitzsch was carried to extremes by N. Weck-lein.[3] Assuming the truth of the Roman sarcasm *Quidquid Graecia mendax audet in historia*, he assigned to fifth-century Greeks in general a tendency to moralize traditional anecdotes, to attribute Greek successes to the gods, to invent causes for historical events; and imputes these practices to Herodotus far more generally than his text allows. When Herodotus moralizes, it is in the speeches, not in the narrative; if he is partial, and suspicious of motives, his Athenian sources are responsible. Though there was grateful recognition of divine help, the Persian quarrel was not a crusade on either side; its causes were political, not religious.

Another *a priori* reasoning from an ingenious hypothesis is by H. Delbruck.[4] From a comparison between the Greek armed forces and those of the Swiss cantons in the fifteenth century, the numbers recorded by Herodotus were criticized and reduced, and the military narrative—and much else—was rewritten. The chief value of Delbruck's approach was to challenge the closer examina-tion of strategy and tactics, which was undertaken by Grundy and Kromayer (p. 25), and the more careful study of the text of Herodotus in face of bold assumptions and generalizations. A late sequel to this mode of criticism is by R. Adam,[5] who treats Herodotus' book as a mere collection of amusing stories, still separable.

The first step in constructive criticism is that of A. Bauer,[6] superior in method to Nitzsch and Wecklein, but characteristic of its period. Compilation from drafts, he argues, explains the defects of the work better than deliberate composition. Such separate writings were combined and revised by Herodotus with-out effacing signs of independent origin. The Samian 'story', for

---

[1] 'Das Zeitalter der Novelle in Hellas', *Preuss. Jahrb.* xxv, 1870.
[2] *Volksmärchen, Sagen, und Novellen bei Hdt. u. seinen Zeitgenossen*, Göttingen, 1921.
[3] *Über die Tradition der Perserkriege*, Munich, 1876.
[4] *Die Perserkriege und die Burgunderkriege*, Berlin, 1887.
[5] *De Herodoti ratione historicae quaestiones selectae*, Berlin, 1890.
[6] *Die Entstehung der Herodotischen Geschichtswerke*, 1878.

example, was written in Samos; the Persian war-narrative before the visit to Athens: probably what was recited there was the story of Marathon, or the expedition of Xerxes. From Athens the longer journeys were made later, and recorded there, and the earlier Libyan 'story' was revised. Book II was a separate composition. Frank expression of free-thinking, picked up in Egypt and applied to men as well as to the gods, led to withdrawal from Athens to Thurii, where the general plan of the book took shape, and composition went as far as v. 77. Later Herodotus returned to Athens and continued it there.

Bauer's argument rests on many small inconsistencies, not easily eliminated under ancient conditions of book production. Though rather speculative, it is consistent with Kirchhoff's chronology, based on internal evidence. Bauer recognized that so elaborate a history took time to write, that revision was inevitable but incomplete, and that an order of composition may be established from cross-references, and correlated with the writer's movements and abodes. All later reconstruction rests on Bauer's studies.

The next few years, however, saw an outbreak of violent attack on the competence and honesty of Herodotus, and of reckless speculation about his authorities.

Very different from the scepticism of Niebuhr is the view of A. H. Sayce[1] that Herodotus drew his information from copious written sources, but deliberately concealed his obligations, especially to Ionian chroniclers, while referring freely to poets and a few other writers. Sayce even regarded the professions of eyewitness and personal inquiry as untrue. But ancient views of copyright were lax; and Herodotus does in fact refer to current authorities on Egypt (ii. 20–24) and on general geography (ii. 16) as well as to Hecataeus by name (ii. 143; vi. 137–8). Moreover, of the many fragments of the 'Logographers' hardly any refer to the Persian Wars; most of the few events noted by them are not mentioned by Herodotus; and he expressly regarded his own account of Egypt as supplementary to current literature. Only

[1] *Herodotus I–III*, 1883.

Dionysius of Miletus and Charon of Lampsacus are known to have written *Persica*; the rest compiled town-histories, in which references to the Persian Wars could only be incidental. Herodotus may well have read them, without obligation to quote. The replies to Sayce of R. C. Jebb[1] and A. Croiset[2] are significant and conclusive.

The special debt of Herodotus to Hecataeus is argued by Diels[3] in spite of the doubts of Cobet[4] as to the genuineness of the latter's fragments, first expressed by Callimachus (Athenaeus ii. 70 b; Strabo 7), but later dispelled by Jacoby.[5]

In the same year, H. Panofsky[6] goes farther than Sayce, regarding even the statements attributed to persons as copied from written sources; for example the different accounts of the death of Cleomenes (vi. 75), where Panofsky has overlooked the Spartan story. Yet Herodotus is so careful to distinguish his own rare affirmations that the phrases 'it is said' or 'they say' are best interpreted in their obvious sense.

Out of the story of the prodigy at Eleusis (viii. 65) and the phrase 'Dicaeus son of Theocydes used to say', P. Trautwein[7] even created a whole volume of *Memoirs*. But the words used by Herodotus in quoting Homer, Aristeas, and Hecataeus are different (ii. 23, 53, 116–17, 143; iv. 13; v. 36, 125–6; vi. 137).

It was high time for a general review of this generation of 'higher criticism', when in 1891 the Académie des Inscriptions et Belles Lettres proposed, as the subject for an essay, 'the tradition of the Persian Wars, and the elements of which it is composed, the narrative of Herodotus, and the contributions of other writers'. The prize fell to Amédée Hauvette,[8] who had written on the logographers (1888) and on Herodotus' geography (1889) and had visited the battlefields (1892) just before Grundy's reconnaissance (p. 25). Hauvette's work marks a return to sanity and

---

[1] *Quarterly Review*, Apr. 1884.   [2] *R.E.G.* I., 1888, 154.
[3] *Hermes*, xxii (1887), 411.
[4] *Mnemosyne*, N.S. xi (1883) 1–7.   [5] *R.E.* l. c. 1913.
[6] *Quaestionum de historiae Herodoti fontibus pars prima*, 1885.
[7] 'The "Memoirs" of Dicaeus, *Hermes*, xxv (1890), 527–66.
[8] *Hérodote historien des guerres médiques*, Paris, 1894.

perspective: even Sayce modified his severer strictures.[1] Hauvette restored Herodotus' credit as an observer and historian, and skilfully collected what was of value in the modern criticisms, as contributions to a reasonable estimate. His running commentary on the narrative embodies most of the historical and archaeological material accumulated since Niebuhr's time. He does full justice to the industry, good faith, and discernment of Herodotus, and restates the few trustworthy glimpses of his life and mode of work. In Germany Busolt's second edition[2] and Eduard Meyer's essay[3] mark a further return to appreciation of Herodotus as an historian.

Meanwhile, the new conditions for research in Egypt after 1882 made possible a fresh examination of the special Egyptian problems by A. Wiedemann,[4] and the criticisms of Sayce[5] were set in their proper light by F. Ll. Griffith,[6] C. Sourdille,[7] Vogt,[8] and W. Spiegelberg.[9] More general interest in Greek antiquities, and better facilities for travel in Greece, made possible both the encyclopaedic studies of J. G. Frazer for his edition of Pausanias and the topographical surveys of ancient battlefields by G. B. Grundy, a scholar and field-surveyor with some knowledge of military matters. His reconstruction of *The Battlefield of Plataea* (1895) followed by studies of Marathon and Thermopylae in *The Great Persian War* (1901) superseded the pioneer work of Leake and Gell, two generations earlier, and were in due course incorporated in the *Antike Schlachtfelder* of J. Kromayer (1924–31). There was severe criticism of Herodotus for military inexperience, and failure to see into the minds of commanders; but here, too, closer study of the text and better appreciation of his difficulties and his sources have on the whole restored his credit. Other

[1] *The Egypt of the Hebrews and Herodotus*, London, 1895.
[2] *Griechische Geschichte*, ii, Berlin, 1895.   [3] *Forschungen*, ii, 1899.
[4] *Herodots zweites Buch.*, Berlin, 1890.   [5] *Herodotus I–III*, 1883.
[6] In *Authority and Archaeology*, ed. D. G. Hogarth, London, 1899.
[7] *La durée et l'étendue du voyage d'Hérodote en Egypte*, 1910; *Hérodote et la religion d'Egypte*, 1910.
[8] *Herodot in Aegypten*, 1919.
[9] *Die Glaubwürdigkeit von Herodot's Beschreibung von Aegypten*, 1921, 1926[2]; E.T. by A. M. Blackman, Oxford, 1927.

studies of warfare are by Admiral Sir Reginald Custance, *War at Sea*[1] and Sir Frederick Maurice on 'Marathon'[2] and on 'The Army of Xerxes'.[3]

From a predominantly literary standpoint, and with a more favourable estimate of the good faith, intelligence, and originality of Herodotus, R. W. Macan in his edition of Books IV, V, VI (1895) and Books VII, VIII, IX (1908)—planned to follow that of Sayce for Books I, II, III (1883)—regarded the last three books as the earliest and previous to the travels (the extent of which Macan thought had been exaggerated); the earlier books as composed at various times (i, ii, iii. 1–119 before the visit to Thurii, iii. 120–v. 76 in the West); and the whole work as enlarged, annotated, and edited at Athens in the first years of the Peloponnesian War. For the priority of vii–viii–ix he relied on ix. 75 (cf. vi. 92, Sophanes); vii. 163 (cf. vi. 23–24, Scythes and Cadmus of Cos); viii. 104 (cf. i. 175, the priestess of Pedasa); vii. 133 (cf. vi. 48, the Persian heralds at Athens and Sparta); viii. 137–9 (cf. v. 22, Macedonian pedigree); on the lack of reference in vii to the Aeginetan War; and on the notices of peoples and tribes in Xerxes' army in i–iv. He laid stress on the pause between iii and iv, as though the original arrangement had been in three sections, i–iii, iv–vi, vii–ix. He recognized the great variety of Herodotus' sources, the wide differences in standpoints and historical value—especially in relation to controversial personalities like Cleomenes, Demaratus, and Miltiades—and the difficulty of distinguishing oral from written information. He stressed the wide range of reading as well as of inquiry and observation, in spite of the devastation of older books by the wars; and he emphasized Herodotus' mastery of his materials, and permeation of them by his own outlook and thought. The influence of Macan is ubiquitous in the useful commentary of W. W. How and J. Wells.[4]

It was a fresh turning-point, of great significance, when F. Jacoby[5] made a fresh examination of all the sources and of the

---

[1] 1925.   [2] *J.H.S.* lii (1932), 13.   [3] *J.H.S.* l (1930), 210.
[4] 2 vols. 1912; 2nd ed. 1928.   [5] In Pauly–Wissowa, *Real-Enc.*, Suppl. ii. 1913.

critical literature. He rejected many of the reconstructions of Bauer and Macan, and in particular showed that Books V–IX were composed later than I–IV. The threefold grouping of the books does not accord with the subject-matter; the main pause is after v. 27 when the northern adventure of Darius has won for Persia, in Macedon, a land-frontier with a Greek state. Herodotus began as a traveller, with an interest in ethnography. His regional *logoi* were composed separately, perhaps as the foundation of lectures in Old Greece, where he continued to collect information about the leading states, and learned much from Delphi, especially about Lydia. His visit to Athens, later than the travels and the *logoi*, gave him new acquaintances and that historical outlook which inspired the eventual *Histories*, into which his *logoi*, or sections of them, were incorporated. After his migration to Thurii there were no western travels or inquiries; but the book was not completed till the early years of the Peloponnesian War. Jacoby did not think that Herodotus returned to Athens, and regarded the final episode as unrevised.

What is here found to be original and characteristic in Herodotus is the combination of wide travels and regional sources with a deliberately historical account of the Persian Wars and their causes. The composition is inspired by epic, but the multifarious material compelled an original treatment by digressions.

Side by side with the epic technique noted by Jacoby, the influence of Attic tragedy on Herodotus' art was studied independently by Myres, 'Herodotus the Tragedian',[1] and attributed to the sojourn in Athens; and later by H. Fohl.[2] Another literary aspect is illustrated by the speeches, in E. Schulz, *Die Reden im Herodot*, and A. Deffner, *Die Rede bei Herodot und ihre Weiterbildung bei Thukydides*, both in 1933. But Herodotus' book was published before the visit of Gorgias of Leontini which introduced Sicilian rhetoric to Athens.

Jacoby's close analysis of text and sources closed a period of

[1] *Mackay Miscellany*, Liverpool (1914), 88.
[2] *Tragische Kunst bei Herodotus*, Rostock, 1932.

criticism; but his theory of disconnected *logoi* was challenged by G. de Sanctis,[1] who propounded an original *Persica*, not a world-history, amplified with separate studies of peoples encountered by the Persians. The Lydian story was expanded by the tragedy of Croesus. The Assyrian *logoi* were written for Book III, but transferred to Book I and then omitted. The Persian story preceded the Lydian, and was linked with the *Prologue* and the *Epilogue*. Later[2] de Sanctis presented the *logos* of Croesus (following Regenbogen and Hellmann below) as an allegory of divine retribution, independent of either Greek or Persian history.

The next generation turned to interpretation. O. Regenbogen[3] emphasized the political interests of Herodotus; E. Howald[4] his human interests and Ionian background; F. Focke[5] his Athenian predilections and interest in the unusual; he was not looking for connexions but for divine interventions. H. Bischof[6] stresses his belief in free will and responsibility.

On the other hand, F. Hellmann[7] regards Herodotus as maintaining by historical instances a belief in divine predestination and the 'cycle of human affairs'; setting out to understand the book as a whole, and discover the writer's outlook. What is fundamental is his view of fate. To this the story of Croesus is introductory, closely connected with the *Preface* and the search for causes. Epic and tragic reference of all human action to the will of God is combined with Ionian concentration on discovering what is knowable. This gives the book its form and unity, neither political nor military but a demonstration of the 'cycle'. Herodotus is mainly interested in *how* things happen. Within apparent confusion, there is plan and balance. Intervention of divine order in human affairs is unpredictable, but resembles the order of nature. Yet there can be warnings. Stress is on the failure of human reckonings, and retribution for aggressors. When Croesus

---

[1] 'La composizione della storia di Erodoto', *Riv. fil. ital.* liv (1926), 289.
[2] 'Il logos di Creso', *Riv. fil. ital.* lxiv (1936), 1–14.
[3] Herodotus in seinem Werke', *Die Antike*, 1930.   [4] *Hermes*, lviii.
[5] 'Herodotus als Historiker', *Tübinger Beiträge*, 1927.
[6] *Die Warner bei Herodotus*, Marburg (Diss.), 1932.
[7] 'Der Kroisos "Logos" ', *N. Phil. Unters.* ix, Berlin, 1934.

realizes that the Persians too have a destiny, he goes beyond Solon, to recognize that the divine order is not malevolent, but providential. To reveal this order is 'history'. Hellmann, however, does not discuss passages where Herodotus puts responsibility on human actors, only noting objections to Bischof's contention that in Herodotus 'man is free'. This treatment is typical of much recent German work.

Whereas Jacoby distinguishes between an earlier ethnographical and a later historical phase in Herodotus' development, M. Pohlenz[1] contends that the 'great design' set out in the *Preface* (i. 1) was present in Herodotus' mind throughout, but that he was distracted by his wider human interests, so that 'history' and *logoi* took shape concurrently, and the causes of events are narrated episodically after the events themselves (vi. 51, 77–83; vii. 204; viii. 131); even the longest digression, on Egypt, follows the announcement of Cambyses' invasion. This was his conscious method, if not always his intention (iv. 70, vii. 171) and is a legacy from the Epic (e.g. *Odyssey* vi. 4–12). Thus the history of Cyrus follows the conquest of Lydia : 'my story goes on to inquire who Cyrus was . . .' (i. 95).

This larger view of Herodotus' outlook and purpose supplies a reason for his travels, or at least for the use he made of them; it explains the persistent search for the 'reason why?', not only in history, but in nature: to account for Egypt and the Egyptians, one must go back beyond the Pyramids and Menes, to the silted sea-gulf which is the 'gift of the Nile', and the climate which brings about the inundation. It is compatible with critical conclusions as to the order of travels and compositions; but presumes also revision, and especially cross-references, over a long period. And in criticism it marks a return from analysis of the form, and the order of composition, to deeper appreciation of purpose and artistic achievement. In this direction there is indeed still much to be done. But the present stage, and immediate prospects of the study of Herodotus, must take account of the course of inquiry during more than a century, and of the main results, as well as

[1] *Herodot, der erste Geschichtsschreiber des Abendlandes*, Berlin, 1937.

the mistakes and failures, of which only an outline has been attempted here.

At what stage in his career Herodotus conceived the project of a history of the struggle between East and West and of its causes is thus disputed. Jacoby thought that he began as a geographer and student of peoples and customs, and was inspired by his experiences in Athens to the larger enterprise, in view of the part played in it by the Athenians. Pohlenz believed that he had the design implicit throughout. J. Enoch Powell argues that Books I–IV[1]—except for a few digressions—were composed as a self-contained 'Persian History' before Herodotus went to Thurii; that the 'Persian Wars' in Books V–IX were written (and perhaps published) shortly before the Peloponnesian War, to refute current misinterpretation of Athenian policy and history, and that Books I–IV were then remodelled and prefixed as an historical introduction to the Eastern Question, including the sections on Athens, Sparta, and Samos, but omitting the 'Assyrian story', and presenting Croesus as responsible historically for the clash between Persia and Greece. This reconstruction he supports by many cross-references and inferences from the order of the travels; and especially by the disparaging reference to Persian informants (i. 1, 4, 5) which was to have prepared for a 'true story' not of Lydia but of Persia, such as stands now at i. 95, with a similar reflection on Persian court-chroniclers. Powell thinks that Athenian influences began early, before the Scythian journey and a second visit to Egypt; that the first draft of the 'Persian History' was published before the migration to Thurii; and that the revision after return to Athens about 432 B.C. was hardly finished when Herodotus died of the plague. Thus both the 'Persian History' and the 'Persian Wars' would mark stages in the advance from Ionian local chronicle to a mature conception of history. All this reverts to a kind of analytical speculation to which Jacoby seemed to have put an end.

In the introduction to his translation of Herodotus[2] Powell concedes that the 'Persian Wars' had taken shape before the

[1] *The History of Herodotus*, Cambridge, 1939.　　　[2] Oxford, 1949.

return to Athens, that only a few 'Athenian' passages were then added, and that the whole work was never finally revised.

In retrospect, then, modern criticism of Herodotus may be summarized as follows. Two generations ago men argued, from omissions and mistakes, that he had compiled his information from gossip and from other travellers. His habitual silence about the sources of his knowledge was imputed to deliberate plagiarism. It was inferred, from errors, that he had not visited the places or seen the objects that he describes. This was perhaps an inevitable phase of critical study, and certainly not peculiar to critics of Herodotus. It challenged more careful examination of the book itself, of the circumstances of its production, and of the personality of the writer, revealed in it unawares; and it has been followed by a general reversion towards respect for the honesty as well as the industry of Herodotus, and recognition of his difficulties; above all, by methodical distinction between the materials collected from sources good and bad, careless and prejudiced, and his employment of them to illustrate his own historical studies. His information is seen now to be such as an intelligent and observant man, of his age and upbringing, might reasonably accept, on eyewitness and hearsay, as true. The presentation of it all, as the record and interpretation of great events, is his own.

III

THE WORLD OF HERODOTUS

A MODERN author—still more, a modern editor of 'literary remains'—has all the facilities of modern typography to distinguish footnotes from text, appendixes from chapters, and chapters from one another. Since printed copies are mechanically uniform, a page-reference connects one passage accurately with another; paragraphs and sub-titles clarify the general arrangement. Verbal descriptions of sites and monuments are 'illustrated', and may be replaced, by pictures; geographical passages by diagrams and maps as mechanically accurate as the letterpress.

In all these matters an ancient writer was at the mercy of the scribe. When Herodotus wishes to explain the size, shape, and geographical relations of the continents he has to dictate 'what each of them is like, *to draw*' (iv. 36), and the reader has to follow his 'measurement' (iv. 99); a river may have to flow 'upwards' (i. 72). Even when there had been an engraved map, it had to be dictated in the same way (v. 49, 52–54). The later *codex*-form of book, with its pile of flat pages, mitigated these difficulties; but it is certain, from the displacement of the Pyramid Kings (ii. 124–37: see p. 4), that the archetype of our text was on rolls.

It was difficult to record buildings and works of art without illustrations. The offerings of Croesus at Delphi (i. 50) lay 'in the Corinthian treasury', at Thebes in the temple of Apollo; if you want details, go and see them. At Athens the Boeotian–Chalcidian trophy was on the Acropolis 'in front of the westward hall' (v. 77). A very complicated building, the Egyptian Labyrinth, was narrated as a personally conducted visit (ii. 148) when 'we went through and saw' the painted courts and corridors (p. 156).[1]

Herodotus the Geographer

To describe places and countries was harder still. Ancient 'geometry' was literally land-measurement, by rectangles with

---

[1] Myres, *Liverpool Annals*, iii. 134.

co-ordinate sides. Even in Babylonia angular measurements were confined to the skies; in the *Meno* Socrates uses a triangle only to bisect or to double a square.[1]

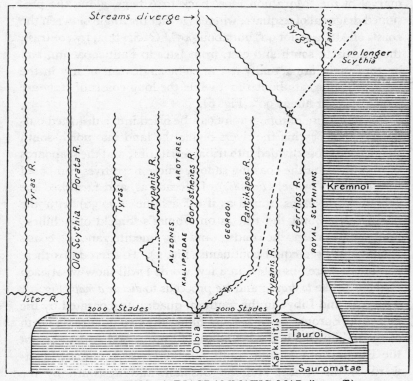

FIG. I. SCYTHIA: A DIAGRAMMATIC MAP (iv. 99 ff.)

The dotted line represents the route indented in iv. 16–20, as follows: Olbia [*three days*]–Pantikapes ford–[*fourteen days*: no Hypacris ford]–Gerrhos ford–[days not given]–Tanais ford–thence beyond 'no longer Scythia' (iv. 21 ff.).

Geographical Journal, viii (1896), 607.

The '*Scythian Square*' is an example (iv. 100: Fig. 1). Scythia fills the space between two pairs of parallels, in latitude and in longitude; eastward and southward are similar squares of sea; and as squares on the sides of the same square are equal, Lake

[1] Myres, 'On the Maps used by Herodotus', *Geographical Journal*, vi (Dec. 1896), 606–31.

Maeotis is equal in area to the Euxine, and there were presumably other such compartments beyond. This 'grid' covers the map: Attica and South Italy are similar squares. Hence the marvel of the 'Marathon race' back to Athens, along the presumed diagonal of a square, whereas in fact the angle between the coasts of Attica is not 90° but about 45°.[1] Of Scythia, by contrast, the sea coasts, south and east, from Ister to Panticapaeum, and on to Tanais, are actually not at right angles but nearly in the same direction, at about 180°; while the long coasts of Italy are like Attica, at about 90° (Fig. 6).

But much useful topography can be fitted into a distorted outline. Within Scythia the rivers divide the land into north–south strips, each cross-divided into tribal territories; and the seaboards were plotted by the coasting sailors, whose narratives composed the 'Round Voyage' (*Periodos*) of Hecataeus, and furnished the Ionian world-maps 'round as if off a lathe' (iv. 36) with the ocean river round the rim as on Homer's 'Shield of Achilles', and 'our sea' in the midst, and its 'mediterranean' coasts frontaging three equal continents (Fig. 2). To Herodotus these continents were obsolete: 'in a few words I will show what each of them is like *to draw*'; and he proceeds to *dictate a map* (Fig. 7), with Asia and Libya in the southern quadrants separated by the Nile, and Europe 'twice as long' filling the two quadrants north of them. This made the boundary of Europe and Asia to be not the Tanais, from north to south, but the Phasis,[2] continued eastward by the Araxes and the Caspian, and westward by the Pontus, Propontis, and Hellespont (Fig. 3).

The *Map of Aristagoras* was a bronze plate engraved with 'all the sea and all the rivers' (v. 49). From Miletus or Ephesus, by Sardis, to Susa, the 'Royal Road' was axial, as on an eighteenth-century road-book; up the middle of Asia Minor—an obvious rectangle (iv. 38–39) between a square Pontus, as in the Scythian map, and a square Levant, recognizable because 'it has Cyprus in it', whereas Pontus is islandless—up a river, the Maeander,

[1] Myres, 'The Ancient Shape of Attica', *Greece and Rome*, xii (1943), 33–42.
[2] Aeschylus, *Prom. Sol.* fr. 191, Murray.

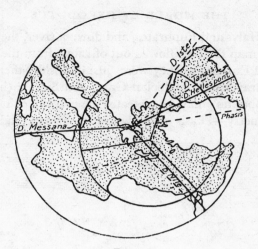

FIG. 2.

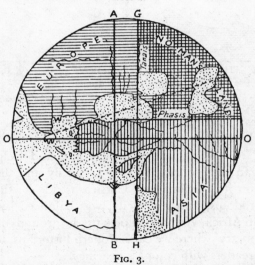

FIG. 3.

FIGS. 2, 3. EMPIRICAL BASIS OF THREE EQUAL CONTINENTS

Small circle: Primitive Aegean geography with Delos (probably) central: the angles
  subtended by the three continents were actually 120° each.
Dotted line: the same with Crete (Phaestus) central.
Large circle: Hellenic geography with Delphi as centre.
Dotted lines: Delos–Ister; Tanais; Hellespont: early stages of the Phasis–Tanais
  controversy.
Shaded map: later stage of the Phasis–Tanais controversy: the 'no-man's land' or
  fourth quadrant assigned by Hecataeus to his *wide* Asia, by Herodotus to his *long*
  Europe.   *Geographical Journal*, viii (1896), 626–7.

across the Halys and Euphrates, and down a river, the Choaspes. On such a map the Nile flowed out of Libya from the south, the Ister out of Europe; as they were 'just opposite', their common longitude traversed the Cilician Gates and Sinope (ii. 34), and similar 'opposites' may be detected elsewhere, enhancing this axial symmetry—Phasis and Pyramus; Sigean and Triopian

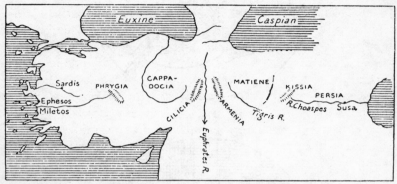

FIG. 4. THE MAP OF ARISTAGORAS 501 B.C. (v. 49 ff.)
An earlier edition of the 'Ionian' map.

Geographical Journal, vi (1896), 611.

promontories; Hermus and Maeander (Figs. 4, 5). Produced westward, this 'Ionian' axis probably followed the later 'line of Eudoxus'[1] from Sunium by the Isthmus and Delphi to the Acroceraunian ridge north of Corcyra: Sicily and the Balearic Islands lay on it; Sardinia and Corsica astride it: the 'square' Italy of Herodotus, north of Sicily, was balanced by a square Carthaginian Africa. We have to pick up the grounds of this 'doctrine of symmetry' where we can. Modern historians, too, do not worry their readers with compass-bearings.

Within Asia Minor, on the meridian or longitude-line of Sinope, the Halys, descending from Armenia (i. 72), turned 'upwards'—for rivers cartographically were arms of the sea (cf. iv. 34, Phasis and Araxes); in ii. 34 the distance is wrongly given as from Sinope to the Cilician Sea. This was the 'neck of the whole

[1] Strabo 391.

country', five days' march in width, by which Alyattes attacked Cyaxares in May 585 B.C., as the course of the eclipse shows, whereas Cyrus came through Cappadocia and crossed the Halys by the bridge, where the river had already turned north by Pteria, 'opposite' to Sinope, i.e. on the same meridian (i. 76). When Herodotus says 'upward' here he means 'northward' on his map, adding that it flowed towards the north wind.[1]

The Alternative Map. But there was another version of the world map (iv. 36–44; Fig. 7, 8) which Herodotus uses without perceiving its discrepancy with the 'Ionian'. As it is primarily a map of the Empire of Darius, we may call it the 'Persian' map, and perhaps attribute it to Scylax of Caryanda, who navigated the 'Indian river' and returned by the Red Sea. The instructions for 'drawing' the continents are precise (iv. 37). Set four nations—Persians, Medes, Saspiri, Colchians—in column from south to north, from sea to sea. From this meridian or prime longitude two promontories project westward embracing the 'Midland' Sea. The northern, Asia Minor—no longer axial as in the 'Ionian' map, for the axis bisects the Levant, with Cyprus central, and then Crete—begins at the Phasis; its north coast 'is extended along' Pontus and Hellespont to Sigeum, and its south coast from the Myriandic Gulf, between Cilicia and Syria, to the Triopian Cape. It contains thirty nations. The 'other promontory' extends along the 'Red Sea'—the southern ocean—from Persia to the Isthmus; only ending there 'conventionally' because Darius had cut his canal from the Nile; in nature, Libya is 'in this other promontory'. Its north coast lies from the Isthmus to the root of the first promontory. This is a remarkable distortion of rectangular Arabia—containing also Babylonia and Syria, three nations only—slewed round from a south-easterly to a westerly axis, enclosing the Levant with its central island Cyprus, bringing the Nile-mouth 'opposite' to Rhodes and the Hellespont instead of the Cilician Gates and Sinope, and destroying its symmetry with the Ister. The Arabian Gulf, our 'Red Sea', now lay north

[1] An Oxford historian wrote that in Balkan lands 'frontiers are more often horizontal than vertical'.

and south, parallel with the lower course of the Nile, and the
Palestine–Syrian coast lay east and west, a perversion easily
overlooked because all its harbours open north, and the north

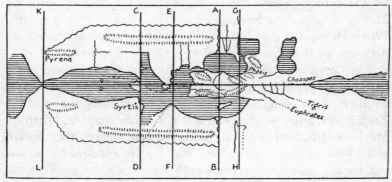

FIG. 5. THE 'IONIAN' MAP, RECONSTRUCTED
With the principal meridians drawn straight north and south.

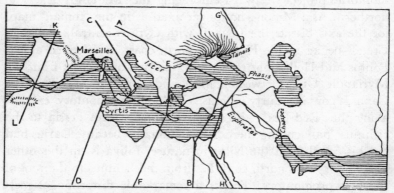

FIG. 6. THE 'IONIAN' MAP, ON MERCATOR'S PROJECTION
With the principal meridians bent at junction of sections.

Geographical Journal, viii (1896), 612.

wind of the Aegean sailing-season swerves so as to blow on-shore
east of the Isthmus. But we know how deep-seated was this
presentation of the Levant, from the interest taken by geographers in comparing the solar meridians of Alexandria and
Rhodes—sea-reckoning by water-clocks, confronted with the

military 'foot-sloggers' (*bématistai*) let loose by Alexander along the land-routes. West of Rhodes we lose sight of this 'Persian' map: it probably merged in the other. On the 'Persian' map the

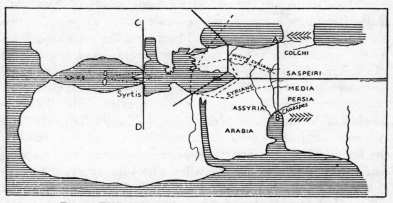

FIG. 7. THE 'PERSIAN' MAP, RECONSTRUCTED
With the principal meridians drawn straight north and south.

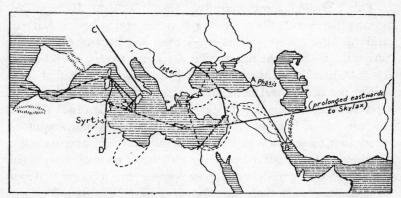

FIG. 8. THE 'PERSIAN' MAP, ON MERCATOR'S PROJECTION
With the principal meridians bent at junctions of sections.

Royal Road approached Susa from the north—probably its actual curvature was summed up in a right angle at the Euphrates. Beyond this 'Nearer East', Asia extended eastward 'ever so far'. Scylax had descended 'an Indian river'—not necessarily the

Indus: probably it was the Ganges, for its crocodiles, being sacred, were comparable with those of the Nile. Sailing down it eastward to the eastern sea, he had returned to the Isthmus in the thirtieth month, justifying the comparison of Asia with Africa 'in other respects' (iv. 44) since Africa too was circumnavigated in the third season, and India and Ceylon extend south of the equator. There was much more, unexplored, beyond the 'Indian river', but not enough to outflank Europe, which stretched from west to east over all, though not so wide from inner to outer sea as the two southern continents. The original threefold dissection of Mediterranean coastlands, by Hellespont, Nile, and Western Strait, had been modified, when Pontus was explored, by the discovery of an outer Bosporus—the Cimmerian—and of the Tanais beyond it; and this was the boundary for Hecataeus—whereas Aeschylus,[1] like Herodotus, set the limit of Europe at the Phasis. His devious route for Io is an attempt to make her cross both 'Oxfords' in the same journey.[2]

The *Hyperborean controversy* (iv. 32–36) reflects discrepancies among travellers' tales of the north. Some, going by the Adriatic and the Alpine passes—then easier than ever because the climate was milder—brought names like *Alpis* and *Carpis*, mistaken for Danubian streams: they reported Europe not very bróad, with sea to the north, and land 'overnorth' beyond that—the Baltic and Sweden. Others, by Pontic ports and Scythian rivers, found the air full of 'feathers' and 'bees'—snowflakes or mosquitoes, according to season—and the land interminable and shoreless, for they travelled east of the Baltic and found no northern sea (iii. 115). Herodotus, in default of observations, has recourse to design and symmetry: if there are Hyperboreans there should also be Hypernotians 'farthest south'; *and there are not.*

The famous *Circumnavigation of Africa* (iv. 42–43) is most credible where Herodotus doubts it. For a west-about journey, the monsoon, the southern trade-winds, and the Benguela and Guinea currents are alike favourable: the climates permit a

---

[1] *Prom. Sol.* fr. 191.
[2] Myres, *Classical Review*, lx (1946), 2.

wheat-crop; and the apparent reversal of the course of the sun is what disconcerts all new-comers in South Africa—rising on your right, as you face midday, and setting on your left after going round by the north. If Scylax circumnavigated Asia from the Ganges, the same observation would confirm the 'close resemblance' of its southern promontory to Africa. On the west coast, the misfortunes of Sataspes (iv. 43) are sufficiently explained by the south-east trade-wind and the northward Benguela current inshore.

Nile and Ister. The symmetrical comparison of the rivers reveals ignorance of the river-systems of Europe and Africa alike. The eastward-flowing river with crocodiles beyond Sahara may well have been the middle Niger, and the Nile source between two rocks—a genuine Egyptian belief—may be faint hearsay of the Ripon Falls, with the Victoria Lake as 'ocean' beyond. It was at all events confirmation of the tricontinental scheme—though Herodotus rejects it—if the Nile did, after all, rise in the ocean[1] (ii. 21).

In Europe the Ister rises at 'Pyrene'—probably the Pyrenees, as counterpart of Atlas—and there is no knowledge of the Rhône, or even of the Eridanus (Po) which some travellers had confused with the northward-flowing Rhine; though he recognizes the name *Eridanos* as Greek, and the stream of this name as the source of amber, actually transalpine (iii. 115). All that he denies is a *north*-flowing Eridanus. Strabo goes much farther (215). The name recurs in the Rhône, the Apennine 'Reno', and elsewhere. Similarly Herodotus does not deny that Cassiterides exist; only that the sources of tin are islands (iii. 115).

The Nile Valley. To the geography of Egypt Herodotus gives especial attention. That it was the 'gift of the Nile' in its alluvial lower course was no new discovery, but the contrast of this and of the rocky plateau through which the river breaks at Elephantine (Assuan) (ii. 25) with the Ethiopian country (Nubia) round Meroe beyond were worth study in connexion with Cambyses'

---

[1] For this whole question see G. A. Wainwright, *Sudan Notes and Records*, xxviii (1947), 11 ff.; *J.H.S.* xlvii. 42.

expedition; and a newer southern source and watershed are
rejected in favour of the long equatorial stream inferred from
symmetry with the Ister (ii. 34), and supported by the Nasa-
monian travellers beyond the Sahara (ii. 32, 33).

The discussion of the Nile flood throws some light on the physical geography of Herodotus (ii. 24–27). The normal sun's course,
for him, is equatorial, along the earth's east–west axis. But cold
north winds blow the sun out of its course—more in winter than
in summer—so that inland Libya has always summer heat, while
Europe has summer rains. Moisture evaporated thus by sun's
heat is scattered by winds—the heaviest Mediterranean rains are
cyclonic, the 'black Auster' of the Romans. Of the equatorial
rains of Abyssinia and Sudan, Herodotus knows nothing.

The deposition of Nile-silt, he observes, is continuous (ii. 10–12)
and can be perceived off-shore. Had he himself reached Egypt
from oversea? It is only a matter of time for the Nile-mouths to
be blocked, so that the river overflows—along the canal of Necho
and Darius—and creates a second Egypt in the Red Sea. Twenty
thousand years would suffice for this, and geological time must be
longer than that, for there are sea-shells and efflorescent salt on
the hills through which the present Nile valley has been cut and
alluviated; and the depth of the alluvium is increasing (ii. 14),
without geological changes (ii. 142), though the sun has 're-
versed its course' four times. Geological time was indeed of
enormous length for Herodotus, and human history was com-
mensurate, though briefer: 17,000 years since the Egyptian
Heracles made the eight older gods to be twelve (ii. 43); 15,000
from Egyptian Pan to Amasis (ii. 145); 11,340 from the first
known King to the 'priest of Hephaestus' (ii. 142). Outside
Egypt, ancient dates are much lower; 'Golden Ages' and historical cycles are mere incidents; Tyre is 2,300 years old (ii. 44);
Dionysus, son of Semele, was born 1,600 years ago; Cadmus
therefore about 2,000; Heracles, son of Amphitryon, 900; Pan,
son of Penelope, 800; the Trojan War therefore about 830 (or
1280 B.C.). These lower dates for Greek gods show when their
names became known and worshipped; in Thasos, five genera-

tions before the birth of Amphitryon's son. The Greeks had already gods without names, nature-powers who 'set everything in order' as the name *theos* seemed to imply (ii. 52) : on the other hand, Egypt knew neither Poseidon nor the Dioscuri (ii. 43). But Minos and any earlier sea-kings are excluded from the 'human generation' within which Polycrates was the first to 'rule the waves' (iii. 122): the Trojan War apparently opening the new era, while the birth of Pan completes the *Theogonia* (ii. 145), though Herodotus himself doubts his godhead. Evidently there was controversy, and a horned and goat-footed god could hardly be Olympian. It is to this 'human generation' with its recurrent pattern of pride and fall, under the rule of *moira* (p. 48), that Herodotus limits his search for historical 'causes' (i. 5) ; and his Persian friends, too, made the Trojan War the 'beginning of enmity'. His proposed review of 'all cities of men' echoes the experience of Odysseus. These geographical parables set the stage for successive encounters between the Persians and other peoples.

Anthropology has the same limits, and Herodotus is in the same sense 'father of anthropology' as he is 'father of history'. Between Homer and Herodotus Greek reason had come into the world. In Ionia Anaximander, and Archelaus a little later, were replacing the folk-lore of Homer and Hesiod, which derived early man from trees and rocks—or from ants, as in Aegina[1]—by evolutionary observations on larval marine forms, or animal embryos, unhindered by religious scruples.[2] Man has become the measure of all things; and things are 'worth recording' according as they amplify existing knowledge or guide attempts to classify and interpret it. In this high meaning of the word, all Greek thought and record was utilitarian.

In the collection of facts about *Man*, and in the interpretation of them, Herodotus is the only 'pre-Socratic' writer who is preserved in full. And for commentary, apart from the Tragedians and Pindar, there are only fragments and excerpts until the days

---

[1] Hesiod, fr. 76 (Rzach).

[2] Plutarch, *Mor.* 908 d; Eusebius, *Praep. Ev.* i. 8; Hippolytus, *Refut. Haeres.* i. 9.

of Hippocrates. Hesiod presents us already with a scheme of archaeology, in which the Ages of gold, silver, and bronze, classified by their respective artefacts, are succeeded first by an Age of Heroes—an anomaly, partly of Homeric authority, partly tradition of the Sea-Raids and the Minoan débâcle—and then by the present Age of Iron. The further observation that primitive man was a forester, sprung from oak or crag, who lived not on grain but on nuts, was easy among Balkan peoples, and not far beyond the common folk-lore about human origins.

But in space, as in time, there were wide limits to the 'human generation', beyond which lay heroes and gods (iii. 122). 'Farthest north' were (perhaps) Hyperboreans;[1] farthest south, Aethiopians[2] beyond Egypt[3] and Libya; farthest east, and west, more Aethiopians, for here the Sun rested his horses[4] and blazed at ground-level. Beyond ethnological Man are the Amazons,[5] monstrous Arimaspi (iii. 116; iv. 27), and other monsters. Some of their diversities were climatic, sun-heat blackening faces (vii. 70) and hardening skulls (iii. 12), but for an explicit doctrine of inheritance and variation we must wait till Hippocrates.[6] Herodotus was saved by his Egyptian studies from reliance on the short Greek pedigrees (ii. 143); moreover, 'anything could happen if you gave it long enough': the Sigynnae on the Danube might be 'colonists of the Medes' (v. 9). So too, for Aeschylus, the great continental peoples are distinguished by their dress, Persian or Greek:[7] the Danaids are recognized by their costume[8] like the Sigynnae, and only secondarily by their complexion.

Herodotus makes significant advances. The Athenian's definition of nationality (viii. 144) rests on blood-kinship, speech, cults and rituals, and mode of life, in that order. To this, modern ethnology adds only that religion is a peculiarly refined test for community of culture. As a field-observer, Herodotus classifies similarly: the Argippaei (iv. 23) are (1) bald, snub-nosed, and bearded; they (2) speak a distinct language; (3) wear Scythian

[1] Aeschylus, fr. 197.　　　[2] Aeschylus, *Suppl.* 286; *P.V.* 808.
[3] Fr. 300.　　　[4] Fr. 192.　　　[5] *Suppl.* 287; *P.V.* 723.
[6] *Air, Water, and Places*, 24.　　[7] *Suppl.* 234–44.　　[8] *Suppl.* 287.

clothing; (4) live, unlike Scythians, on tree fruit—each character introduced by 'but' as a species of the previous genus. The plum-tree itself, on which they live, is defined by similar specification, like the hippopotamus and the crocodile. His account of the Amazons (iv. 110, 112–15, 117) anticipates the more methodical treatment of Hippocrates;[1] but his Colchians are related to the Egyptians not by skin—or hair—colour, but by customs (ii. 104–5). The beardlessness among the Scythians at Ascalon (i. 105), though ascribed to divine wrath, had its counterpart among the peoples of Scythia: for its significance we have again to wait for Hippocrates:[2] 'displaced persons', like the Sigynnae, were no rarity in the ancient world.

But whatever their origin, each regional variety of man had its own process of growth (*physis*), as well as its modes of behaviour (*nomoi*) conforming to its habitat—again a Hippocratic doctrine. Knowledge of the *physis* and *nomoi* of the Egyptians refutes Greek fables about their behaviour (ii. 45) and explains their thick skulls (iii. 12). It is as 'natural' for Callatian Indians to eat dead parents as for Greeks to cremate them: as Pindar said, 'custom is king of all' (iii. 38); Cambyses was mad to deride it. But custom was not immutable. The Pelasgians in prehistoric Attica somehow 'relearned their language' (i. 57) while they were 'turning into Hellenes'. It was left to Thucydides[3] to put the problem one stage farther back, by deriving the Greeks from the intercourse between Pelasgian aborigines and a specific minority of 'sons of Hellen' from elsewhere. Breed, however, counted for much. In the story of Pytheus (vii. 181) the implied contrast is between the 'gadgets' of Persian surgery and the physical fit-ness of a Greek, though 'mangled to butcher's meat'.

It is in accordance with this anthropological theory that Hero-dotus devotes so much attention to food supply and to marriage customs. It is hardly by chance that each of the strange customs which he mentions happens to be typical of a widespread type of observance, outside patriarchal society. Aeschylus was asking in

[1] *De Aëre*, 17, § 42.
[2] *On the Sacred Disease*, ed. Kuhn, p. 561.   [3] i. 3.

the *Eumenides* whether a man was nearer akin to his father or to his mother. The *Andromache* and the *Medea* of Euripides present already another point of view, and in the *Republic* of Plato the equality of the sexes is proclaimed: social organization, like all else, has become an adaptation of natural means to cultural ends.

NATURE, GODS, AND MEN

Herodotus seldom affirms his own beliefs. Often he makes general statements either 'in character'—as Solon or Croesus— or in the course of his story, with the risk that they may be accepted as his own; and the probability that he intends them so is increased by what he affirms expressly and personally.

While he asserts that 'all men have equal knowledge' about the gods (ii. 3), he records different opinions, and states his own (ii. 146). Great misdeeds bring great punishments from the gods (ii. 120)—the earthquake at Potidaea (viii. 129), the vengeance of Talthybius after two generations (vii. 137), the storm which reduced the Persian fleet towards equality with the Greek (viii. 13), Demeter defending her sanctuary at Plataea (ix. 65; cf. 101 at Mycale), and other examples. The gods send warnings of evil to come (vi. 27); it was 'not unlikely' that Delos was shaken at a crisis (vi. 98). He cannot dispute oracles, or allow others to do so (viii. 77), though oracles may be false, or perverted (ix. 43), or misunderstood.

In general, he agrees with Pindar that 'custom is king of all' (iii. 38); but what the customs are which govern events can only be ascertained by observation and comparison; this is ἱστορίη ('research'), to record and preserve events, and to discern their causes (i. 1). The example of Croesus shows that a man may 'initiate wrongdoing' (i. 5) and be responsible for his acts, in great things or in small; Aristagoras *ought not* to have told the truth' if he wished to convince Cleomenes (v. 50). There is a 'cycle in human affairs' (i. 207) and 'well-being never stays in one place' (i. 5).

These examples are sufficient to exhibit the principles and beliefs of Herodotus, which are implicit in his 'histories'. Like all the earlier Greek thinkers, he has his own vocabulary, derived from common speech. From these leading terms his notions about the world, the gods, and the place of men in nature have to be derived. They are not always consistent: in particular he seems to have combined beliefs in an immutable order of nature and human fate, and in human initiative and responsibility; a moral order as well as a physical nature. That the world is intelligible, admitting analysis by human reason, and synthesis by human imagination, was no discovery of Herodotus. But the background of early Greek thought, against which he should be displayed, is fragmentary, like his own statements.

In all periods of advancing knowledge each pioneer has his own set of terms, drawn from everyday speech, and contributed to a standard idiom. In a popular and general writer like Herodotus, words which become technical in Heracleitus and Anaxagoras are still used more freely, and more nearly in their primary sense.

We see, therefore, most clearly where Herodotus stands— what his philosophy, his *creed*, is—if we study his usage of a few cardinal terms: φύσις, τύχη, μοῖρα, τίσις, τὸ θεῖον, δίκη, ἀρχή, and above all αἰτίη—'the reason why they fought with one another' (i. 1).

Of external nature he has not much to say, except to describe curiosities. It is built on a plan, with extremes of climate, and rarer products afar off (iii. 106); but 'God's own country' is in Greece, and especially in Ionia (i. 142). He is sceptical about the 'Ocean River' of the geographers (iv. 36; cf. ii. 21), and his notions of symmetry between north and south (ii. 33) are compatible with extension eastwards 'ever so far' (iv. 20). The Gorge of Tempe is 'the work of an earthquake' (vii. 129), but if anyone believes that Poseidon shakes the earth, here is a piece of his work. Rain 'comes from God' in its season (iii. 117), but the rains which cause the Nile-flood are drawn up by the sun (ii. 24) which is itself a god and the 'cause' of this (ii. 24, 26).

Physis in Herodotus retains its original verbal sense (vii. 134). The world is in process of growth, well seen in the 'outpouring' of Egyptian silt, the 'gift of the river' (ii. 5). The characteristics of the crocodile (ii. 68), the hippopotamus (ii. 71), and the trans-Caspian plum (iv. 23) are given in the order of their appearance, like Homer's *môly*-plant;[1] and the 'growth' of wheat begins with the manure on the field (iii. 22). The Apis bull also has its specific process of growing (ii. 38; iii. 28). A great part of physics has been formulated by man's observation and reasons into *nomoi*[2] (ii. 45): it is also expressed in the *idea* (ἰδέα, specific appearance) of anything (ii. 71). All this is in full accord with the usage of the dramatists[3] and of contemporary physicists.[4]

Moira, 'fate', necessarily calls for consideration at this point. In Herodotus it is frequent, in its popular meanings: (1) a *share* of anything, like *meros* (i. 146, 204; ii. 17; iv. 145; viii. 129); (2) a part of a territory, or people, or army, and so a political 'party' (iv. 148; v. 69; vii. 157); (3) a proportional estimate of value (ii. 172); and finally (4) in four passages only, the fated end of a man, 'assigned' by the personified *Moirai*: i. 91 (Croesus); i. 121 (Cyrus); iii. 142 (Polycrates); iv. 164 (Arcesilaus 'either voluntarily or involuntarily' fulfilled his *moira*). Even a god cannot vary this (i. 91). The usage is that of the physicists and dramatists. At first sight, it is sheer mechanistic fatalism; yet personal *Moirai*, at Apollo's request, postponed Croesus' fate for three years.

At first sight also *tychê*, 'chance', looks like the direct personal negation of *moira*; a world in chaos, where things just happen, without form, and also void—the 'atoms' and 'space' of Anaxagoras, ἄτομα καὶ κενόν. Occasionally in Herodotus κατὰ τύχην is quite neutral (vi. 70; vii. 10; viii. 87); or it is disastrous (vi. 16; viii. 87); but usually τύχη is favourable (θείη, i. 126; iii. 139; iv. 8; v. 92: χρηστή, i. 119; vii. 236); and when a god offers his help (χρᾷ) it is for man to accept it (χρᾶσθαι). This is probably nearer to the primary meaning; for the stem τυχ- means 'to hit the mark';

---

[1] *Od.* x. 302.
[2] Myres, *The Political Ideas of the Greeks*, 154–60.
[3] Aeschylus, *Ag.* 633; Sophocles, *O.C.* 1295; *Ant.* 346; *O.T.* 334–5, 869–70; Euripides, *Bacchae*, 891–6.
[4] Empedocles, frr. 8 and 63; Heracleitus, fr. 1: cf. Hippocrates, *Peri Diaitas* i. 11.

in this sense τύχη is the opposite of ἁμαρτία, 'a bad shot'—the nearest word in Greek for 'sin'. When a man has done his best, within his *moira*, there is still something, like a veering wind for an archer, which makes him either 'hit' or 'miss' (i. 118, 124). Thus the best-laid plans 'gang aft a-gley' (vii. 10); yet it is no credit to the man of evil counsel, but a windfall (εὕρημα εὕρηκε) if he makes a 'hit'; his evil mind is evil still. *Tychê*, like *moira*, is some-times almost personified (i. 32; ii. 10). In Thucydides[1] redressing human impotence it is confronted with φύσις ἀναγκαία to con-strain even τὸ θεῖον.

Similarly *'coincidence'* (συμφορή, i. 32, 35; vii. 49) is primarily neutral, like its verb (i. 19; ii. 111; iii. 10; iv. 157; vi. 86; viii. 86), but the adjective σύμφερον (viii. 60) is in a good sense 'con-venient'. Like *tychê* it is beyond human control or anticipation; but it is no negation of *moira*.

Nemesis only occurs once: 'a great *nemesis* from God' fell on Croesus for his pride (i. 34). Elsewhere Herodotus uses *phthonos*. The verb is Homeric, though not the substantive; it is the corre-lative of μεγαίρειν (from μέγας) and ἄγαμαι (from ἄγαν), both meaning to 'think excessive'.[2] It is especially characteristic of 'the divine' (τὸ θεῖον πᾶν ἐὸν φθονερόν τε καὶ ταραχῶδες, i. 32). But what had originally been conceived as a moral statement (viii. 10) was coming to be the expression of a physical reaction or restoration of balance, in nature and in human affairs (i. 32–34; ii. 120; iii. 40; viii. 109). In man, however, the offence is still a state of mind, a moral not a physical derangement.

For this reaction the regular word in Herodotus is *tisis*, 'retribu-tion' (i. 13; v. 79; viii. 76) in its primary meaning, moral and judicial, linked with τιμωρίη, 'penance' (vii. 8), and ποινή, 'penalty' (iii. 14; vii. 134–6). Thus Arabian snakes kill their mothers, as Orestes did, to avenge their sire (iii. 109); Darius requites Oroetes' crime (iii. 127); and Cyrus fears retribution, if he kills Croesus (i. 86). The oracle states the rule: οὐδεὶς ἀνθρώπων ἀδικῶν τίσιν οὐκ ἀποτίσει, 'no unjust man shall fail to pay the

---

[1] v. 104 τῇ τύχῃ ἐκ τοῦ θείου.

[2] For its long history see S. Ranulf, *The Jealousy of the Gods* (Copenhagen).

penalty' (v. 56). Examples are the fate of Leotychides (vi. 72), of Cyrus (i. 214), of Cleomenes (vi. 84), and of Panionius (viii. 105–6), whose 'avengers' are plural, like those of Oroetes (iii. 128) and the *erinyes* of Aeschylus. It is not always easy to decide whether Herodotus is speaking 'in character', or recording popular opinion, or is giving his own judgement. But *phthonos* (φθόνος) seems always to occur in reported speech, and for 'retribution' not 'envy' (i. 32; iii. 40; vii. 10, 46; viii. 109). Occasionally, however, he is explicit: 'for great wrongs there are also great penances (τιμωρίαι) from the gods' (ii. 120); Troy was devastated 'after divine plan' (τοῦ δαιμονίου παρασκευάζοντος, ii. 120); and Demeter avenged Persian outrage (ix. 65).

What is it, then, that brings *tisis* and *timôria*? Do they come by *tychê* or by *moira*, or 'from the divine'? For the Arabian snakes it is 'divine providence, wise as we should expect' (iii. 108), concerning the plan of the world as we know it: there is 'design' in nature, and it is the gods, as their name was held to imply (ii. 52), who 'set all things in order' and can give preknowledge of that order to men (i. 209–10). It is τὸ θεῖον which protects 'righteousness' (τὸ δίκαιον), which is in accordance with the 'custom' or observance of that plan (cf. θεοὶ νόμῳ δικαίῳ χρώμενοι, viii. 106) and imposes penalties (ii. 210).

It is easy to dispute, when Herodotus says that 'all men know equally about the gods', whether he means 'equally much' or 'equally little'. That he believed himself to have been entrusted with knowledge which he would not divulge (ii. 47, 51) helps to explain his habitual tolerance and reserve, in face of foreign cults and beliefs, and his independent effort to clear his own mind about the nature of all gods alike, a pre-Socratic research anticipating the 'history of religions' ascribed to Posidonius, and elaborated for Roman religion by Varro, but itself anticipated by Aeschylus[1] with the same equation of *gods* with *laying down* and *ordinance*: θεοί—θέντες—θεσμοί. The relation between actual Greek gods with personal names (θεοί), the nameless gods of the Pelasgians, and an impersonal and immemorial 'Godhead' (τὸ

---

[1] *Eumenides* 391.

θεῖον), was clarified by his discovery in Egypt that the world was incomparably older than Greek belief conceived (ii. 145). Just as it took long ages to fill the Nile Gulf with silt, and would take 20,000 years more to fill the Red Sea, so there had been no god in human form in Egypt for 11,300 years. In comparison, the Greek 'golden age' and the Hesiodic 'birth of the gods' were but as yesterday. And not all Greek gods went back even to the beginning of the present cycle: hence the significance of his discussion of Pan and Heracles (ii. 46, 145–6) and his restriction of his own inquiries to the 'human generation' (iii. 123), discarding mythology and the longer genealogies, and concentrating like Odysseus on the 'cities of men' (i. 5; cf. *Od.* i. 1 ff.). With his references to the gods are to be compared his presentation of heroes—Orestes (i. 67–68), the Tyndarids (v. 75), Argos (vi. 80), and the Aeacids (viii. 83–84), and the rival cults in Sicyon (v. 67, 82–83). The line is not very clearly drawn (ii. 45); Helen at Therapne is 'the goddess' (vi. 61).

In no point is Herodotus more 'like Homer', as Longinus says,[1] than in his references to Olympian intervention in human affairs. Such reputed intervention he records often. Gods record their will, and give warnings by oracles and dreams, through seers and visions of all sorts (i. 209–10). Apollo, in person, defended his treasures at Delphi (viii. 35–39 and ix. 42). The storm wrecked Persian ships 'to make that fleet equal to the Greek' (viii. 13). While Xerxes' dream left the King free to choose, Artabanus was threatened for trying to prevent 'what was bound to happen' (τὸ χρεὸν γενέσθαι). He too was free to act, but was brought to admit that there is a 'god-sent impulse' of destruction (δαιμονίη τις γίνεται ὁρμή . . . φθορὴ . . . θεήλατος), to attack and defeat the Greeks. Yet Xerxes, if he would, might still fly in the face of providence (vii. 14–19).[2]

But these narratives of divine action are always 'on information received', never given as historical 'causes' (αἰτίαι), and sometimes expressly as antecedents (vii. 189, Boreas; ii. 181, Ladice).

---

[1] xiii. 3.
[2] G. C. J. Daniels, *Religieus-historische studie over Herodotus*, Antwerp, 1946.

So too the rain came *after* Croesus' prayer; the calm *after* the Magians' howling (vii. 191); the Greeks thanked Poseidon, not *for* the storm, but *after* it. At Delphi (viii. 37–39) what was certain was that the rocks fell, for there they lay: it was Mys himself, not a god, who understood the oracle in Carian speech (viii. 133–5): the tragic fulfilment of Solon's warning was the proof that it was the 'word of God' σὺν θεῷ εἰρημένον (i. 86). All such incidents are carried to the credit side of an unbalanced account (iv. 152; vi. 27; vii. 57). But his belief in the prophecy of Bacis (viii. 77) is his own, like his general acceptance of oracles (i. 26), though he admits that there are 'counterfeits' (i. 66–75; cf. v. 65, 91; vii. 6). And in general his estimate of the gods is higher than Homer's: no god in Herodotus, even a foreign one, is described as doing anything inhuman or improper. Misdoings at Delphi are noted on hearsay only (v. 90; vi. 75). 'The unworthiness of the minister affecteth not the efficiency of the sacrament', as the canon says.

Like some of his contemporaries, Herodotus had learned from Persians of a god who was 'the whole circuit of the sky'; and of others who, though they had personal names, had no temples nor altars (i. 131–2). His own notions of the divine (ὁ θεός, τὸ θεῖον, τὸ δαιμόνιον) lie close to those of Xenophanes and Heracleitus, and to the Samothracian cult of the 'great gods', into which he seems to have been initiated (ii. 51). Twice he describes, among foreigners, a belief in immortality (iv. 94) and transmigration (ii. 123).

But, like Homer's 'Purpose of Zeus' (βουλὴ Διός), Fate and Chance, for Herodotus, are above the gods; only in the second oracle to the Athenians (vii. 141) Zeus still plays the part of Fate, and repels Athena's plea. Apollo can only foresee the future (i. 91); he cannot change it. By revealing something of the full facts he can 'offer his help'—knowledge which man is free to accept or refuse. It was consistent with the 'Purpose of Zeus' as revealed at Delphi that Themistocles should hit on the favourable meaning of the second oracle, convince his colleagues, and save his country (viii. 143–4); whereas Cambyses, 'mistaking wholly what was to come', killed his brother, lost his kingdom, and only at the last accepted the place of his death, because 'it is not in man's nature to avert what is about to come' (iii. 64). So, too, Croesus' precautions miscarried for his son and for his kingdom (i. 34–45, 47–56).

Such a theology was compatible with beliefs about τύχη and συμφορή, with an 'ordained lot', πεπρωμένη (εἱμαρμένη) μοῖρα, and an equilibrium or cycle in nature and men's affairs which 'the divine' maintains and redresses. Common to the Ionian philosophers and to Attic tragedy is the notion of 'insolence', ὕβρις, leading to 'infatuation', ἄτη, and disaster. It is conspicuous in the story of Croesus; perceptible also in the Scythian story, where Artabanus gives the repeated warning, and Darius so narrowly escapes disaster, only because this episode has become incorporated in the larger theme of Persian expansion, which is to meet its fate under Xerxes, as the Lydia of Gyges and Alyattes, in spite of warning (i. 13), encountered 'requital' under Croesus. It underlies the whole planning of the expedition of Xerxes, the warnings of Artabanus (vii. 10–46), Demaratus (vii. 101, 209, 235), and Artemisia (viii. 68); his deception by the Dream (vii. 16 ff.) and by Sicinnus (viii. 75), and his persistence in the policy of Mardonius, his evil genius throughout. But it comes to Herodotus, ready made, in the stories of Croesus, Polycrates, and Periander, and is applied to the historical narratives of Cyrus and Cambyses.

Man.—So, between τύχη, μοῖρα, and τὸ θεῖον stands *Man*: ἡ ἀνθρωπείη λεγομένη γενεή (iii. 122). Each breed of men (p. 45) has its own φύσις, like the land of Egypt and the crocodile, influenced by surroundings and upbringing. From their φύσις men themselves, intelligent observers, formulate their respective νόμοι and νόμιμα, which everyone but a lunatic like Cambyses respects (iii. 38), without necessarily either approval or obligation to conform. As with Sophocles,[1] 'many strange things there are, and none is stranger than Man', πολλὰ τὰ δεινά, κ' οὐδὲν ἀνθρώπου δεινότερον πέλει.

---

[1] *Ant.* 332–3.

Now in nothing do men, and peoples, differ more strangely than in their ability to take the initiative, to alter and dominate their circumstances. This is essentially the 'strangeness', δεινότης, noted by Sophocles; and from Homer onward the most frequent word for this quality is ἀρχή, another loan from common speech which never wholly loses its original sense of 'initiative' or its correlation with τέλος.[1]

So far as we can judge from fragments, the logographers had arranged their gatherings in an order of time or of space, of chronicle or locality; they had selected certain kinds of events— reigns or priesthoods—as a framework; but they had not done more. In this they had been outrun by the physicists, who sought for *causes* and *effects*—though a king or a priest is an ἀρχή because an αἴτιος—illustrating the larger processes of nature by homely experiments with earth, water, air, and fire, elements which could be brought under man's control, and by comparisons with human passions, efforts, and will. But in themselves alone had they direct experiences of a cause and its effect. Their use of the popular words ἀρχή ('initiative') and αἰτίη ('responsibility') for physical causes is typical, and their extension of the terms φύσις and νόμος, ἔρως and ἔρις from human nature to physics: Heracleitus[2] spoke of the ἐρίνυες, Δίκης ἐπίκουροι—'the very devil of a police'—which keep the sun in its course.

Ἀρχή. In his opening words Herodotus applies this search for causes to human affairs; and this search for causes dominates his thought throughout. The word ἀρχή he uses seldom, usually in its popular sense of 'beginning' or 'initiative'. The Scythian, strangling an ox, pulls on τὴν ἀρχὴν τοῦ στρόφου, the beginning'— or, as we say, the *end*—'of the rope' (iv. 60). Only rarely is it the 'occasion' rather than the 'cause' of events (i. 5; v. 82, 89, 97; viii. 84; with τέλος, 'conclusion', vii. 51). Usually it is personal 'initiative' or the occasion for its exercise, in political office or territorial dominion. Deioces, founder of the Median kingdom, 'fell in love with power' (ἐρασθεὶς τυραννίδος, i. 96) and 'courting initiative', practised justice—the way things normally happen—

---

[1] Myres, *The Political Ideas of the Greeks*, 80–97.   [2] Fr. 94 Diels.

till he attained this freedom of action, and could impose his abnormal will on his neighbours. Later the Medes exercised such 'higher initiative', ἐπ-αρχή, over other peoples. Such achievements Herodotus revels in describing, and the greatest of these 'wonderful works', and most 'memorable', is the Empire of Cyrus and of Darius, whose ghost in the *Persae* is the true εἴδωλον, 'image', of the great king as Herodotus portrays him, whose 'will of one' (ἀνδρὸς ἑνός, iii. 82) is the essential motive force of the Empire. Only the seed of Otanes remained exempt from that ἀρχή: καὶ ἄρχεται τοσαῦτα ὅσα αὐτὴ θέλει under the laws of Persia (iii. 83). Here in a parable is human freedom within the natural and the political world.

Aitia, αἰτίη. Unlike the physical philosophers, however, searching in nature for ἀρχαί—'first causes'—and perennial entities, Herodotus is concerned with αἰτίαι, 'responsibilities', and therefore with αἴτιοι, 'responsible' people. Like ἱστορίη and ἀρχή the word αἰτία is taken from common speech, and must be considered with its cognates; αἰτεῖν, 'to ask for something from somebody'; αἰτιᾶσθαι, 'to ask on your own behalf' (i. 90, vi. 139). Among simple folk, as has been said,[1] 'when something happens, somebody must be at the bottom of it'. All animism, and all history, rests on this assumption. A person is αἴτιος when you may ask from him that he shall recompense you for the consequences of an act of his; when you impute initiative, responsibility, and most commonly blame. This is ἐν αἰτίῃ ἔχειν τινά (v. 106), and αἰτίη is my initiative (ἀρχή) regarded from another person's standpoint. Abstractly τὸ αἴτιον is used with the genitive (iii. 108; ix. 93). The imputation may be unjustified, a mere pretext (iv. 167), the judgement of an interested person; and thus Herodotus inquires δι' ἣν αἰτίην ἐπολέμησαν ἀλλήλοισι (i. 1); regards the ships sent to raid Sardis as ἀρχὴ κακῶν (v. 97); designates Croesus as πρῶτον ὑπάρξαντα ἀδίκων ἔργων (i. 5); and writes ἤρχετο τὸ δεύτερον ἐκ Νάξου τε καὶ Μιλήτου Ἴωσι κακὰ γενέσθαι (v. 28). Here again no agreed terminology had yet come into being; but it was coming.

The word αἰτία does not occur in Homer, but the adjective and

[1] W. R. Thayer, *Atlantic Monthly,* cxxii (1928), 68.

the verb are frequent. Zeus complains that θεοὺς βροτοὶ αἰτιόωνται,[1] and of a slippery fellow it is said : δεινὸς ἀνήρ·τάχα κεν καὶ ἀναίτιον αἰτιόῳτο[2]—'the man is slim; he might put the blame on a blameless man'. Aeschylus elaborates the strict legal sense ;[3] Pindar, the moral sense of 'responsibility' ;[4] Thucydides, the responsibility for good as well as evil.

The physicists offer graduated usages, from quite popular idiom (αἰτίη ἁμαρτίης Democritus), to abstract generalization (Thrasymachus, Anaxagoras, Democritus). Natural causes may be αἰτίαι (Anaxagoras, Archelaus, Hippocrates, Philolaus); and in general (says Empedocles) ἀνάγκη is an αἰτία χρηστικὴ τῶν ἀρχῶν, 'a cause employing the elements'. The αἰτίαι of Democritus are 'without origin' and 'come from above (οὐράνιαι) out of limitless time' : to discover one such αἰτιολογία was better than to be King of Persia. Beyond all special αἰτίαι Parmenides conceived of one 'universal cause', which was a deity (δαίμων) ; what is αἴτιον is τὸ ποιοῦν—'that which makes to be'—contrasted with inert and irresponsible 'matter', ὕλη. Anaxagoras had identified this 'cause' with the 'infinite' (τὸ ἄπειρον); Leucippus with 'being and not being' τὸ ὄν τε καὶ μὴ ὄν; Metrodorus with fullness and emptiness, and also with τὰ ἄτομα, 'indivisible' corpuscles moving in space. Here again an agreed terminology is only coming into being; we are still far from the 'four causes' in the philosophy of Aristotle, in whose time αἰτία had been almost wholly superseded by ἀρχή.

What sort of αἰτίαι might an historian expect to find for political events ? Herodotus distinguishes expressly between πρόφασις, the 'pretext asserted', and αἰτία, the real 'motive' to which ἀρχή gives initiative and occasion. Most frequently αἰτία has its popular judicial sense of 'responsibility' (i. 45; ii. 91; iii. 59, 60; v. 70, 71, 106; vi. 115; viii. 99) which has outlived the philosophic and technical senses (i. 35; cf. Thuc. ii. 48; v. 60). For Herodotus all αἰτίαι alike are themselves historical events—or what his authori-

---

[1] Od. i. 32; cf. Il. iii. 164 θεοί νύ μοι αἴτιοί εἰσιν; Il. xix. 409–10 θεός τε μέγας καὶ μοῖρα κραταίη.   [2] Il. xi. 654.
[3] Cho. 68, 273.   [4] Nem. 7. 16–17.

ties accepted as such; human acts, or responsible opinions leading
to action (i. 2, 4; ii. 91; ix. 42). There is no Διὸς βουλή behind the
Persian Wars, as there is in the *Iliad* and *Odyssey*, except in the
popular oracle (vii. 141); nor, with very few exceptions, is even
αἴτιος used except for human and responsible acts, and αἰτία
never. The Gorge of Tempe may be Poseidon's 'work' (ἔργον:
ποιῆσαι, vii. 129) but it is the physical effect of a physical cause:
you cannot ask *why* Poseidon did it. Yet exceptionally Herodotus
does allow himself to 'wonder' what was the cause (αἴτιον) which
'compelled' lions to ravage only the camels of Xerxes (vii. 125):
it is by 'divine foresight' that the unborn lion-cub is αἴτιον of
its mother's death (iii. 108) like the Arabian snakes in the same
context. The Etesian winds are said by some to 'cause' the Nile
flood (ii. 20), as Herodotus believed the sun did, swerving southwards (ii. 25–26). So too a physical 'cause' is given for Sataspes'
failure to circumnavigate Africa (iv. 43), and for the hardness of
Egyptian skulls (iii. 12). All these are variations of the order of
nature, and in one of them Herodotus explicitly detects divine
intervention. The Nile itself was in some sense a god.

With whole societies it is the same as with individuals; for a
society consists of individuals, and is energized—as Thucydides
knew—πρώτου ἀνδρὸς ἀρχῇ (ii. 65), 'by the initiative of the first
man'. So it is in full consciousness of the effects of his words on his
public that Herodotus delivers his ἐπίφθονος γνώμη (vii. 139), that
if the Athenians had surrendered to Xerxes there would have been
no Greek resistance at sea, and consequently Peloponnese would
have been indefensible. To whichever side they turned, the scale
would sink. Again the phrase is 'repelling the king, if the gods
willed', and on this point their faith held, and their free choice,
whatever Delphi might say; for them, one god at least was *not*
'playing fair'. Those words were written by no Ionian fatalist;
and what precedes about men's manifold 'study' of the oracle—
it is the same word διζημένων as Heracleitus uses of his examination of himself—leads deliberately up to the presentation of
Themistocles, a new personality, whose scholarship refuted the
seers, whose common sense convinced his fellows, and whose

'other decision before this' had been justified already, in the building of the fleet (vii. 144). Reassured about the oracle, relying (at long last) on the god, and using their ships and their common counsel, the Athenians made the crucial decision. It was τύχη that the ships, built to fight Aegina, were ready. It was μοῖρα if 'black blood fell on the house-roofs', and Apollo cursed and warned. As for the gods, Pallas herself—so Delphi said—had failed to change the counsel of Zeus, βουλὴ Διός. But the Athenians made their choice, *and won*; δεσπότῃ νόμῳ χρώμενοι . . . βουλῇ πείθεσθαι ἑνός.

Than the βουλὴ ἑνός, then, the motive force of a great empire, only one thing is greater; the δεσπότης νόμος of a free state, as Demaratus displays it to Xerxes; the rule of law over men who individually are free, ἐλεύθεροι, literally 'grown up', like Roman *liberi*. In a Greek city νόμος expressed the φύσις of the citizens, and 'commands always the same', unlike the whimsy orders of Xerxes; it was usually κατὰ τὰ πάτρια, 'in accordance with the ways of old': but occasionally the citizens κοινῷ λόγῳ χρώμενοι, 'employing mutual reasoning', made it to be otherwise, and then the individual citizen, if he acts κατὰ νόμον, is not αἴτιος; no 'claim' can lie against him. So far, the subject of a despotism, too, 'obeying the will of one' is ἀναίτιος, like a docile horse. But to Heracleitus was attributed the saying[1] that it is νόμος καὶ βουλῇ πείθεσθαι ἑνός. And so Thucydides describes Athenian democracy.

Miltiades, addressing Callimachus at Marathon (vi. 109), says 'It is *in thee*, either to put Athens in slavery, or to make her free'. That was τύχη, and his name, 'fine fighter' was a good omen; for Callimachus was commander *by lot*. On the other hand, 'if the gods play fair' we shall win—that is τὸ θεῖον. But 'all these point to thee, and depend on thee' (ἐς σὲ νῦν τείνει καὶ ἐκ σέο ἤρτηται). Callimachus was *free*; and 'with the decision of the polemarch added, it was confirmed' to attack. Callimachus, though the word is not used, was αἴτιος: what mattered, for Ionian physicist alike and for lover of Athens, was 'reasoned decision', and the 'will of one man' which resulted.

[1] Diels, B. 33 [110].

Themistocles, too, at Salamis (viii. 60) addresses Eurybiades in the same terms: ἐν σοί ἐστι, 'it is *in thee*, to save Greece'; and he succeeds, where his previous threat of desertion had failed, adding, less confidently than Miltiades, that probability is the guide of life. Even God does not maintain the improbable.

Here, once again, is reason and judgement, γνώμη and a βουλὴ ἑνός. It is a hard saying; but it is part of every Greek man's μοῖρα that he is ἐλεύθερος, 'grown up' and free to choose. And with that discovery, Herodotus stands revealed to us as the Father of History.

IV
THE FATHER OF HISTORY

'THE project of Herodotus is to write history'; and the plan of the whole work is simple. It consists of two main parts: a narrative of the struggles between Persians and Greeks, from the Ionian Revolt of 500 B.C. to the defeat of Xerxes' invasion in 480–479 B.C. (v. 28–ix), preceded by a retrospect of the origin of the quarrel between East and West, and the Rise of the Persian Empire and of the leading Greek states, Athens and Sparta (i–v. 27). From back references it is clear that the later part presumes acquaintance with the earlier, or sections of it; and from allusions to events between 432 B.C. and 429 B.C. that Herodotus was still working on it in those years. On the other hand, there is no certain allusion in i–v. 27 to any event later than the foundation of Thurii (443 B.C.) and the departure of Herodotus for the West.

Whereas the story of the 'Persian Wars' (v. 28–ix) down to the Persian conquest of Libya is only interrupted by the digressions into Athenian and Spartan history (v. 39–42, 55–96; vi. 51–93) supplementary to those on Athens (i. 59–64) and early Greece (i. 56–58), and on Sparta (i. 65–70, 82), the 'Persian History' —to use Powell's general name for i–v. 27—includes, in addition to an outline of the rise of the Persian people under Cyrus, Cambyses, and Darius (i. 95–140; iii. 61–105, 118–19) long descriptions of Lydia, Ionia, Egypt, Scythia, and Libya, with a shorter note on Thrace and Macedon, and what may be extracts from a longer description of Assyria (i. 106, 178, 184–7, 192–200 especially i. 193; iv. 198). The digressions on Athens (i. 59–64), Sparta (i. 65–70, 82), and Samos (iii. 39–60, 120–8, 139–49), like the account of Cyrene (iv. 145–67, 200–5), are insufficient Greek counterpart to Persian achievements to justify the wide, balanced claim of the Preface (i. 1) 'some displayed by Greeks, some by foreign folk' or the further phrase (i. 6) 'reviewing small and large cities alike'. On the other hand, the repeated disparaging references (i. 1, 4, 5) to Persian sources of information prepare the reader for an alternative history not of Lydia but of Persia and Persian conquest such as is given in Books I–IV.

Our prime concern, however, must be with the *Histories* as Herodotus left them, as a work of art and of research. Their purpose is twofold: to preserve the record of great deeds, whether of Greeks or of Persians, and to discover the reasons for the quarrel between them. Apart from speculative and prehistoric motives, the first wrongdoer was Croesus—not because he attacked Greek cities: his predecessors since Gyges had all done that—but because, having exacted tribute, he failed to protect them. This did not need to be stated explicitly; in ancient empires, as in medieval feudalism, service and security went together. At the summit of Lydian prosperity stand the twin digressions on Athens (i. 59–64) and Sparta (i. 65–70), linked by a note on the diverse origins of the Greek peoples (i. 56–58).

Since Croesus is represented as the offender, the formal introduction of Cyrus could be postponed till the Lydian story was ended (i. 94). The antecedents of Cyrus (i. 95–130) include a retrospect of the Median dynasty which he overthrew, and so his defeat of Croesus completed his conquest of western Asia (i. 130). A description of Persian customs (i. 131–40) is balanced by a retrospect of the Greek cities of Asia Minor (i. 142–57), and followed by their subjection, revolt, and reconquest by Harpagus (i. 152–77) together with their coastland neighbours.

The further expansion of Persian rule is the main theme of Books i. 178–216 (the conquest of Babylon by Cyrus); ii. 1; iii. 1–38 (the conquest of Egypt by Cambyses), iii. 61–87 (the Magian revolt and usurpation of Darius) and iii. 88–138 (his reorganization of the empire); iii. 150–9 (Darius' conquest of Babylon); iv. 1–144 (his expedition into Scythia); iv. 145–205 (operations in Libya); v. 1–27 (his settlement of the north-western frontier in Thrace and Paeonia). But whereas the accounts of Scythia and Libya are counterparts and balanced, and the long digression on Egypt which fills Book II was at one time balanced by the lost 'Assyrian story' (p. 99, the Persian sections of Book III are alternated with the rise, the glory, and the fall of Samos under Polycrates (iii. 39–60, 120–8, 139–49). This antistrophic structure of pendant narratives resembles that of tragic *strophe* and *antistrophe* so closely that Herodotus may well have adopted it during his residence at Athens, where all this part of his work seems to have been taking shape. A conspicuous example on a smaller scale is the pair of digressions on Athens and Sparta in Book I; and the same principle inspires the narratives of the visits of Aristagoras, with similar pendant digressions (v. 38–97) and Paeonian 'epode' (v. 98); Persian and Greek preparations in 480 B.C. (vii. 19–138, 138–74); and the dissection of the Lydian and Samian episodes into a 'rise' and 'fall' of Croesus and Polycrates respectively. Within the Lydian tragedy, the story of Solon (i. 29–33) is balanced by that of Atys and Adrastus (i. 34–45); the invasion of Cappadocia by Croesus (i. 71–77) by the counter-attack of Cyrus on Sardis (i. 78–81). Some of these antitheses, like this last, are inherent in the course of events, but Herodotus has made full use of them in a formal scheme.

But in these passages, and even within some of the balanced episodes, there is a quite different principle of composition, which can best be described as 'pedimental'. Whereas, in a romance or a drama, event follows on event, in an order of time, to a final climax or catastrophe, in 'pedimental' composition, whether in narrative or in sculpture and painting, the climax is central and episodes are ranged on either hand—or, in narrative, before and after—to prepare for it or reveal its consequences. The pediments of the temple in Aegina, a war-memorial from the years after Salamis, display the Greek victory by setting triumphant Athena in the midst of a convergent mêlée of Greeks and Persians.

This kind of composition is very ancient and widespread; in the 'heraldic' grouping of men and animals on engraved seal-stones, from Minoan times onward, and on the 'Lion Gate' relief at Mycenae; in early bronze-reliefs and vase-paintings; on parts of the 'Chest of Cypselus' seen by Pausanias at Olympia;[1]

---

[1] Paus. v. 17–19: Myres, *J.H.S.* lxvi (1946), 122.

on the 'Shield of Achilles' in *Iliad* xviii,[1] and the Hesiodic 'Shield of Heracles',[2] where it is the antithesis to the 'progressive' or 'frieze' order, in which one group or episode follows uniformly on another. Frieze-episodes, however, may be confronted pedimentally in converging movement either about a central figure or group, or directly, as in a battle-scene. In the sixth and fifth centuries pedimental compositions were combined in the same larger design with friezes as on the Parthenon; and in the Parthenon frieze itself the long processions converge on the pedimentally grouped deities on the east front, with the most important in the midst. Thus in Book V, after a balanced account of the consequences of the Scythian Expedition (1–27), the outbreak and first success of the Ionian Revolt are separated by the balanced appeals of Aristagoras to Sparta and to Athens—with explanations of his reception at each—from the collapse of the movement (v. 97–vi. 47) and the Persian reprisals which were frustrated at Marathon (vi. 48–140), are interrupted again by the long account of the reign of Cleomenes in Sparta, essential to the course of events in Athens.

A fresh composition fills Books VII, VIII, IX. The prelude sets Xerxes on the throne, and launches the Persian Empire into war (vii. 1–19). It is itself symmetrical about the dreams of Xerxes and Artabanus (vii. 12–18). The preparations at the Hellespont and Mount Athos, and the advance of the army to Therma in Macedon (vii. 132–7), are balanced by Greek preparations at Athens introducing Themistocles (vii. 138–44), the mission of spies to Persia (vii. 145–7), the appeals for help to Argos (vii. 148–52), Syracuse (vii. 153–67), Corcyra (vii. 168), and Crete (vii. 169–71), and the decision to evacuate Thessaly and defend the pass of Thermopylae (vii. 172–5), while a Greek squadron held the strait between Thessaly and Euboea to cover the sea-flank of the land-force (vii. 176–95). The defeat of Leonidas at Thermopylae (vii. 196–239) and the retreat of the ships from Artemisium (viii. 1–25) are presented in parallel narratives, balanced by the subsequent land-battle at Plataea (ix. 1–89) and

---

[1] Myres, *Who were the Greeks?* (1930), 519.   [2] *J.H.S.* lxi (1941), 17.

sea-fight at Mycale (ix. 90–113), on either side of the central
struggle at Salamis (viii. 40–144). In all, it is a fivefold composition:

land and sea defeat—crucial struggle—land and sea victory

enframed between the prelude in Susa (vii. 1–19) and an epilogue,
also centred in Susa (ix. 115–22), revealing the collapse of
Persian morale, while the Greek capture of Sestos completes the
expulsion of the invader from Europe.

This is a literary composition, of wide scope and exceedingly
varied content. Like an ode of Pindar, or an Athenian tragedy, it
has 'a beginning, a middle, and an end'. The main story,
enunciated in the Preface (i. 1–5), is clearly articulated, and interspersed with what Herodotus himself calls 'insertions' ($\pi\alpha\rho\epsilon\nu$-
$\theta\hat{\eta}\kappa\alpha\iota$, vii. 5, 171) which illustrate or explain its turning-points,
like the choric odes of tragedy and the myths introduced by
Pindar to enhance his themes. What has seemed to many critics
of Herodotus to be irrelevant is revealed by closer study of the
subject-matter and clearer appreciation of his constructive skill
to be deliberate and experimental, and to mark a turning point
in Greek prose literature, the significance of which can best be
seen in the Hebrew *Books of Kings* and *Chronicles*. Though Herodotus occasionally breaks his narrative to explain his method,
these scattered points tell us little about his literary art, or about
the principles which guide him in assembling, selecting, and
arranging his information. To recover these, and reveal Herodotus at work, we have to proceed by inference from what he has
written; when we understand the structure of his book, we may
learn from it *how* it was composed, and perhaps even *why*.

'Muses', Books, and Chapters

The customary division of the text into 'chapters' is no older
than the printed edition of 1608, and illustrates the literary
practice of the Revival of Learning and the first generation of
printers and publishers. Even the separation of the *Histories* into
nine books under the names of the Nine Muses is as arbitrary as

the division of the *Iliad* and the *Odyssey* into twenty-four, under the names of the twenty-four Greek letters. Probably it perpetuates a librarian's fancy, inspired by some edition which happened to fill nine boxes of rolls, or nine 'tomes' (*tomoi*) or 'sections' in codex form, like the famous three *Tomes* of Manetho's *History of Egypt*. In the King's Library of the British Museum the books are catalogued under the names of the Twelve Caesars, whose busts adorn the bookcases. The first references to these 'Muses' are in Lucian, *de Hist. conscrib.* 42, *Herodotus*; the first references to books in the Lindian Chronicle[1] (not later than 99 B.C.), and in Diodorus xi. 37. 6.

Though the 'Muses' are of various lengths, this ninefold division does not always accord with the pauses in the narrative. In Book III, chapters 1–38 are the direct sequel of Book II. Book V 1–27 are the sequel of the Scythian story in Book IV, and are separated by an emphatic interval of time from the Ionian Revolt. Book VI 1–47 completes the narrative of that Revolt, and is followed by the new enterprise of Darius which was shattered at Marathon. In Book VII, chapters 1–174 are the story of Xerxes' preparations and advance as far as Thessaly: then come the Greek preparations (175–95) and the story of Thermopylae (196–239); but the pendant narrative of Artemisium begins Book VIII 1–39 before that of Salamis: and Book IX is shared between Plataea and Mycale. But it is the coincidence of a principal pause in the narrative with the conventional break between Books VI and VII which has tempted some scholars to regard Books VII–IX as in some sense a separate work; and the similar pause between Books III and IV has contributed to the illusion that Herodotus planned his *Histories* in three 'triads', regardless of the complete break emphasized by Herodotus himself (in v. 28) between the conquests of Darius (Books III and IV) and the Ionian Revolt with its sequel at Marathon (v. 28–vi. 48; vi. 48–140). We may therefore discard wholly the traditional division into 'Muses', and examine the text as if it were an unpublished manuscript awaiting a modern editor.

[1] ταῖ β τᾶν ἱστο[ρι]ᾶ[ν], referring to ii. 182.

But it was recognized in antiquity that the work was composed of distinct parts. Its title is usually quoted in the plural.[1]

Herodotus himself, moreover, frequently refers to this or that *logos*. Most of these cross-references are identifiable in our text; but his promise (i. 184) to record the Kings of Babylon 'in the Assyrian *logoi*' is unfulfilled (see also p. 94).

THE ART OF HERODOTUS

History is only one of the historical sciences which study the sequences of events. It is also one of the liberal arts, Man's attempt to ascertain, record, and understand his own past, to determine, in Ranke's phrase, 'what actually happened', and why. This is explicit in the Preface of Herodotus—the three propositions of which are best displayed as a title-page.

1. Men's deeds have intrinsic value for Man, and are worth saving from oblivion.
2. Great deeds are no monopoly of any people: there is an 'other side' even to the Persian Wars.
3. Such deeds are not chance occurrences; they spring from motives, which may be ascertained. The present has its causes in the past, and the past has value for the present as a guide to the future.

But this threefold notion of history was of complex and recent growth in Greece. On Herodotus' formulation of it, and his own achievement, rest his claim to be the 'Father of History'.

Primitive man, if we may judge from description of modern savages, has little historic sense. He lives in and for the present. He answers historical and physical questions alike impersonally and intransitively—'it rained', 'it happened'—or assigns both natural and social events to a personal cause: 'He maketh His sun to rise.' Even genealogy, beyond its practical use to define a man's place in the community, has little content; anecdotes enshrine wit and experience, but have no coherence. In the theocratic 'dynasties' of the Near East, persons and events were

---

[1] Pliny, *N.H.* xi. 18 *auctor ille historiarum.*

ΗΡΟΔΟΤΟΥ
ΑΛΙΚΑΡΝΗΣΣΕΟΣ

ἱστορίης ἀπόδεξις

ἥδε, ὡς

μήτε τὰ γενόμενα ἐξ ἀνθρώπων τῷ χρόνῳ

ἐξίτηλα γένηται,

μήτε ἔργα μεγάλα τε καὶ θωμαστά,

τὰ μὲν Ἕλλησι, τὰ δὲ βαρβάροισι ἀποδεχθέντα,

ἀκλεᾶ γένηται,

τά τε ἄλλα καὶ

ΔΙ᾽ ἭΝ ἈΙΤΙΗΝ

ἐπολέμησαν ἀλλήλοισι.

recorded for administrative use and for eternal comfort of great
souls. But there was no *history*, for the same reason that there was
no *science*. The 'ways' of a Master, in heaven or on earth, were
'past finding out': his moods, like those of Cambyses or Cleomenes,
were incalculable; it was useless to collect or classify experience.
Nor had even the Hebrews any reasoned view of the value of
science or of history. They applied their theocratic philosophy to
events and actions alike: 'shall not the Judge of all the earth do
right?' But the theory did not fit the facts. Only an indomitable
hopefulness—for 'against hope they believed in hope' (Rom. iv.
18)—brought in at last a new world to redress the balance of the
old. Their 'teaching by example' was not philosophy but prophecy; the results were not history but theology.

In early Greece, two aspects of the matter emerge. The name
of Clio among the Pierian Muses takes us straight back to the
'deeds of man'[1] with which Achilles beguiled his leisure, singing
to his lyre, and forward to the project of Herodotus. This is the
supreme reward promised by Zeus for Achilles; if he does the
right thing, he shall have his Homer.[2] But the *end*, which gave
value to the rehearsal of great deeds, appears more explicitly in
Hesiod's account of another Muse, Calliope—'fair speech'—
whose special care for epic is an aspect of her as source of effective
utterance in general, to sway opinion, abate dissension, and
soothe the troubled heart, like David before Saul, putting things
'the right way round'.[3] Conversely, the soul of Agamemnon
would 'groan aloud' if Gelo made a disastrous choice (vii. 159).

Under inspiration of Calliope, mere *saga*—stories of heroes—
become built up into compositions around some larger theme; a
'Wrath' as in the *Iliad* or in the lay of Demodocus,[4] or a 'Return'
as in the *Odyssey* and the minor 'returns', inlaid in it, of the Argo
and of Nestor, Agamemnon, and Menelaus; interwoven now
with another 'Wrath' against the suitors, and another wandering
'search', of Telemachus for his father. And in the *Odyssey* as we
have it, there are minor 'characters', neither from saga nor prose

---

[1] κλέα ἀνδρῶν: *Il.* ix. 186–9.   [2] *Il.* xxiv. 110–11, 116.
[3] *Theog.* 89.   [4] *Od.* iii. 135.

folk-tale, but inventions of a more spontaneous and original kind, Nausicaa and Eurycleia, Eumaeus and Melanthius, Telemachus himself, and Patroclus. In the *Iliad* it has even been suggested by Rhys Carpenter[1] that the contrast between Achilles and the other heroes marks him too as a poetical invention.

Only as daughters of 'Remembrance' (*Mnêmosynê*) are the nine Muses of Pieria related at all to Hesiod's other three, the Muses of his own Helicon, un-Olympian, and perhaps pre-Olympian 'powers', like the three *Charites* ('Graces') of Orchomenos, and the three *Moirai* ('Fates'). Like these, they were functional: Memory (*Mnêmê*), Practice (*Meletê*), and Expression (*Aoidê*). The man 'whom the Muses love' is known by the range and accuracy of his knowledge of the 'deeds of former men'; by the thoroughness and reasonableness of his treatment of them; and by the facility of his presentation. As *Memory* stands to the 'eyewitness' and 'hearsay' of Herodotus, so *Practice* stands to his *historia* and *gnômê* (iii. 115; vi. 105); and Heliconian *aoidê* is Herodotean *logos*. As the 'deeds of former men' obliterate the 'cares of an evil mind', so Herodotus the historian can say 'I choose to forget' (iv. 43).

To Epic, the art of Herodotus is allied not only by his frequent use of Homeric words and phrases, and his respect for Homeric authority, but by his kinship with Panyassis, the 'seer' of Halicarnassus, who tried to 'resuscitate epic' in the same generation;[2] and by his principal literary artifice (p. 81) which appears already in much of the structure of the *Iliad* and in less degree in the *Odyssey* also.[3]

Narrative, whether oral or written, ranks among the arts with music, and with modern film-technique, rather than with the graphic and glyptic arts which present their subject in two or more dimensions but are debarred from temporal changes. Rhetoric, dance, and drama alone command both time and space. Yet Greek critics use 'rhythm' (*rhythmos*, 'impulse') for a

---

[1] *Folklore, Saga, and Fiction in the Epic* (1946), 70 ff.
[2] Kinkel, *Epicorum Graecorum Fragmenta*, 5, p. 253.
[3] Myres, *J.H.S.* lxxii (1952). 1–19: lxxiii (forthcoming).

quality which they perceived, and were aware that an artist could create, in a statue or a vase-painting, as well as in a pattern, a dance, a melody, or a poem. Was there also 'rhythm' in prose composition? Certainly orators practised it, and Aristotle's *Rhetoric* analyses and rationalizes their technique. All this is part of Calliope's task. Early examples of what Hesiod meant by 'memory' are the two 'Catalogues',[1] Odysseus' visions of departed heroes and heroines,[2] the Hesiodic *Eoiai*, an anthology of similes commemorating famous women; and his own *Theogonia*, reducing to a genealogical diagram the legends of gods and heroes, many of local origin and interest. Hesiod was also a pioneer in didactic science in *Works and Days*, and in descriptive art, though no mortal could have wielded his *Shield of Heracles*.

Logos. But the next steps were taken not in Greece but in Ionia; not in verse but in prose; a great variety of *logoi*, all alike attempting to describe and explain—for the word has both meanings—the natural world or some aspect of it; what Heracleitus called 'that which surrounds us, being rational and congruous with our minds' ($\lambda o\gamma\iota\kappa\acute{o}\nu$ $\tau\epsilon$ $\mathring{o}\nu$ $\kappa\alpha\grave{\iota}$ $\phi\rho\epsilon\nu\mathring{\eta}\rho\epsilon\varsigma$)—just what the disordered wits of Cambyses (iii. 25) and Cleomenes (v. 42) were *not*.

The word *logos*, $\lambda\acute{o}\gamma o\varsigma$, a verbal substantive, stands to $\lambda\acute{e}\gamma\epsilon\iota\nu$, 'to say', as $\psi\acute{o}\gamma o\varsigma$ to $\psi\acute{e}\gamma\epsilon\iota\nu$, 'to blame', and the like: it means simply 'what is said'. Between Homeric and classical Greek it has changed meanings with *mythos*, but not precisely or universally.

Its use implies nothing as to the truth or significance of 'what was said'; only that this was how the tale was told. To tell 'the actual story', $\tau\grave{o}\nu$ $\acute{e}\acute{o}\nu\tau\alpha$ $\lambda\acute{o}\gamma o\nu$, was to conform to the facts, and must be expressly stated, not assumed. Nor is the teller responsible: it is his part to repeat the tale 'as it is told', and his hearers may hold him to the traditional version. But any *logos* may be told in various contexts. The same incident may be attributed to different persons or be nameless; and a story-teller may group tales of different origins about a 'famous' person—meaning just this, that many tales are told about him. But for lack of a standard text a tale varied, from mouth to mouth, and from place to place,

[1] *Il.* ii. 484–779, 816–77. [2] *Od.* xi. 225–332; 385–640.

acquiring details and enhancements, a moral, or application to fresh circumstances.

According to their subjects, *logoi* may be ritual or religious myths, historical legends about particular persons or occasions, 'fables' obviously fictitious, such as animal stories, or mere folk-tales in which the same story or plot persists among many variations of detail, often over great intervals of space or time. In immense numbers and endless variety, they are an essential part of the 'tradition' or 'culture' which is the common inheritance of a people and shapes the mental habits of each new generation; but the 'tale that is told' is always coming into being or passing away. It is no man's property, but a common possession of all who have memory and observation. Like a picture or a melody or a dance, a tale gives precision and vividness to an experience, and collectively to the significance of life. Inevitably, therefore, Herodotus, 'the most typical Greek all round that ever lived',[1] is a supreme artist in story-telling, and is rightly described as *logopoios*, whatever he may have achieved besides. But by the conditions of his art the story-teller makes his stories his own, by his manner of telling and his outlook on life. As long as the *logos* remains oral, it is told anew on each occasion. If, and when, it is written down, its form is fixed, and it passes out of folk-lore into literature; often only to perish in archetype or be survived by another oral version.

Thus only the fittest *logos* survives, and fitness is determined by the taste and memory of the hearers. All the Muses alike are daughters of Memory. Essential to survival is clear and vivid presentation; for, as Longinus says, 'art is perfect when it seems to be nature', and the *logopoios* 'makes hearing sight'.[2] Personages are typical characters, without psychological elaboration. Direct speech is used without thought of historical accuracy. Conformity to familiar phrases gives a conventional and even archaic air to the diction. Sentences are short and simple; digressions and repetitions are frequent, and sustain the attention of an audience, whereas they confuse a reader.

[1] Thompson, J. A. K., *The Art of the Logos*, 143.　　[2] *De Sublim.* 22. 1, 26.

The earliest Greek *logoi* dealing with the 'way things grow' (*physis*) hardly concern us; but Hecataeus of Miletus wrote a *Periodos* (*Journey round the World*). Our fragments of it are mainly topographical, and it included such facts (frr. 284, 286–7, 291–2) as furnished Aristagoras with his map (v. 49; p. 34). His *Genealogies*, without chronological frame, included his own (Hdt. ii. 143), traced to the foundation of Miletus about 1030 B.C. Based on such genealogies, codifying the aristocratic families whose privileges of birthright were being challenged, and also being claimed by pretenders, were the genealogies of Acusilaus of Argos (*c.* 500 B.C.) and Pherecydes of Athens (*c.* 460 B.C.). They included official lists of kings and priestesses, reinforced from victory monuments and other dedications. Numerous *Foundations* and *Chronicles* of single cities—of Lampsacus and Sparta by Charon, of Miletus by Dionysius, of Athens by Hellanicus— found room for descriptions of resources, institutions, and historical events; and were linked together in guidebooks (*Periodoi*, *Periêgêseis*) like the *Periplus* of Scylax of Caryanda, and memoirs of residence abroad (*Epidêmiai*). Larger themes were only attempted when Persian aggression linked the fortunes of cities and peoples in a common resistance and revealed a national cause and ideal. Xanthus wrote a history of Lydia; Dionysius compiled *Persica*, Charon both *Persica* and *Hellenica*, and Damastes of Sigeum wrote on *Events in Greece*. A long extract from Xanthus[1] in Ionic dialect and simple diction may be taken as typical: it includes romances, folk-tales, and customs as well as events.[2]

Collectively these early prose-writers are described by Thucydides as 'writers of *logoi*'.[3] Herodotus describes Hecataeus, like Aesop, as *logopoios* (ii. 143); and is himself classed with 'Ctesias and the *logographoi*' by Theopompus.[4]

From its primitive sense (p. 70) many shades of meaning

---

[1] In Nicolas of Damascus, *F.G.H.* ii. A. 90. 47.

[2] For details see Pearson, L. J., *Early Ionian Historians*, 1939; Jacoby, *F. G. His.* (in progress).

[3] Cf. Plato, *Phaedrus*, 257 c.

[4] Fr. 1. Compare λογοποιέω Thuc. vi. 38; Andocides, iii. 35; Lysias, xvi. 11; λογοποιική Plato, *Euthydemus*, 289 c: λογοποιΐα in Theophrastùs, *Charact.* 8 is mere 'newsmongering'.

emerge. In Homer it is rare; for the cheerful 'patter' of a surgeon at work[1] or the beguilements of Calypso.[2] Later, and more seriously, it is an argument;[3] but the regular Epic word for the latter is *mythos*, only rarely depreciated a little.[4] Long sections in the earlier books of Herodotus are typical *logoi* in form, only slightly edited to fit their place in his general design.

Topics	Egypt	Babylon	Scythia	Massa-getae	Thrace	Libya	Persia
	II	I	IV	I	V	IV	I
Origin and Mytho-logy of the people	12–14	..	5–15	..	3	..	..
Geography	5–9	193–4	16–35	202	10	181	..
Rivers	10–34	..	47–57	..	..	..	..
Criticism of cur-rent theories	15–16	..	37–45	..	..	..	..
The Ocean	21, 23	..	36	..	..	..	..
Causes of floods	20–27	..	50	..	..	..	..
Customs	35, 36	195–7	46,64–6, 70	216	6	187, 189–91	133–9
Religion and ritual	37–76	..	59–63	216	7	188	131–2
Divination	82, 83	..	67–69	..	..	..	140
Burials	85–90	198	71–75	216	4, 5, 8	190	140
Resistance to foreign influences	91 (cf. 79)	..	76–80	..	..	..	..

Their principal topics are similar—geography, natural history, ethnology, religion, and miscellaneous curiosities (*thaumata*, i. 93) —and these tend even to occur in the same order. Whether Herodotus lectured publicly or not, he marshalled his material on a system already conventional; and since in these sections there is little or no reference to the main theme of the *Histories*, it has been inferred that, when they were being compiled, that theme did not yet dominate Herodotus' thoughts. Fragments of such *logoi* are detached, and even dissected, for insertion in another context: for example, the story of Periander (v. 93 continued iii. 50–53).

The relevance of anecdote to context varies. The tale of Glaucus son of Epicydes, told by Leotychides (vi. 86) to put Athenians to shame, is mere parable, like Nathan's tale of the

---

[1] *Il.* xv. 393–4.   [2] *Od.* i. 56–57.   [3] *Batr.* 144–5.   [4] *Il.* iii. 212.

ewe lamb: it has no historical content; the situation is immemorial, applied to an event of today: at most, verisimilitude is
added by putting Glaucus three generations before the speaker.
The story of Periander (v. 92) illustrates the behaviour of tyrants
in general, to dissuade Cleomenes from restoring Hippias, but
part of the tale is about Cypselus, not Periander, Pindaric in its
double meaning; for what Corinthian or Athenian could forget
that the tyrannies had broken the old régimes and led to present
greatness? But another part, in another context, is about Corinthian relations not with Samos (iii. 50–53) but with Corcyra, a
burning question still in Herodotus' time, and a real digression
into causes of the political anomalies of Greece. The irony is even
sharper in the story of Peisistratus (i. 59–64) and in the comparison of Cleisthenes with his grandfather in Sicyon (v. 66–69),
where every incident goes wrong.[1]

But most of these *logoi* stand where they do as Herodotus'
answer to the same question '*Why?*' The story of Candaules shows
why the Mermnad dynasty replaced the Lydian Heracleids (i. 7–
14); the stories of Solon (i. 29–33) and Atys (i. 34–45) illustrate
the infatuate pride of Croesus, impervious to warnings; and so
forth.

Mythos, too, in its long history, has shifted its meaning, but in
the reverse direction. In Epic, it is speech with a view to action,
not like *logos* contrasted with it.[2] Empedocles insists on the truth
of his 'myths' about nature and the gods,[3] unlikely as they
sound; and so, too, Parmenides; but Pindar speaks of myths
'decorated with varied lies beyond the true tale',[4] which appeal
to the 'blind heart' of the mob. In Aeschylus the connexion
between speech and necessary action remains;[5] but it is lost in
Sophocles[6] and Euripides.[7] When Critias, however, speaks of

---

[1] Myres, *Mélanges Glotz*, ii (1932). 657–66.
[2] *Il.* ix. 443; xvi. 83; xvii. 200; *Od.* ii. 137; xiii. 19; xvii. 177.
[3] Diels, i. 1 B, frr. 62, 114.
[4] *Ol.* i. 29 μῦθοι, δεδαιδαλμένοι ψεύδεσι ποικίλοις, ὑπὲρ τὸν ἀληθῆ λόγον: cf. *Pyth.* ix.
76; *Nem.* vii. 23.
[5] *P.V.* 664; *Ag.* 1368–9; *Cho.* 314.
[6] *Ajax*, 865.
[7] *Iph. Aul.* 799; *Ion*, 196–7.

'shameful myths'[1] it is *malice* not *untruth* that he condemns; they are *meant* to lead to bad acts.[2]

Herodotus uses *mythos* rarely. A 'silly *mythos*' about the Ocean river, or about Heracles in Egypt, fails to stand the test of reason (ii. 23, 45); and παραμυθέομαι is used once, quite popularly (ii. 121). His habitual word for his own and other people's writings is *logos*.

Thucydides distinguishes from history the indemonstrable statements of poets and chroniclers (*logographoi*, i. 21), which have 'won their way to the myth-like' (*mythôdes*); but if his criticism is aimed at Herodotus, it is not that his story is untrustworthy, but that it is tendentious.

This will become clear by comparison with fourth-century usage. Plato uses *mythologia* for 'conversation', the clearing-house of thought;[3] Aesop's animal-fables, though beyond experience, are *mythoi*, with meaning and utility; it is proposed 'to make a *mythos* of the State', μυθολογεῖν τὴν πολιτείαν,[4] in parable and diagram; Socrates doubts whether his story will be accepted, but (like Empedocles) he can no other.

Aristotle, distinguishing the elements of tragedy,[5] describes as *mythos* 'the imitation of the action', and explains it as 'the way the acts are put together';[6] he has already defined 'diction' (*lexis*) as 'the way the metres are composed'. Both are distinct from the course of the dialogue (*dianoia*) in which the characters 'converse and announce and express an opinion' on those acts. And of all these elements of tragedy, 'the greatest is *mythos*'. It stands here for the 'plot', the setting of acts or incidents in relation to one another, the *scenario* for which *lexis* and *dianoia* provide the *libretto*: and on this all else depends. In this dramatic usage *mythos* is the precise equivalent of the Latin *fabula*, standing to *fari* as μῦθος to μύζω and οὐδὲ μῦ, with much the same emergence

---

[1] Diels, ii. 1, B. 6–10.
[2] This meaning persists in παραμυθοῦμαι (*Il.* ix. 417, 684; xv. 45; *Aesch. P.V.* 1063; Soph. *Ant.* 935; Hdt. ii. 121; Thuc. ii. 44, iii. 75; Plut. *Mor.* 2. 2486 παραμυθεῖσθαι τὸ μυθῶδες).   [3] *Laws*, 752 a.
[4] *Rep.* 379 a.   [5] *Poet.* 1450ᵃ5.
[6] τῆς πράξεως ἡ μίμησις, τῶν πραγμάτων σύστασις, 1450ᵃ16.

of meanings. Aristotle, indeed, probably canonized, as a term of criticism, what was current among poets and *chorêgoi* as a bit of stage-slang, inherited from the primitive religious drama (*mystêrion*) to denote the spoken part of the ceremony, while *drama* meant the ritual acts (*drômena*). Both alike are aspects of the action (*prâgma*).[1]

But it was in the *mythos* that the marshalling or composition of such actions found its significance, and this explains the freedom with which Athenian dramatists handle the characters and episodes of traditional subjects, as in the *Prometheus* or the *Persae*, or the three *Electra*-plays. Here the special use of the word *mythos* by the physical philosophers finds its explanation: they, too, are 'putting together the facts' of sense-perception, in compositions as surprising to contemporaries as those of Einstein or Jeans to us. When Aristotle, then, calls Herodotus a *mythologos*, he has hit upon the same peculiar quality in his work as had aroused the protest of Thucydides.

It is probably not by accident that this dramatic 'mythical' structure is most clearly displayed in the earlier part of the *History*: but it is perceptible also throughout. The 'Lydian story' (i. 6–94) is the prose *scenario* for a tragic 'Capture of Sardis', like the 'Capture of Miletus' which brought Athenian censure on Phrynichus (vi. 21), and the celebration of 'good things that were their own'[2] in the *Persae* of Aeschylus. Studied in this aspect, the sketch of the rise of the Mermnadae stands for the *Prologos*; the dialogue between Croesus and Solon is ironic counterpart to the scene between Creon and Teiresias in *Antigone*, followed by the death of Atys, as by that of Haemon. No Herald, as in *Agamemnon*, is needed for the battle on the Halys, for Cyrus 'announces himself';[3] and when Croesus is on the pyre, and the fire is alight, as we see it on the Louvre vase-painting, comes Apollo, *deus ex machina*: in Euripides' words, 'so ended this act'. Between these *epeisodia* the digressions on Athens and Sparta fall into place as

---

[1] In Euripidean choral phrase, τοιόνδ' ἀπέβη τόδε πρᾶγμα, 'here endeth this act' of a trilogy, the *actus* of Horace's paraphrase (*Ars Poet*. 189, 194).

[2] οἰκήια ἀγαθά.   [3] αὐτὸς ἄγγελος, i. 79.

antistrophic *stasima*, as who should sing πολλὰ τὰ δεινά, κοὐδὲν
Ἑλλήνων δεινότερον πέλει.¹ So, too, the earlier war, with the eclipse
of Thales (i. 72–74), the tragedy of Thyrea, announced by
'messenger' (i. 82), and the retrospect of Lydian glories, inventions, and dedications: 'and so the Lydians had been subjected
to the Persians' (i. 94). Throughout this 'Lydian story', phrases
in iambic rhythm are frequent: especially in the dialogue with
Solon.²

Herodotus loves a hero. In the 'Lydian story' Croesus fills the
part; in the latter half of Book I the fortunes of Cyrus assign him
the same role. Marvellously preserved, like Oedipus, in infancy,
accepted as his people's leader, he dominates their Median kins-
men, and chastises Croesus' insolence; then conquering Ionia
and Babylon, he falls at last through his own confidence, in
defiance of the warning of Tomyris. Cambyses' tragedy is shorter
and simpler; Polycrates is another typical victim. Darius, after
unprecedented successes, and a plain warning in Scythia, tempts
fortune too far and is defeated at Marathon. But by this time
history has begun to take over control from tragedy; the 'hero'
of Books V and VI is not Darius but Cleomenes, in the dramatic
'myth' of *Kleomenés mainomenos*, a pendant to the Sophoclean
Ajax. And in the last three books, while the King is the overt

---

¹ Myres, 'Herodotus the Tragedian', in *A Miscellany presented to J. M. Mackay*, ed.
O. Elton (Liverpool, 1914), 88–96.
² Iambic lines can be formed by minor transpositions.

    i. 30   νῦν ὦν ἐπειρέσθαι σ' ἐπῆλθέ μ' ἵμερος,
              πάντων [Σόλων] τίν' εἶδες ὀλβιώτατον.

              κοίη δ' κρίνεις Τέλλον ... ὀλβιώτατον

              Τέλλος γὰρ εἶχεν εὖ μὲν ἤκουσαν πόλιν,
              παῖδάς τε καλοὺς κἀγαθοὺς [παιδοτρόφους]

    31   τούτοις γὰρ ἦσαν οὖσιν Ἀργείοις γένος
              ἀρκῶν βίος καὶ σώματος ῥώμη τοίη.

    32   ὦ Κροῖσε, πᾶν τὸ θεῖον ἐξεπίσταμαι
              φθονερόν τε καὶ ταραχῶδες ἀνθρωπηίων.

Cyrus too, i. 79:   ὡς ταῦτ' ἔδοξε κατὰ τάχος ποίει [τάδε] ...
              ἐλάσας γὰρ εἰς γῆν Λυδίην [πολὺν] στρατὸν
              ἐλήλυθ' αὐτὸς ἄγγελος [Κροίσου πόλει].

sufferer, the sinner and tragic hero is not Xerxes but *Mardonios hybristês*, the son-in-law of Darius, who began so well in the appeasement after the Ionian Revolt (vi. 43), but failed to learn from the warning storm off Mount Athos (vi. 44), and became the evil genius of Persia from the accession of Xerxes to the field of Plataea, in spite of the tragic warnings of Artabanus and Demaratus.

It is probably to Athenian influence that Herodotus owes his debt to the literary technique of tragedy. His residence at Athens comes midway in his career and affected him profoundly in other ways. His Egyptian and Libyan section shows little of this influence; the Scythian rather more, in its 'myth-like' narrative and frequent speeches; the Lydian story is saturated with it; Books V and VI, with the problem of Cleomenes, and Books VII–VIII–IX, with that of Xerxes and Mardonius, apply the same method so as to compose episodes and situations in wider and wider compositions; with speeches, and pairs of speeches, to mark statically the crucial moments, and with the main narrative broken into episodes by self-contained descriptions, or incidents relevant to what precedes and follows. Sometimes two such digressions are linked together, like the *strophê* and *antistrophê* of a tragic chorus: the Athenian and Spartan sections (i. 59–64, 65–68), between the rise and the fall of Lydia, have a brief introduction to emphasize their parallelism (i. 56–58); the visits of Aristagoras to Sparta (v. 39–54) and to Athens (v. 55–97) serve as the frame for explanatory retrospects of both cities: and the preparations of Persia (vii. 20–137) and of the Greeks (vii. 138–71) for the invasion of Xerxes, between the King's decision to attack (vii. 1–19) and his entry into Thessaly (vii. 196). The long accounts of Scythia (iv. 1–144) and of Libya (iv. 145–205) are similar counterparts, each swollen by internal digressions on the regions and their peoples; but here the Libyan story is enfolded between the Scythian reconnaissance of Darius and his annexation of Thrace (v. 1–27); and the latter includes yet another pair of geographical appendixes, on Thrace (v. 3–10) and on Paeonia (v. 12–17).

In Book III the structure is still more involved; for the story of Polycrates of Samos (iii. 39–60, 120–8, 139–49) is told in 'alternate chapters' with that of Cambyses and of Darius' reorganization (i. 38, 61–119, 129–38, 150–9); so that interest is maintained in what is in effect a double-plot; for Polycrates very nearly achieved a policy of national defence for Greece. The Persian narrative is, however, structurally, the main story; for it begins in continuation of Book I, and is itself continued by Book III: it is the Samian story which is 'inlaid', a *parenthêkê*, like the sections on Athens and Sparta in Book I, and the section on Cyrene (iv. 145–67). For these digressions Herodotus expressly apologizes (iv. 30, 145), at the same time calling attention to them as a literary device for co-ordinating so vast a range of materials.

Statical and Kinetic. Another characteristic akin to Attic tragedy, and partially suggested by it, is the alternation of what may be described as statical and kinetic elements. When an army is on the march there is no unity either of place or of time. The order of events in time is a function of the order of places on the ground; and the reason for the army's movement is that by leaving one place where it has halted it may in due time arrive at another, where it comes to a standstill again. Such a literary narrative may be compared to a sculptured frieze, and to those intervals between the dialogues of a tragedy during which some event occurs off-stage, altering the whole situation, 'advancing the plot', and giving the speakers in the following stage-scene something fresh to talk about.

The structure of a canal or a bridge, or the muster-roll of an army—still more (as in tragedy) an 'episode' of dialogue or debate—has an internal unity of time, place, and content, like a metope of a temple or a painted group on a vase. It may also, like a vase-painting or a pediment, have its inherent composition and a balanced 'rhythm' of its parts; but though in this respect it may be composite, it does not contribute to the course of events, but completely arrests it, on the literary or the pictorial plane. Examples of such 'metope' or 'pilaster' elements are the single figures of Chilon and Amphilytus in the story of Peisistratus (i. 59, 62), the description of the Canal and the Bridges (vii. 22–25; 33–36), the two halves of the story of Pythius the Lydian (vii. 27–29, 38–39), and the dialogues of Xerxes with Artabanus (vii. 46–52) and with Demaratus (vii. 101–5).

By alternating statical 'metope' compositions with kinetic 'friezes' or processional pageants Herodotus achieves within the compass of a continuous 'roll of a book' an articulated structure, each element in which stands clearly defined; and his frequent catch-phrases, introducing such passages and cross-referring them, are evidence that this procedure was deliberate.

From tragedy—inherited, however, from epic—comes also the use of speeches, and especially of pairs of speeches, to punctuate the narrative and emphasize its turning-points: examples are in the Scythian Expedition and during the march of Xerxes. There is no pretence that the record is verbally correct. The points of view are stated vividly, 'in character' as Herodotus conceives them; and on occasion he defends his record against criticism: compare the establishment of democracies by Mardonius (vi. 43) with their advocacy by Otanes (iii. 80). They may consist of formal *logoi*; the geographical lecture of Aristagoras (v. 49), overflowing into formal commentary (v. 52–54); the moral tale of Glaucus (vi. 86); the political story of the Corinthian tyranny (v. 92).

Akin to this is the brilliant portrayal of character, especially on the first appearance of a personage; and herein Herodotus makes good his claim to present both Greeks and foreigners in their deeds (i. 1). With the large-scale portrait of Darius, to which many episodes contribute, we may compare the retrospect of him in the *Persae*; that of Cyrus recalls Arrian's analysis of Alexander's career,[1] perhaps suggested by it. Notable also are other great Persians: Otanes, rheumatic but incorruptible (v. 25); Megabazus, too keen-eyed to be left on the West Front (v. 26); Artaphernes, who must always 'ask his brother' (v. 31); Artabanus of the old guard; Mardonius (vi. 43)—and among Greeks, Cleomenes, Demaratus, and Themistocles.

[1] *Anabasis*, vii. 1, 4.

Pedimental Composition. But this debt to the tragedians is not the end of the literary development of Herodotus. Drama, as Aristotle puts it, has a beginning, a middle, and an end. So also has history, which studies the sequence of events in time. But history goes farther; it distinguishes events by their values; above all, it seeks for causes, those events or circumstances from which other events follow, and on which they depend.

In a Latin 'period' the subject stands first, conditions, accessions, even subordinate agents, are enunciated next, in order; the principal verb comes at the end, immediately preceded by the object and its attributes and qualifications. In unconstrained Greek, as in English, normal syntax places the verb between subject and object, but a more significant word may be substituted in the central position. In the motto of the Academy

$$μηδεὶς ἀγεωμέτρητος εἰσίτω$$

the significant word could be central without disturbance of normal syntax. In the English line

All hope abandon, ye who enter here

normal order is inverted to centralize the significant word *abandon*. But complete the iambic line

$$μηδεὶς ἀγεωμέτρητος εἰσίτω, Κλέον$$

and it becomes part of a larger composition—a comedian's snub to a rabble-rouser, presuming either a previous question, or a retort such as

$$ὁ Νικίας δ' ἄπειρός ἐστι μουσικῆς$$

which is in the same 'pedimental' form, and balances it in the whole couplet around the significant words *Κλέον* and *Νικίας*.

Herodotus was not the inventor of this mode of composition. It is in the genius of the Greek language and of Greek art. In Greek verse the hexameter and the iambic line are balanced about their *caesura*; in the geometric art of the Early Iron Age, centre-piece and pendant side-panels are fundamental. The structure of the *Iliad* and of the *Odyssey* has similar culminations

and counterparts.¹ The same design is characteristic of the
dithyramb, and fundamental in another archaic survival, the
stichomythia of tragedy; not only in Aeschylus² with whom it is in-
variable, but, with growing laxity, in Sophocles and Euripides.
Aeschylus also employs this structure in his choric odes. It
reappears, after Herodotus, throughout the formal prologue of
Thucydides.³ In the graphic arts, rhythm and balance dominate
vase-painting; their simplest expression, 'heraldic symmetry',
goes back indeed both into Minoan and into Oriental design; it
is frequent on the 'Chest of Cypselus' at Olympia,⁴ on the engraved bowls known as 'Phoenician',⁵ and in the Hesiodic
'Shield of Heracles'⁶. Its best-known expression is, of course, in the
pedimental sculpture of Greek temples; at Aegina it is employed
in commemorative designs of Greeks and Barbarians in combat
about the central figure of Athena; this was evidently a war-
memorial, like the *Preface* of Herodotus. In sculpture and painting
there is the advantage that all parts of the composition can be
seen together and compared. In music and poetry they are
presented in an order of time, and must be compared in retrospect. An elementary example is in quarter-chimes, where, however, the hour-stroke normally comes at the end: strike the hour
after the half-hour, and you have a pedimental composition.
Only slightly more complicated are tunes like *Now the day is over*
and *O God, our help in ages past*—so effective as bell-chimes: and
there are melodies in which the last half of the notes are in
inverse order to the first half, like the letters in an *abracadabra*
charm.

There is therefore nothing improbable in such a mode of
composition: how Herodotus makes use of it, to arrange and
enhance his materials, is a matter of observation. Though it does
not seem to have been studied hitherto, it is employed by him on
every scale, small and large. Examples follow:

¹ Myres, *J.H.S.* lxii (1942), 204 (*Iliad*); *J.H.S.* lxxii (*Odyssey*): lxxiii (*Iliad*).
² Myres, *Proc. Brit. Acad.* xxxv (1949).
³ i. 1–23. E. Täubler, *Die Archäologia des Thukcydides.*
⁴ Myres, *J.H.S.* lxvi (1946), 122.
⁵ Myres, *J.H.S.* liii (1933), 25.   ⁶ Myres, *J.H.S.* lxi (1941), 33.

1. Leotychides, demanding the restoration of Aeginetan hostages (vi. 86), puts Athenian behaviour to shame by the cautionary tale of Glaucus, son of Epicydes. The *logos* is immemorial, though Leotychides lends it historical credence (p. 74). Herodotus retells it in three scenes, of which the second is the significant centre-piece; it is not the curse of Delphi, but the sin of Glaucus, that is the 'cause' of his fate; Delphi only reveals the connexion.

2. To Periander of Corinth, Thrasybulus and his Milesians owed their release from Lydian blockade (i. 21–22). But who was Periander? To answer this question (i. 23–24) Herodotus tells the story of 'Arion and the Dolphin'. But as retold by him, and heard by him (so he says) both in Periander's Corinth and in Arion's Lesbos, the hero is not Arion but Periander, so great a sea king that he will see justice done to a Lesbian, even if the villains are Corinthian. Corinth's repute for safe transport is at stake. 'That's the kind of man Periander was', and a good friend for all who used the sea, in Lesbos or in Miletus. It was indeed during the tyrannies of Periander and Thrasybulus that Corinth temporarily deserted its normal friendship with Samos (iii. 48) and was keeping the sea-ways open for its normal rival, Miletus, on the occasion of the Lydian war and the momentous peace-treaty thereafter, which fixed the political position of Miletus, apart from the rest of Ionia, until the Ionian Revolt. But all *that* the audience is presumed to recall while Herodotus is telling of Arion: the historical *mythos*, the 'putting together of the actions', we come to appreciate while our integration of Greek history matures.

The story of Arion was old and popular, but Herodotus has retold it in a formal scheme as well as a new context. What is central and crucial is still (2) the shipmen's crime, and the dolphin's rescue; but this stands supported and enhanced by side-panels, like those of a triptych: (1) Arion prefers a Corinthian ship for his return from the West; (3) Arion stands before Periander, confronted with the convicted crew. And it is only by this latter that the anecdote is connected causally with the main story: the change of emphasis has not remodelled the narrative, and Herodotus insists that he heard it in this form both in Corinth and in Arion's own city, Lesbos.

3. The other stories about Periander and his father Cypselus (iii. 50–53; v. 92) do not show this symmetry; they are unedited *logoi*. But both are parts of a longer chronicle, incorporated without change, and on separate occasions,[1] and their episodes follow straight on like those of the story of Gyges quoted from Xanthus,[2] and the topics of Egyptian and Scythian geography.

4. The political reforms of Cleisthenes at Athens are illustrated (v. 66–71) by those of his grandfather, Cleisthenes of Sicyon. In every point of comparison, the story fails (p. 81). But as told by Herodotus—ironically or not—it is the reputed 'cause' and inspiration of the Athenian reforms. Accordingly the description of these is in two parts (66, 69) and the causal anecdote is central.

5. More formal and more elaborate are the pendant retrospects of Athens and Sparta (i. 59–68). The popular account of Peisistratus was that of an ogre-tyrant, like Periander and Polycrates, whose dynasty was brought to a bad end by Harmodius and Aristogeiton. And so, ironically, Herodotus sets out to tell how the Athenians were 'oppressed and harried' by him. Between the prologue at Olympia, and the 'Cleansing of Delos' in the epilogue, there are three episodes, and of these the second is central, the recognition of Peisistratus as Athena's choice, between the threefold strife of partisans, and the eventual return of Peisistratus and his sons. But in the pageant of Phye—'the silliest affair ever' though it imposed on the grandparents of his own Athenian public—Herodotus has retained Megacles to balance Peisistratus on the other side of Athena's car; and in the third episode his introduction of Hippias and Hipparchus is counterpart to the *pas-de-trois* of the three party-leaders. Further, as Chilon stands at Olympia, breathing threats over the sacrifice of Hippocrates in the prologue, so the blessing of Amphilytus marks the junction of the restoration-scene with the epilogue of achievements, culminating in the great benefaction to Apollo.

---

[1] Powell, 48, 56. [2] Nic. Dam. *F.G.H.* 90. F 47.

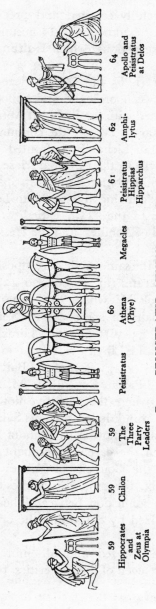

| 59 | 59 | 59 | | 60 | | | | 61 | 62 | | 64 |
| Hippocrates and Zeus at Olympia | Chilon | The Three Party Leaders | Peisistratus | Athena (Phye) | | | Megacles | Peisistratus Hippias Hipparchus | Amphilytus | | Apollo and Peisistratus at Delos |

FIG. 9. PEISISTRATID ATHENS (i. 59–64)

| Lycurgus and the Pythia | Spartan advance | | Mêlée | | Spartan prisoners | | Lychas and the Blacksmith |

FIG. 10. SPARTAN WAR WITH TEGEA (i. 65–68)

Clearly, in a composition so carefully selected and precisely marshalled, to cavil at omissions or symmetries is to misunderstand that 'putting together of the actions' which is dramatic *mythos*.

6. In the Spartan counterpart (i. 65–68), three frieze-like scenes are similarly enframed between prologue and epilogue. In the prologue, Lycurgus, confronted with the Pythia at Apollo's tripod, is saluted as Apollo's emissary, to create the conquering people. In the epilogue, the Spartan Lichas is confronted with the blacksmith of Tegea, at his anvil. In the threefold frieze, the central mêlée is preceded by the confident march-out from Sparta, and followed by the same warriors, 'dancing in fetters' into Tegea town: compare the presentations of the 'Two Cities', which punctuate the scenes on the Shield of Achilles[1] and the Hesiodic Shield of Heracles.[2]

On a larger scale, illustrations of the same mode of composition are frequent: in the story of Polycrates (iii. 39–60, 120–49); in the 'Scythian Expedition' in Book IV where the scenes are punctuated with speeches and pairs of speeches; in Xerxes' crossing of the Hellespont (vii. 53–56); in the Thracian–Macedonian *Epilogue* to Scythia and Libya (v. 1–25); in the accounts of the death of Cleomenes (vi. 73–84), of the Battle of Marathon (vi. 94–120), and of the Parian Expedition (vi. 132–6). Even in the last three books, where the narrative flows so consecutively and historically, the grand design presents Salamis as the central episode, preceded and followed by pairs of land and sea fights—enframed between the carefully wrought and wholly symmetrical prologue in the Councils of Xerxes (vii. 1–19) and the triptych epilogue (ix. 107–22), with Xerxes once more the centre figure. And the connexion between Thermopylae and Artemisium is emphasized by enframing the one in the other.

This pedimental structure, deep-seated and all-embracing though it is, has escaped the notice even of literary critics, prob-

---

[1] *Il.* xviii. 490–540.
[2] *Scut.* 237–85; Myres, *J.H.S.* lxi (1941), 33; cf. *Who were the Greeks?* 519–21.

ably because the literary skill of Herodotus has so completely united the substance of history with its form. It is rather a habit of mind than an artifice or *memoria technica*. He was seeking for causes, for significance and values, and it was as natural to him to group his characters and incidents in this way as to a contemporary sculptor or painter. We have lost the contemporary representation of Marathon in the Painted Portico at Athens, but from the notes of Pausanias[1] the balanced 'rhythm' can be recovered (pp. 203-4); and the same traditional setting is preserved in the 'Darius Vase' two generations later,[2] allowance being made for the spatial limits of the vase-surfaces which superposed tiers of figures instead of extending them laterally in a frieze or a narrative. In the latter, their places would have to be found in 'insertions', *parenthêkai* (vii. 5, 171) and *prosthêkai* (iv. 30) which are Herodotus' confessed expedients. In the pediments of Aegina and Olympia, presiding deities are central in what is conceived as a mêlée of combatants; on the Parthenon they are central among personifications of land and sea, mountain and river, which are their actual background; sun and moon enframe the whole group instead of looking down upon it. Relative significances could only be expressed by grouping, and above all by balance and rhythm. In Attic art the device goes back to the superposed lines of mourners, and the displayed equipment of the funeral car, on the great geometric vases. In his use of essentially the same technique Herodotus achieves verbal perspective and that amplitude of scene which is his distinction and charm: things and events are 'worth relating' (v. 47) and 'worth seeing' (iv. 85), as they approach or recede around the centre of interest, the *aitia* of the historical composition.

This is a 'putting together of the actions' of great originality and boldness. In the strictest sense, it 'rose towards the *myth-like*', and as such Thucydides condemns it. He perceived the technical artifice, and was trying himself to write history without it, though still within the metope-rhythm of winters and summers.

Considered simply as narrative, and still more as an attempt to

---

[1] Pausanias i. xv. 4.   [2] Furtwängler–Reichhold, ii, pl. 88.

discover causes and to write history, the work of Herodotus owes so much to deliberate artifice that it is worth while to analyse it all, and discover the main lines of its structure, in accordance with the claims of his Preface. Like the *Iliad* and the *Odyssey*, the *Histories* consist of major compositions separated by the chief pauses in the action. These in turn consist of episodes in which that action is developed, sometimes in a single narrative-order, sometimes in alternate chapters (iii, v, vi), or parallel narratives (iv) only loosely connected in time. But except in explanatory digressions, on Persia, Egypt, Scythia, or Cyrene, the narrative never harks back, from the accession of Gyges to the retreat of Xerxes. These episodes again are composed of events, each traced from its cause—as Herodotus detects it—and developed into its consequences: and these in turn are grouped around more significant incidents, as already observed.

V

THE STRUCTURE OF THE *HISTORIES*

IN Book I. 184 Herodotus promises to give, in his 'Assyrian stories', an account of early kings of Babylonia. This promise is not fulfilled. If it had been, the 'Assyrian stories' would have been a counterpart to the 'Egyptian stories' in Book II which is now so disproportionate an appendix to Cambyses' conquest of Egypt. It has been disputed whether the 'Assyrian stories' stood after the description of Babylonia and Assyria (i. 192–200) appended to the capture of Babylon by Cyrus (i. 177–91) or before the capture by Darius (iii. 139–49). On the general ground of symmetry, the former is more likely (p. 94).

Apart from this loss, and the accidental displacement of a section of Egyptian history (ii. 100–37) which should follow ii. 136 not 99, there is no reason to doubt that we have Herodotus' book essentially as he left it. The order in which he may have composed its principal sections, and any changes which he made in an earlier order—for example, making the story of Croesus into a prelude to the whole—can only be discovered by comparison of references backwards and forwards and occasional inconsistencies, and do not affect the structure of our text. But the structure of our text always helps to explain why an episode stands where it does.

The Prologue (i. 1–6), which states the purpose of the work, and rejects inadequate 'causes' for the Persian Wars, leads directly to the *Rise and Fall of Lydia* (i. 7–94), Croesus being presented as the 'first wrongdoer' against the Greeks on his coast; he exacted tribute, but failed to defend them. At the centre point of this tragic composition stand counterpart-presentations of Athens and Sparta, which had promised help to Croesus, but failed to save him.

The Rise of the Persian Empire (i. 95–ii, iii, iv, v. 1–27) is an elaborately balanced composition, from the origin of Cyrus the

Persian and his supremacy over Media (i. 95–130), with an appendix on Persian customs, to the pacification of new European provinces by Darius (v. 1–28) whereby his Empire gained a land frontier with the Greek king of Macedon. Principal stages in Persian conquest are the *Second Conquest of Ionia* after the Revolt of Pactyas (i. 141–76) introducing the Greek cities of Ionia, Aeolis, and Caria; the *Conquest of Babylon by Cyrus* (i. 177–201), with the incomplete account of Mesopotamia; the *War of Cyrus with the Massagetae* on his north-eastern frontier, leading to his death (i. 201–16); and the *Conquest of Egypt by Cambyses* (ii, iii. 1–38) with the *description of Egypt* (ii). Central is the dream of Cyrus about his eventual successor Darius (i. 209–10), and the sequence of episodes goes on to v. 28 as follows:

In Book III two narratives are alternated: (*a*) the *Magian Revolt, Death of Cambyses*, and *Accession of Darius* (iii. 61–87), followed by a geographical *Description of the Empire* (iii. 88–117), by the episodes of Intaphernes (iii. 118–19) and Democedes (iii. 129–38) and by the *Second Conquest of Babylon* (iii. 150–9) which completed Darius' consolidation of the Empire in Asia: (*b*) the *Rise and Fall of Polycrates of Samos* (iii. 39–60, 120–8, 139–49), the only leader of a Greek defensive sea-power after the Conquest of Ionia (i. 141–76). This tale of pride and fall balances the tragedy of Croesus.

In Book IV, similarly, *Persian aggression in Europe* (iv. 1–144) and in *Libya* (iv. 145–205) is described with full geographical commentaries, and a retrospect of Persian relations with Cyrene (iv. 145–67, 200–5), a counterpart to those with Samos (Book III). In v. 1–27 Darius pacifies his new European dependencies and reorganizes the western provinces of Asia Minor. Thus ends the 'Persian History' as some have called it; and the stage is set for a second quarrel with the western neighbours.

In the *Ionian Revolt* (v. 28), this new struggle breaks out, led by Miletus, discountenanced by Sparta (v. 49–54), but supported by Athens (v. 55–94); both decisions require historical inquiry into causes (v. 39–41, 55–96). The suppression of the Revolt occupies the first half of Book VI (1–48), followed by further examination of the relations between Sparta and Athens during the reigns of Cleomenes (vi. 48–93) and Leotychides.

The *Campaign of Marathon* (vi. 94–120), which is Persian reprisal for the Ionian Revolt, requires several footnotes and appendixes, especially to complete the story of Miltiades (vi. 121–39).

The last three books (VII–IX) are more closely connected: the story of Artemisium passes over from vii. 178–95 to viii. 1–23: that of Salamis ends at viii. 107, but that of Plataea does not begin till ix. 19 after a consecutive narrative of negotiations and intrigues. The structure is also more closely wrought. Between a *Prologue* in which Xerxes decides to attack (vii. 1–19) and an *Epilogue* (ix. 107–22) illustrating Persian demoralization stand, first, contrasted reviews of the Persian and Greek preparations (vii. 20–130, 131–71); then the fivefold composition of battle narratives: land and sea fights, Thermopylae and Artemisium preceding, and Plataea and Mycale following, the crucial struggle at Salamis (viii. 49–107).

Within this general plan, each section has its own structure and rhythm, which must be set out separately hereafter, if its historical perspective is to be appreciated, and allowance also made for omissions. Herodotus is no less memorable for his silences than for his garrulity.

BOOK I. CROESUS OF LYDIA AND CYRUS OF PERSIA

The Rise and Fall of Lydia (i. 7–94)

The structure of the 'Lydian story' is simple. Straightforward narrative, a chronicle from the earliest times to Gyges, Alyattes, and Croesus, is elaborated with self-contained anecdotes (*novelle*) —the romance of Candaules and Gyges (i. 8–12), the war of Alyattes with Miletus (i. 16–22), incorporating the folk-tale of Arion and the Dolphin (i. 23–24), the wisdom of Bias (or Pittacus, i. 27), and a geographical sketch of the Empire (i. 28). The centre-piece (i. 46–56) is preceded by a pair of warning episodes—Solon (i. 29–33) and Atys and Adrastus (i. 34–45)—

followed by another pair, about allies who defaulted—Athens under Peisistratus (i. 59–64) and Sparta confronted with Tegea (i. 65–8)—linked by an analysis of the composite Greek people (i. 56–58).

The centre-piece reveals the self-confident misinterpretation of the oracles by Croesus (i. 46–56).

The counterpart of the rise of Lydia opens with the rejection of the advice of Sandanis (i. 71) and a review of the strategical and historical background (i. 72–74) introducing Alyattes again; then follow rapidly the Cappadocian fiasco (i. 75–77); the counter-attack of Cyrus (i. 78–87); the failure of Sparta to help Croesus; and the capture and rescue of Croesus (i. 86–88), a folk-tale pendant to that of Gyges (i. 8–12).

The appendices i. 93–94 on Lydian customs, on the origin of the Etruscans by migration from Lydia, and on the invention of coinage, are all that is left of an enframing anthropology of Lydia, balancing the ethnology and earlier history before Gyges (i. 7): compare the similar frames of Persian history and culture (i. 95–106, 131–40).

This 'Lydian story' is not only the historical occasion of the collision between Persians and Greeks, but a first exemplification of the 'cycle in human affairs', and of the responsibility of man for his use of wealth and power, which it is Herodotus' purpose to investigate. The historical frieze of narrative is subordinated to a tragic *peripateia*, rising and falling fortunes, weak and strong characters, divine providence and human will, centred on the offence of Croesus, from which the greater tragedy is to proceed.

Cyrus and the Persians

The story of Persia and the Persians (i. 95–140) has a similarly balanced structure. Its components are, as in the 'Lydian story', (a) an historical retrospect, carrying back the chain of causes to the self-determined Deioces, a type-specimen of the Oriental rule of force (*despoteia*) as instrument of national unity, and of a conquest-state. The threefold progression—Deioces, Phraortes, Cyaxares—is centred on the set-back of the Scythian invasion, like the Cimmerian invasion in the 'Lydian story'; and the capture of Nineveh (i. 106), which closes this composition, is deliberately postponed to another context, those 'Assyrian stories' which have not been preserved (p. 94). The part played by Nabopolassar (Labynetus) in the destruction of Assyria is also reduced to a phrase (i. 106), as it belonged to the lost story of Babylonia. The death of Cyaxares set Astyages on the throne of Media. (*b*) The reign of Astyages (i. 107–30) has, as sole incident, the emergence of Cyrus. This is central, and is analysed below. (*c*) A systematic description of Persian manners, like those of Egypt, Scythia, and Thrace, and in much the same order of topics; save that deities and ritual precede social customs and are thus separated from burials and the Magi; and there is no geographical preamble. This confirms the probability that Herodotus had not himself visited Persia (pp. 6–7); and conversely that when he does describe a country, it is from his own observation.

Between these two accessory chapters, (*a*) for history and (*c*) for ethnography respectively, stands (*b*) the story of Cyrus and the Persian Revolt, in a form deliberately preferred, as the 'real story', to more romantic and exaggerated versions (i. 98; cf. 122) such as attracted Ctesias. That there were also *less* marvellous versions we know from the *Cyropaedia* of Xenophon, who, like Herodotus, had Persian friends. The two visions of Astyages about Mandane (i. 107–8) are the counterpart of Croesus' dream about Atys (i. 34). Again the composition is threefold, the historical 'cause', the conspiracy of Cyrus and Harpagus (i. 123–6) (*b*) standing between (*a*) the romance which introduces the two leaders (i. 107–22) and (*c*) the transfer of supremacy from Medes to Persians (i. 127–9). In the *History* as we have it, the Medo-Persian conquest of Lydia has been already narrated as the 'cause' of the clash between Persians and Greeks, so Herodotus can 'return to the former story' without further ado (i. 140).

The Second Conquest of Ionia (i. 141–76)

This section, like the 'History of Persia', consists of three episodes: (*a*) Ionian negotiations with Cyrus and with Sparta

(i. 141–53); (*b*) the revolt of Pactyas, after Cyrus had withdrawn to deal with troubles elsewhere (i. 154–61); this is the 'cause' of the 'second conquest'; (*c*) the consequent reconquest of Ionia by Harpagus, with severer repression, and diverse fates for Phocaea, Teos, and Miletus (i. 162–70). Of these the second, (*b*), is central, and the 'cause' of the subsequent troubles. In (*a*) is inlaid the history and description of Ionia and Aeolis (i. 142–51); at the end of (*c*) stands the pendant account of Caria and Lycia (i. 171–6) on the annexation of those districts. The whole is a well-wrought pedimental composition, centred on the expulsion of Phocaeans and Teians to new homes oversea.

The Later History of Cyrus (i. 178–214)

The remainder of Book I is at the same time the end of the story of Cyrus and the opening section of that general history of Persian conquests which ends in Book V. 27. Following the 'Second Conquest of Ionia' (i. 141–76) it balances the earlier story of Cyrus which precedes; and this threefold composition is itself a pendant to the 'Lydian story' (i. 6–94). It is moreover isolated from the rest of the Persian conquests by the disproportionate 'Egyptian story' which fills Book II, an unbalanced excrescence, as it stands, in contrast with the pendant stories of Scythia and Libya in Book IV.

This ambiguous position of the later history of Cyrus bears directly on the problem of the lost 'Assyrian stories' promised in i. 106, 184, 192. It is natural to suppose that these sections were connected with the geographical and ethnological description of Babylonia (i. 178–200): they included a history of the Babylonian kingdom, and an account of the Fall of Nineveh in 612 B.C. to which Aristotle alludes (p. 18 n.). All we learn from these references is that the last section stood later, not with the description of Babylon (i. 178–87): but they need not have been far off. The general announcement of 'many other things' (i. 192) separates these from the special account of the Persian administration of Babylonia, with the satrap's stud-farm and kennels, and may simply refer to what follows (i. 185–99). Cross-references to

Egypt (i. 193, 8, ii. 100) and to Libya (i. 193) prove nothing about omissions.

Powell[1] has followed Kirchhoff and de Sanctis[2] in the view that the lost passage followed or preceded the *Second Capture of Babylon* (iii. 150–60) and suggests that it was displaced to make room for the story of Samos. But this takes no account of the larger construction of Books I–III suggested here.

In the extant text, the forward-reference (i. 192) to 'many other things' is immediately followed by a description of the climate, river-system, crops, boats, dress, social customs, medicine, burials, and religious ritual, with a note on tribes of fish-eaters (i. 200). These topics, which Powell now accepts (1949) as part of the *Assyrian Stories*, follow much the same order as for Egypt (ii. 2–91) and Scythia (iv. 16–75) except that worship and divination are omitted before burials, and there is no introductory archaeology, Babylon itself having been already described (i. 178–83) with forward-reference for dynastic history. For Egypt, the dynastic history follows the geographical description (ii. 99 ff.); and there is nothing to preclude such a history of Babylonia after i. 200. It seems therefore simplest to suppose with Powell that chapters i. 199–200 are themselves the earlier part of the *Assyrian stories*—but (against him) that the lost historical section followed immediately, before the back-reference to 'this nation' in i. 201.[3]

The Death of Cyrus in war with the Massagetae (i. 201–16) has its own balanced structure, beginning with geographical description (201–3) and ending with ethnographical (215–16). This is the same common form as in the stories of Lydia and Persia but more concise. Within this frame, the project is discussed in speeches from Queen Tomyris (206) and Croesus (207) and set

---

[1] *Hist. Hdt.* 19–23.

[2] *Riv. fil. class.* liv (1926), 289–309; lxiv (1936), 1–14.

[3] To the disappearance of a whole section of a book there is a recent parallel. In the preface to his *History of Sicily* Edward Freeman stated that he had already written the account of the Norman Kingdom. But his executors could not find it (vol. iv, preface). Freeman, still working, died of smallpox, alone, in a hotel at Alicante: γένοιτο δ' ἂν πᾶν.

going (208) : but between this and the disastrous sequel (212–14) with more speeches from Tomyris stands the vision of the young Darius, revealed to Cyrus as his successor (209–10). Only the death of Cyrus saved the young man from an early and igno-minious fate. The central position of this episode between the 'Lydian story' and the accession of Darius in Book III, with its romantic and rhetorical handling, is emphasized by Herodotus' selection, among 'many stories that were told', of what he con-siders the 'most probable' (214), which makes Croesus, the first victim of Cyrus, to be the cause of his undoing, as well as mouth-piece of a warning like that of Solon to himself.

Standing, as it does, between the *Conquest of Babylon* and the pendant *Conquest of Egypt* (ii. 1, iii. 1–38), this episode further premises an extended description of Babylon before 201, to balance Book II, and it will be seen later (p. 97) that this sym-metry may be traced even farther forward into Book III. The 'first empire' of Persia, created by Cyrus and so nearly ruined by Cambyses and the Magian Revolt (iii. 61–79), reaches its supreme moment at the death of Cyrus; and the Rise of Samos (iii. 39–60) follows the Conquest of Egypt, as the Second Con-quest of Ionia (i. 141–76) precedes the Conquest of Babylon. The central apparition of Darius thus points forward to his accession (iii. 85–87) and reorganization of a second and greater Empire, after the defeat of the Magi (iii. 61–79).

BOOK II. EGYPT

The Description of Egypt in Book II has little trace of balanced composition. It is a *logos*, a scientific survey, the main topics of which are arranged on the same general plan (p. 73) as for Scythia and Libya in Book IV, and less fully for Persia (i. 131–40), Babylonia (i. 178–87), the Massagetae (i. 201–3, 215–16), and Thrace (v. 1–8).

All these descriptions may therefore be regarded as based on independent drafts, of earlier dates than their present contexts, and as illustrating the method of Ionian 'logographers' (p. 72). Probably they were composed respectively soon after the journeys which they record, except the account of the Massagetae, obtained from Persian informants.

From a similar Lydian *logos* remain only the historical retrospect (i. 7–25), a few footnotes (i. 92–94), and perhaps the description of dedications at Delphi (i. 14, 50–51).

BOOK III. CAMBYSES AND DARIUS: SAMOS UNDER POLYCRATES

Here is at first sight a collection of disconnected episodes between the Accession of Cambyses and the Second Conquest of Babylon. There is, however, in the first place, a clear attempt at chronological sequence, in phrases linking one incident on to the next, or back to the death of Cambyses. Secondly, three stages of the history of Samos (39–60, 120–8, 139–49) are deliberately interposed between the main incidents in Persian history—the Egyptian and Ethiopian adventures of Cambyses (1–38), the Magian Revolt and Accession of Darius (61–89) and the Second Capture of Babylon (150–9).

But this is not all. Reckoning forwards and backwards from the central episode—the Apparition of Darius to Cyrus (i. 209–10) between the pendant First Conquest of Babylon (i. 177–200) and Conquest of Egypt (ii. 1, iii. 1–38)—the first Samian episode (ii. 39–60) becomes the counterpart of the Second Conquest of Ionia (i. 141–76); and the Magian Revolt and Accession of Darius (iii. 61–87) correspond with the first founding of the Persian Empire by Cyrus on that of Media (i. 95–140). The survey of Persian manners under Cyrus (i. 131–40) is the counterpart of the review of the provinces and resources of the Empire as reorganized by Darius (iii. 89–117). Beyond this, again, the second Samian episode (iii. 120–8), with the *nemesis* on the pride of Polycrates, echoes the prosperity and fall of Croesus (i. 46–94).

But at this distance from the centre-piece, the symmetry is no longer exact; and all episodes after the Accession of Darius (iii. 61–87) are more closely related to this, and to the death of Cambyses, than to any previous events. In particular, there is no explicit comparison of the Second Conquest of Babylon (iii.

150–8) with the First (i. 177–200); their settings and back-grounds are different; and the Second Conquest becomes itself the occasion of yet another character-study of a great Persian, Zopyrus, like Otanes (iii. 83–84), Intaphernes (iii. 118–19), and Oroetes (iii. 120–8). Democedes, too, contrasts with Polycrates and Syloson as types of enterprising Greeks (iii. 129–38). These are 'pilaster' elements, like Chilon and Amphilytus, Lycurgus and Lichas, in Book I.

Samos (iii. 39–60, 120–8, 139–49)

The Samian episode has a threefold symmetry in each of its three parts. In the first, the rise of Polycrates (iii. 39–43) with the appendix on Samian monuments (60), the story of Polycrates and Amasis (iii. 40–43), and the adventures of the exiled Samians (57–59) enframe the Spartan and Corinthian attack on Polycrates (44–56); and inlaid in this are the causes of Spartan and Corinthian enmity respectively. The old quarrel of Corinth with Corcyra (48–53) is a far pendant to the story of Periander and Thrasybulus (i. 20–24) and to another tale of Periander later (v. 92). The final note on Samian marvels is confessedly an anomaly, but it resumes the opening theme of Polycrates' achievement, and thus is an epilogue to the whole story.

In the second Samian episode the death of Polycrates (123–5) is enframed in the story of Oroetes (120–2, 126–8), which ranks this story with those of Intaphernes (118–19) and Zopyrus (153–8). In the third, the capture of Samos by Otanes is preceded by the anecdote of Syloson (139–40) and followed by the visit of Maeandrius to Sparta (148–9), the counterpart of the Spartan dealings with Polycrates (44–47, 52–56). The whole Samian incident is thus interconnected, and linked with the general course of western events. Moreover, between the second and third Samian episodes stands the adventure of Democedes; and similarly the later Libyan story is enframed in Persian relations with Cyrene (iv. 148–67, 197–205).

On the other hand, the second (and central) episode is at the same time a chapter in the history of Darius, the intrigues of

Oroetes like those of Aryandes (iv. 165-7, 200, 203) illustrating administrative difficulties with former officers of Cambyses, and ranking among the portraits of great Persians (p. 98).

Within the larger structure already noted as centred on the Apparition of Darius (i. 209-10), between the successes of Cyrus and the failure of Cambyses, we have therefore a balanced composition centred on his accession (iii. 85-87), flanked by the Conquest of Egypt (iii. 1-38) and the Second Conquest of Babylon (iii. 150-9) and implemented by the earlier and later Samian episodes (iii. 39-60, 120-49) and by the twofold reconstruction of the Empire by Darius: (*a*) political, after the Magian Revolt, centred on the Essay on Government (iii. 80-82), and (*b*) economic (iii. 89-117), centred on the finances of Persia itself and the Gold-supply (iv. 97-105). The portraits of other great Persians, already noted (iii. 118-59), are pendant to the account of the Seven (iii. 80-84); as those of Maeandrius and Democedes (iii. 129-44) are to Polycrates and Periander (iii. 39-43, 48-53).

It must be noted, finally and in prospect, that up to the end of Book III all has gone well with Darius. In Book IV he receives warnings, in the Scythian adventure and the resistance of Cyrene. In Books V and VI the quarrel with the Greeks breaks out anew with another warning at Marathon, and in Books VII-IX Xerxes pays the penalty for the unprecedented successes of Darius.

SCYTHIA AND LIBYA
(Book IV (with V. 1-27))

The story of Democedes (iii. 129-38) had shown Darius exploring the heart of the Greek world as far as South Italy; and the attack on Samos resumed his aggression against the nearest and most powerful Greek state. In Book IV great reconnaissances, right-handed through Thrace and Scythia into the hinterland of Olbia and Panticapaeum, and left-handed behind Cyrene, served to ascertain its breadth from north to south, and to assure the King-of-kings that there were no remoter dangers to be feared. With the opening chapters of Book V (1-27) the story is brought back to the newly conquered Thracian province, to the first land-contact with a Greek state, in Macedon, and to a 'remission of troubles' like that which had followed the twin victories over Samos and Babylon in Book III.

Each of these reconnaissances is a self-contained episode, but also a stage in the march of empire. As an episode, each has its structure and development, and it is significant that the Scythian story, which has its sequel in the Ionian Revolt, is constructed to embrace the Libyan, which was already a closed chapter. For the real break between Books IV and V comes at the 'remission of troubles' (v. 28) and the Thracian epilogue is itself the counter-part of the long prologue about Scythia (iv. 1–82), before the expedition of Darius begins. Only with this symmetry recognized is the structure of the Scythian story itself appreciable, with the adventures of Darius as its centre-piece.

The Scythian Story

As some of the speeches are summarized in oblique construc-tion, the whole story, as we have it, may be an abridgement; and the same need for brevity may explain the lack of counterparts to the three long notes on the earlier part: (*a*) on the peoples of Thrace (iv. 93–96, amplified in v. 3–10), (*b*) on the map (iv. 99–101), and (*c*) on the neighbours of Scythia (iv. 103–9) all derived from *logos*-material like the other geographical notes. The Amazon story (iv. 110–17) is so loosely attached to the last of these that it may be an afterthought.

With these qualifications, the Scythian story is revealed as a concerted whole, with a central episode, prologue (iv. 1–82), and epilogue (v. 1–2). All these sections are composite, instalments of narrative being punctuated by explanatory notes.

The Prologue briefly sets out the purpose of the expedition, punitive and preventive (p. 121). The general arrangement is in the same mode of composition as the accounts of Egypt and Libya, and what is left of the descriptions of Lydia, Persia, and Babylon.

The Epilogue (v. 1–27), though shorter, is more elaborately con-structed, with its own prologue (v. 1–2) and epilogue (v. 23–25).

The centre-piece (v. 3–22), too, is composite, exhibiting the successes of Megabazus in Paeonia (14–15) enframed between the
Paeonian incident (12–13) which attracted the attention of
Darius to this region, and the Macedonian fiasco (17–20) which
not only extinguished Persian intrigue west of the Strymon, but
demonstrated that in Macedon the royal house at least was
Greek: so that here East and West stood face to face at last. The
prologue (v. 1–10) introduces the description of Thrace (3–10)
by an initial success at Perinthus (1–2); in the epilogue, Darius'
organization of the western frontier region is closed by the sub-
sidiary operations of Otanes.

Inlaid in this composition we see Darius (a) rewarding Ionian
and Aeolian loyalty and conferring on Histiaeus a charter to
exploit the Strymon valley, (b) retrieving that false step by withdrawing to Susa both Histiaeus, who was betraying him, and
Megabazus, who (like Oroetes earlier) was too active an officer
to be left in an independent command; moreover, though
Artaphernes and Otanes were absolutely 'safe' men, civil and
military authority was better in separate hands.

This highly wrought construction is set out on p. 122.

The description of Thrace (3–10), like that of Scythia and the
Scythians (iv. 96–109), survives from an original *logos*, and is
balanced at the end of Megabazus' successes by the account of
the lake-dwellers (16). The Paeonians (v. 1) balance the Pelasgians of Lemnos (27). The enthroned Darius recurs as a statical
component between the scenes of vigorous action in Thrace,
Paeonia, Macedon, and Hellespont. The ominous figure of
Histiaeus points backward to the Ister Bridge (iv. 118, 137, 141)
and forward to the Ionian Revolt (vi. 1–5). The Paeonian 'trap
to catch a King' (12–13) is balanced by the King's own 'trap to
catch a Greek' (24).

The Centre-piece between Prologue and Epilogue is the Scythian
Expedition itself, in five episodes of advance and of retreat,
punctuated by pairs of speeches, and by descriptive notes. The
two crossings of the Ister are counterparts (97–98, 140–2), and
so too are the two Scythian counter-measures (102–9, 136–42).

Darius reaches the Oarus (124) and withdraws from it (135); between these crossings is the crisis (129–34) with five speeches: Darius, Gobryas, Scythians, Darius, Gobryas, like a sequence of speeches in the *Odyssey*[1], between the ruse of the asses (129) and that of the rear-guard (135): outside these stand the two Scythian strategies (120–35, 136). Other pairs of speeches are only reported; from Artabanus and Oeobazus (83–84) and from Darius and Artabanus (143–4); (*b*) from Coes and Darius (97–98) and from Miltiades and Histiaeus (139).

Here is the *scenario* for a drama, which we might entitle *Darius, or the Scythians*, with its *peripateia* in iv. 131. By the descriptive *stasima* (94–96, 99–100) between its episodes, the action is prolonged on the outward march, and the return is accelerated by the omission of such passages.

The Libyan Story (iv. 145–205)

This is a counterpart of the Scythian story, describing Persian aggression into Africa, an attempt to outflank the Greek world southward, like the conquest of Thrace to the north. But its connexion with the main narrative is looser. But for the later date of its conclusion, it might have been made a counterpart to Cambyses' invasion of Ethiopia from the same Egyptian base. Its achievement is less significant, and its structure much simpler.

The narrative is divided by the long geographical description (168–99) which is a normal *logos* (pp. 72–73). Before the break, the causes of Greek enterprises in Libya are traced down to the conflict between Cyrene and Egypt (165–7); after it (200) this conflict is resumed and continued to the devastation of Barca and the fate of Pheretima. Cyrene alone is spared (203), the counterpart of its earlier prosperity (159–65), where the catchword *prophasis* connects with 145 and 200.[2] What is central and causal is the appeal of Pheretima to Aryandes (165–7, 200).

The foundation of Thera is narrated on Theraean authority only; preceded by the joint testimony from Thera and Sparta,

---

[1] Myres, 'The Speeches of the Odyssey', *J.H.S.*, lxxii. 1–19.
[2] Compare ἐφρόντιζον οὐδέν (197).

and followed by that from Thera and Cyrene. For the rhythm, compare the central group of speeches (126–34) in the Scythian story.

For the Thracian Epilogue to the Scythian story (v. 1–27) see p. 101 above.

DARIUS AND THE IONIANS: ATHENS: CLEOMENES
(Books V–VI)

The Ionian Revolt (v. 28–38, 99–126; vi. 1–41)

The 'renewal of troubles' which led to the Ionian Revolt of 500–494 B.C. is narrated in two sections, separated by the long digressions explaining the situation in Sparta (v. 39–54) and in Athens (v. 55–97) at the time of the visits of Aristagoras. Of these sections the first is a *Prologue*, describing the growth of unrest in Ionia (v. 28–37). The Revolt spreads, extends to Cyprus, and causes Darius to restore Histiaeus to Miletus (v. 98–vi. 107). The central episode in this *crescendo* composition is the Burning of Sardis (v. 99–102). This is balanced by the collapse of the Revolt and the fall of Miletus (vi. 6–41): central here is the Battle of Lade. The *Epilogue* of Persian reprisals (vi. 26–41), reforms (42), and precautions by Thrace and Macedon (44–46) balances the *Prologue* of preparations for the Revolt (v. 28–37).

The Retrospect of Athenian History (v. 55–96)

This composition is complicated by frequent marginal notes, but its structure is clear. There are five main episodes. The first and last recount the fall of the Peisistratidae; Hipparchus is murdered by the Gephyraeans (55–62); Hippias, expelled (62–65) and denied all hope of return, becomes a vassal of Persia (94–96).

Within this frame Herodotus reveals three main 'causes' of Athenian policy thereafter. The first is the Democratic Revolution (66–73) supplemented by the antecedents of Cleisthenes, on his mother's (67–68) and his father's (71) side. Isagoras too is traced back 'ever so far' (66). The third is the 'ancient feud' between Aegina and Athens (79–90), which was to drive Athens into sea-power under Themistocles. Between these, as centre-piece, Cleomenes reappears as instigator of Thebes and Chalcis (74–78) and occasion for Athenian reprisals and liberation from enemies on land, the death-blow to Cleomenes' policy of inter-vention (75). Inlaid in this are the domestic 'causes' of Cleo-menes' failure: Corinthian support of Athens, and the dynastic quarrel with Demaratus.

Here are most of the main factors in the politics of middle Greece: only Argos remains to be added, in the later story of Cleomenes (vi. 75–84).

The Tragedy of Cleomenes (vi. 52–60, 61–64, 72, 76–84, 87)

This section is regularly constructed, though five large digres-sions separate its main incidents (52–60, 61–64, 72, 76–84, 87). Amid the preparations of Darius (48–49, 94), the medism of Aegina (49, 89–93) provokes Athens to appeal to Sparta. Cleo-menes intervenes, is opposed by Demaratus, and deposes him (51–61). Central is the medism of Demaratus (67), the conse-quences of which continue through Books VII–VIII. Supported now by Leotychides, Cleomenes imposes his policy on Aegina (73) but loses his reason and dies. The search into causes of his death (76–84) balances that into the double kingship at Sparta (52–60): it is expanded by incidents of the Argive War (76–82). Thereafter Leotychides follows the smaller policy in Aegina (85–87), but Athens recovers freedom of action (89–93 balan-cing 49).

Marathon (vi. 94–139)

The story of Marathon, with the Parian epilogue, falls super-ficially into four sections: (i) the expedition, to the capture of Eretria (94–102); (ii) the Athenian preparations (103–8); (iii) the battle, and return to Athens (109–20), with the note on the Alcmaeonidae (121–31); (iv) the Parian Expedition, and disgrace of Miltiades (132–9). But there are pendants and counterparts which point to a more schematic arrangement, though it has been overlaid, more than elsewhere, with relevant but uncompensated incidents.

Assuming that the battle and forced march back to Athens are central, they are separated by the notes on the Polemarch (110) and on the losses and prodigies (117) from the sections on the council of war (109) and on the return of the Persians (118–19). This composite centre-piece is preceded by convergent frieze-items; the arrival—in time—of the Plataeans (108), with a note on the Plataean alliance, and followed by the arrival—too late—of the Spartans (120). To the Spartan episode are prefixed the notes on the Delian statue (118) and the Eretrian captives (119).

This larger composition is preceded by the account of Miltiades' family (103–4) and followed by that of the Alcmaeonidae (125–31); the presence of Hippias at Marathon (102, 107) balancing the treacherous shield-signal (121).

This leaves, as *Prologue* or leading side-panel, the Persian advance through the islands, the fall of Eretria, and the landing at Marathon (94–102); and, as *Epilogue*, the Athenian advance into the Cyclades and the failure to take Paros (132–9), a tripartite composition. Anomalies are (*a*) the duplication of the Plataean episode by the appeal to Sparta, and (*b*) Pheidippides' adventure (105–6), counterpart partly to the Spartan item, partly to the affair of the Delian statue (118).

THE INVASION OF XERXES

(Books VII, VIII, IX)

The last three books form a single great composition, with a *Prologue* (vii. 1–19), an *Epilogue* (ix. 108–22), and between these (*a*) the dual *Prelude* for the Persian and Greek preparations (vii. 20–138, 138–74) and (*b*) the main narrative, in five episodes, of which Salamis is central (viii. 40–113), preceded by a land-fight and sea-fight, Thermopylae (vii. 198–233) and Artemisium (vii. 179–95, viii. 1–23); and followed by a pendant pair, Plataea (ix. 12–88) and Mycale (ix. 96–106). Between these major narratives are subordinate episodes which link them into a continuous story. Each has its own balanced structure enhancing its centre-piece, which exhibits the 'cause' of the whole, as Herodotus conceives it, between its antecedents and its consequences.

The Prologue, in which Xerxes is introduced, and his mind is made up for him, is more fully dramatized even than the 'Debate of the Conspirators' in Book III. It is also most carefully constructed, with its own historical retrospect and no less than seven antithetical elements (*a–g*) in the dramatic composition, and in the historical retrospect (1–7) of Persia at the accession of Xerxes. These are (1) the external obstacle to the policy of Darius, namely a revolt of Egypt (vii. 1); (2) the internal dispute over the succession; and (3) the intrigue of Demaratus and Atossa which (4) put Xerxes on the throne when Darius died. This, (4), is central. It leads to the forward policy of Mardonius (5), supported by (6) the exiled Aleuadae and Peisistratidae, and (7) the suppression of the Egyptian revolt, balancing (1) as Mardonius (5), is the counterpart of Demaratus (3).

All this presents Xerxes as free, if he wishes, to attack the Greeks, and he is now disposed to do so (8). It is a preliminary self-contained composition, of a familiar type. In the larger scheme of the *Prologue* it is the counterpart of the Magian interpretation of the Fourth Dream (19), which releases the national effort, described in its consequences in vii. 19–138, and summarized (138) as a double enterprise, to punish Athens and Eretria, and to dominate all Greece.

The struggle for the soul of Xerxes is even more dramatic, though less historical (see pp. 217–18).

Structure of Book VII

After this *Prologue* come the pendant preparations (20–138, 145–74), Persian and Greek, centred on the behaviour of the Athenians (138–44); and then the pendant narratives of Thermopylae (198–233) and Artemisium (179–95; continued viii. 1–23).

Persian Preparations (vii. 20–137)

This section is carefully planned, and clearly articulate, though the *Catalogue* of the Persian forces inserted abruptly (vii. 60–100) is disproportionately long (61–99). It opens with a comparison of this expedition with earlier enterprises (20–21) and ends with a shorter estimate of the expedition itself and the apprehensions of the Greeks (138), connecting with the story of Greek preparations (140–75).

The canal at Mount Athos (22–24), the Strymon bridge, and the double bridges on the Hellespont (34–36) were begun three years ahead; the actual 'King's Way' between the Strymon and Acanthus is only noted later (vii. 115); the only other physical obstacle, the frontier range of Olympus, was to be bypassed through the Gorge of Tempe (128–31).

Within this frame, the Persian heralds are sent out from Sardis (32) and return to Xerxes at Therma (131).

The expedition itself is in five sections: Critalla to Sardis (26–32); Sardis to Abydus (33–43); Abydus to Doriscus (44–104); Doriscus to Acanthus (108–23); Acanthus to Therma (124–7). The third is central, with the twofold review of the whole force (44–45, 59–100). Its significance is enhanced by the speeches of Artabanus, reviewing risks and problems (46–52), and of Demaratus, forecasting Spartan courage and Greek 'rule of law' (101–5): compare the use of speeches throughout the Scythian Expedition (p. 101). Dominating this centre-piece, Xerxes on his throne overlooks the strait and the army, 'like Zeus himself' (56, cf. 44–48) for the devastation of Greece: the crucial moment is signalled by the portent of mare-and-hare (57) 'easy to guess' in the sequel.

A curious phrase—at the end of vii. 55—gives a glimpse of Herodotus at work. For formal symmetry, in a pageant of this kind, the King should have been the central figure; and is in fact presented passing over the bridge between advance-guard and rear-guard. But facts are stubborn things. Herodotus' other information was that the King passed over *last*. And so he must have done, if he reviewed his whole force as it crossed the bridge, and *saw* what Herodotus would have his reader see. So he leaves his reader to have it either way.

The symmetry of this large composition is gravely perverted by the inclusion of the *Catalogue*, which precedes the review at Doriscus and is out of all proportion longer than the *Order of Crossing* (54–85) which is its counterpart and follows the review at Abydus. Here again we see Herodotus at his desk. A *Catalogue* there surely had to be, by Homeric precedent, and historical analogy with the lists of contingents at Thermopylae, and Plataea, and of ships at Salamis. And a lordly *Catalogue* he compiled; the sources and historical value of which do not concern us here. But where was it to stand in the book? The voluminous account of Egypt was set at the beginning of Cambyses' conquest, and we know the precise point at which a continuous narrative was unpicked to make room for it, since the opening words of iii. 1 actually repeat those of ii. 1. There was the same problem about the pendant account of Mesopotamia and Babylon (p. 94); and this was perhaps never solved, though we may be sure that the account itself was written, and that it was a worthy counterpart to Book II. With these indications we have only to compare the phrases between which the *Catalogue* stands in vii. 60 and 100 to see that as in ii. 1–iii. 1 the draft has been disrupted precisely at this point, and rewritten, either before or after the interpolated passage, to cover the junction.[1]

Whether the *Catalogue* was expressly written for this place, or was an older draft, there is nothing to show; nor is the question important. It was in any event a distinct composition, as indeed its subject prescribed. We are familiar with the contrast of structure and style, between metope and frieze in architecture, between medallion and zone in vase-painting, and between epic and dramatic literature. The presentation of armed forces, in line or in column, is an exemplary subject for a frieze, or a punctuated list like the Homeric *Catalogues* or the *Heroes in Hades*. Wherever it

---

[1] vii. 60 ends: ἀριθμήσαντες δὲ κατὰ ἔθνεα διέτασσον . . . . vii. 100 begins, after a formal link: Ξέρξης δέ, ἐπεὶ ἠριθμήθη τε καὶ διετάχθη ὁ στρατός . . .

was placed in a pedimental composition, it necessarily interrupted rhythm and symmetry.

For a modern writer, with the expedients of large and small type, page references, footnotes, and appendixes, such a problem is easy to avoid: but neither papyrus-roll, nor (most elementary of all) that oral delivery, of which there are so many traces in Herodotus, permitted these evasions. It was at all events least anomalous, if it stood as near as might be to the culmination of the design, and if the construction of this design was close knit enough to sustain it; and this is the solution contrived by Herodotus. For dramatic parallels, turn to the 'beacon-speech' in the *Agamemnon*, and to the 'wanderings of Io' in the *Prometheus*; and note that, in the latter, Aeschylus has in fact done what Herodotus has but indicated in outline. He has divided the long episode into two pendant passages like the stories of Pythius (vii. 27–29, 38–39) and Periander.

The sections (i) *Critalla–Sardis* and (ii) *Sardis–Abydos* are presented as a symmetrical composition. The centre-piece (iii) is the Bridging of the Hellespont (vii. 33–36), and within this the climax is not the mechanical achievement either of the first bridges (34) or of the second (36), but the magical 'binding' and propitiation by Xerxes. The two side-panels (22–32, 37–43) which precede this centre-piece are interconnected by the pendant incidents of the Benefaction and Disloyalty of Pythius (vii. 27–29, 38–39)—a single moralizing anecdote which Herodotus has deliberately bisected for decorative use, as he bisected the story of Periander in iii. 50–53 and v. 92 in quite different contexts. The whole passage is also bound to its counterpart vii. 108–33 by the mission of the Heralds, who set out from Sardis (32) and rejoin the King at Therma (131). Here the Curse of Talthybius, combining heroism with crime, is a counterpart to the story of Pythius. With the order of march between Sardis and Abydus (40–41) compare the description of the three parallel routes and the course of the fleet between Doriscus and Acanthus (121–3).

Similarly in the counterpart (105–33) the statical description of routes, depots, and commissariat (119, 122–3) separates the

narrative—sections (iv) and (v)—as the description of the Hellespont and its bridges separates sections (i) and (ii). Finally the
description of the natural Gorge of Tempe through the strategical
frontier of Greece balances the account of the artificial breach of
the canal at Acanthus, which precedes section (i); and the raid
of lions on the camel-train (125–6) recalls the transport organization (25). It is hardly possible that all these correspondences are
accidental.

Greek Preparations (vii. 145–71)

This section is the pendant to the *Persian Preparations* (vii. 20–
137) and is as carefully elaborated. Enframed between the account
of spontaneous Athenian courage and loyalty (vii. 138–44) and
the involuntary medism of the Thessalians (vii. 172–4) is the
fivefold 'Narrative of Missions', wherein the Mission to Syracuse
is central, preceded by Sardis and Argos, and followed by
Corcyra and Crete. The Mission to Syracuse is enhanced by
speeches, elaborated by a prologue describing the origin and rise
of Gelo, and followed by his subsequent achievements, which
justify his decision to retain a free hand for defence in the West.

The mission to Argos is elaborated by a comparison between
Argive and non-Argive versions; by the subsequent episode at
Susa; and by Herodotus' own reflections, which expand this
section out of all proportion to its place in the composition in the
light of later history. The opening passage, on the achievements
of Athens, is expanded by the two oracles, and by the introduction
of Themistocles, as author of the successful policy—evacuation of
Attica, and vigorous use of the new fleet. To the behaviour of
Athens, the principal offender against Persia, threatened by
Delphi, and doubtful even of the second oracle's meaning, but
upheld by a leader of genius, the formal counterpart is that of
Thessaly, only accidentally involved in the struggle by its geographical position, supported in principle by the other Greeks,
but betrayed by their inability to defend it, and by the treason of
its own chiefs, the Aleuadae.

Both the Argive and the Athenian elaborations in this design have the appearance of after-thought and deliberate emphasis. The design therefore is premeditated.

The policy of Argos is set out in contrasted detail, with extenuating and aggravating circumstances. Its crucial instance, however, the subsequent mission to Susa, occurred at a time when Argos and Athens alike were confronted with a recurrent danger, the jealous and aggressive temper of Sparta, and were concerned to secure their rear in the event of conflict. So Herodotus acquits Argos, on grounds which excuse also the Athenian mission to Susa, *whatever it was.*

Thermopylae (vii. 196–233)

Realistic and vivid as is the narrative of Thermopylae, it is nevertheless composed on the pedimental scheme already familiar. The short account of Xerxes' march through Thessaly and Achaea (196–201) stands outside it, and consists of a description of the topography of Thermopylae (198–200) between Xerxes' visit to Halos (196–7) and the sketch of the armies in position (201). It marks the arrival of Xerxes in Greece. Similarly the march through middle Greece portends the occupation of Attica.

The Prologue (202–4), like the *Epilogue*, contrasts Leonidas with Demaratus. The history of Leonidas (205) is enframed between the loyal contingents (202–3) and the disloyal Thebans (205–8). Thereafter stands Demaratus, warning Xerxes (209). The pendant to this is his speech after the battle (234–7), followed by Xerxes' revenge on Leonidas (238) and Demaratus' message to Sparta (239). These three balanced episodes (Dem., Leon., Dem.) form the *Epilogue* (234–9).

The Battle itself consists of the central decision of Leonidas (220) enframed by static episodes, the warning and the fate of Megistias (219–21). This is the 'cause' of the whole tragedy. It stands between the *First Three Days* (210–18)—Ephialtes (219), the flank march (214–17), and the escape of the Phocians (218)—and the *Fourth Day* (232–33)—the refusal of the Thespians to retreat like the Phocians (224), the final attack (223–5) balancing the flank march; epitaphs, exploits, and absentees (226–32), and the fate of the Thebans (233) balancing the story of Ephialtes.

Note that what is central and crucial is not the flank-march, nor the final combat, but (as at Marathon) the decision of the responsible commander, and the oracle which it fulfilled.

The *Epilogue* (234–9) needs further treatment below (pp. 254–5). With the repeated statical appearances of Demaratus compare the statical seers, Chilon and Amphilytus in the story of Peisistratus (i. 59, 62), or Artabanus and Demaratus earlier (vii. 46, 101).

From *Thermopylae and Artemisium to Plataea* (viii. 27–29, 107–44)

Between the major compositions vii. 175–viii. 26 and viii. 39, and again between viii. 40–106 and ix. 1–88, the narrative consists of several separate episodes, without major interest. Even these, however, display traces of balance and climax.

The invasion of Phocis and Doris (viii. 27–32) is separated from the raid on Delphi (35–39) by Alexander's protectorate over the Boeotians (34), a characteristic bisection by a contrasted incident.

The sequel to Salamis (viii. 107–44) is more complicated. Counterpart to Alexander's aid to Boeotia (34) is his failure to seduce the Athenians (136–44), itself bisected by the story of his ancestor Perdiccas (137–9): but this is not central.

The whole section is an epilogue to Salamis, centred on the dedications (121–2) and awards after the return of the fleet from the islands (123–5) and the final estimate of Themistocles. The former half gives the retreat of Xerxes bisected by the Greek advance into the islands; the latter gives (a) the doings of Artabazus in the north (126–9) with the establishment of the fleet at Samos (130); (b) the doings of Mardonius in the south (133–5) with the mission of Alexander (136–43), including his pedigree; separated by (c) the spring advance of the fleet to Delos and the loyal mission from Ionia (132), centred on the personality (131) (and pedigree) of Leotychides, who has now replaced Eurybiades. The same threefold rhythm, triply sub-divided, recurs in the *Prologue to Plataea* (ix. 1–18).

Salamis (viii. 40–106)

To tell the story of Salamis, Herodotus had to combine three narratives: the Persian advance, attack, and defeat; the Greek preparations, decision, and counter-attack; and the dispute among the Greek commanders, till Themistocles was able to make them fight where they were, by tempting the Persians to meet them there. He has achieved this by narrating each separately, and alternating the accounts, as he has done in Books III, V, and VI. Between viii. 40 and viii. 106 there are seven sections: A, B, C, D, C', B', A'; of these, A, C, C', A' are the Persian story, though in A (the evacuation of Attica 41, 52–55) is embodied the concentration of the Greek ships at Salamis, and the Greek naval catalogue (42–49); the pendant Persian catalogue (66–68) is in C, and the Persian losses (89) are in C'. Sections B and B' are the Greek story; the preliminary debate, with five speeches—Themistocles, Adeimantus, Themistocles, Adeimantus, Themistocles (58–62); and the sequel to the fight in the bay, Aeginetan and Corinthian doings, and other episodes. Central D (72–82) is partly Persian debates (65–71), partly Greek doings; the crisis (75–76) is twofold, Themistocles' stratagem and Persian response to it. This section is deformed by the catalogues of Persian sea forces (66) and of Greek land forces (72–73), in the light of which, and of the Persian advance on the Isthmus (63–71), the Greek debate is resumed (74). The Persian land advance (71) and sea advance (76) are complementary.

Minor counterparts are the appeal to the Aeacidae (64) and their arrival from Aegina (83); the portents of snake (41), olive (55), and oracle about Cape Colias (96), with the earthquake (64) and the vision of Dicaeus (65). Throughout, the gods are not far behind the scene.

This stately narrative is enframed between the two shorter sections, *Prologue* and *Epilogue*, no less symmetrically composed, which have been analysed already.

PLATAEA (ix. 1–88)

Whatever may be thought of Herodotus' sources, there is no doubt that he believed that they were sufficient for an account of the battle, and that his narrative was intended to be in chronological order. It is therefore less influenced by method and style; and if rhythm and symmetry are detected in it, they must result from deep-seated habit.

The story of the battle, which fills the greater part of Book IX, consists of five sections. The first (1–18) and fifth (71–89) are prologue and epilogue; the second (19–40) gives the preliminaries, and the fourth (58–70) the results, of the decisions to fight, which occupy the third (41–57).

The long *Prologue* (1–18) and *Epilogue* (71–88) are linked by the medizing Theban, Attaginus (15–16, 86–88).

The *Prologue*, between Mardonius' advance into Attica (ix. 1) and his retreat (13), is centred on the Spartan decision to attack (9) between the delays at the Isthmus (10–11) and earlier (5–7). Theban and Thessalian advice to Mardonius (1–3) and his fruitless message to the Athenians (4–5) have their counterpart in the banquet of Attaginus (15–16) and the Phocian episode (17–18).

The *Epilogue* (ix. 71–88) is analysed below (pp. 116–17).

Within each section there is further articulation of incidents, some of which are counterparts: Thorex the Thessalian twice advises Mardonius (1. 55), opening the first and fourth sections; the death of Masistius (20–24) anticipates that of Mardonius (63–64); the controversy between Athenians and Tegeates (26–27) is echoed in their respective shares in the attack on the camp (70) and in the awards for valour (71); the failure of the two soothsayers (33–37) is contrasted with the successful prayer of Pausanias (61); the banquet of Attaginus (15–16) is recalled by his reappearance and escape (86–88); his colleague Timagenides closes sections ii and v (38, 86–87). The Greek advance from the Isthmus (19) is balanced by Artabazus' retreat into Thessaly (66–67). The order of battle (28–31) is recalled by the awards for valour (71–78); though these, with the distribution of booty and thank-offerings, and the story of the Coan captive (76), are delayed to form the epilogue (71–78, 80–81) with notes on the laggard contingents from Mantineia and Elis, and an incident discreditable to Aegina (77–79).

Within the several sections there is less conspicuous structure. In the *Prologue* (1–18) Mardonius advances into Attica (1–2), before the Spartan decision to attack (9), only to withdraw to Thebes (13). The bold advice of Thorex (1) is countered by the apprehensions of Attaginus (15–16) and Mardonius' suspicions of the Phocians (17–18).

The second section (19–40) brings the Greeks into position (28–30) facing the Persians (31–32) after the cavalry action in which Masistius fell, and before the raid on the Greek food-convoy (38–39). Unfavourable auspices on both sides inaugurate the long pause which is ended by Pausanias' prayer (61).

The fourth section (58–70) is the pendant to this phase of preparation, and the sequel to the decisions in the third. What is central is the prayer of Pausanias (61) followed by the death of Mardonius (63) and the Persian retreat (65–70). In the crisis, Pausanias gives the Athenians freedom of action (55), but they are indispensable for storming the camp (70).

The third section (41–57) is the centre-piece of the whole composition, and distinguishes the 'causes' of this decisive land-battle, as the centrepiece of the Salamis story reveals the diplomacy of Themistocles. The dispute between Artabazus and Mardonius (41) has its counterpart in that between Amompharetus and Pausanias. Between these episodes stand the message of Alexander (44) and Pausanias' change of position and revocation of it (46–48); and central between these is the challenge of Mardonius, the actual *momentum rerum*. Where the fighting began results from the decisions, not of Pausanias or Mardonius, but of Amompharetus (53–57) and Artabazus (41–42), both after strenuous obstruction. For while Amompharetus was halted, the Persians were moving into the trap where they were attacked and defeated, under the auspices of Hera and Demeter. This indeed is the significance of the whole incident: whether

Amompharetus was just mule-stupid, or had the better eye for ground, is a question to which there is no answer. But it was his refusal to move, like the concurrence of Artabazus, that let the battle happen where it did.

In the *Epilogue*, the collection and disposal of the booty is central (80–81): it is flanked by the distinctions and rewards (71–75), and by the burials, with the disappearance of the body of Mardonius (84–85). To the disgrace of the laggards (77) and Aeginetan brutality (78–79), the counterpart is the punishment of Theban traitors (86–88). Pausanias' treatment of the Coan suppliant enhances his reply to the Aeginetan. Finally, the northward retreat of Artabazus (89) resumes his withdrawal from the battlefield, and enframes all this supplementary narrative, leading on to the final collapse of Persian morale (107–22).

The story of Plataea is enlivened by no less than twenty 'speeches', most of them quite short, and some mere messages: ten of them are in pairs (7, 25, 44, 76, 79). This is a novelty, and perhaps an experiment, where the details were inevitably copious and involved. Among the leading persons, Amompharetus is recorded obliquely (55), an unconscious Laconism; the advice of Artabazus is also reported (41). Mardonius speaks on four occasions (10, 42, 48, 58), Pausanias also four times (46, 60, 76, 79); and Athenians thrice (7, 27, 46).

MYCALE (ix. 99–106)

Between two debates on policy (96–97, 106) the centre-piece passes from the invitation of Leotychides (98) to the 'second revolt' of Ionia which follows the battle. The fighting is grouped before and after the portent of the Herald's Staff, and the discussion of divine intervention (100–1). The disarmament of the Samians (99) is balanced by the Milesian closure of the passes (104). The long account of Evenius, the father of Deiphonus (93–95), is without counterpart.

EPILOGUE TO THE WHOLE HISTORY (ix. 107–22)

These interpolated episodes are no unfinished or slipshod writing, but an unusually intricate composition, combining the main story with illustrations of Herodotus' verdict on the whole Persian enterprise, and leading to a cross-reference which spans almost the whole extent of his book, and answers his initial question as to 'the reason why they fought with one another'. The second episode (108–13) is central, the personal misbehaviour of Xerxes and his Queen, and his own brother's revenge. The first introduces Masistes and illustrates loss of nerve in the high command (107); the third the demoralization of high civil officers, Oeobazus and Artayctes (115–21); for Oeobazus, who deserted, was in charge of the cables on the Hellespont (115), and Artayctes also introduces Artembares, the companion of Cyrus, who had been an early sample of the same lack of self-control.

TABULAR ANALYSIS OF BOOKS I-IX

I. 1-5. PROLOGUE

I. 5-94. THE RISE OF LYDIA

7.	The older Dynasties.
8-14.	Gyges: first contact with Hellas (14).
15-16.	Ardys: Sadyattes: Kimmerian inroads.
17-22.	Alyattes: collision with Miletus.
23-24.	Corinth helps Miletus: Periander and Arion.
26.	Croesus: policy towards Greeks in Asia.
27.	policy towards Greeks in Europe.
28.	*Geographical Sketch of Western Asia Minor.*
29-33.	Solon: all is not well with Croesus.
34-45.	Atys and Adrastus: the beginning of the end.
46-56.	Croesus consults the Oracles: his mistake.

WHO ARE THE GREEKS? PELASGIAN AND HELLENE, 56-58

59-64.	*Athens under Peisistratus.*
65-68.	*Sparta and Tegea.*

THE FALL OF LYDIA

69-70.	Croesus calls for help from Sparta: in vain.
71.	Croesus enters Cappadocia: advice of Sandanis.
72.	*Geographical War-map of Asia Minor.*
73-74.	*The Former War of Alyattes.*
76.	Cyrus attacks Croesus: the Ionians stand firm.
77-78.	Croesus' eastern allies: Egypt and Babylon.
79-81.	Cyrus in Lydia: surprise: portents.
83.	*Why Sparta did not help Croesus.*
84-91.	Capture and liberation of Croesus.
92-94.	Lydian customs: games: coinage: tombs: Etruscan kinsmen.

I. 95-140. CYRUS AND THE PERSIANS

95-101.	Assyrian and Median Empires.
102.	Deioces: Phraortes. I. Assyrian War: unsuccessful.
103.	Cyaxares. II. Assyrian War: indecisive.
103-6.	Scythian invasion: (cf. iv. 1).
106.	III. Assyrian War: successful.
107.	Astyages: his dream of Mandane.
108-22.	Birth of Cyrus: upbringing: recognition.
123-9.	Conspiracy of Cyrus and Harpagus.
131-40.	Persian manners and customs.

I. 141–III. 158. THE EMPIRE OF CYRUS AND CAMBYSES

III. 61–158. THE EMPIRE OF DARIUS

THE MAGIAN REVOLT AND ACCESSION OF DARIUS

III. 61–148.   *[Counterpart to Cyrus and the Persians.]*

61–67.   The False Smerdis and the Death of Cambyses.

68–84.   The Seven Conspirators.

80–82.   Essay on Forms of Government.

83.   Otanes (Great Persians I).

84–87.   ACCESSION OF DARIUS.

88.   Dynastic arrangements.

89–117.   Provincial administration.

97.   Persia.

98–105.   India and the gold-supply.

106–17.   *[Geography of Outland.*

118–19.   Intaphernes (Great Persians II).

120–8.   *Rise and Fall of Samos—II, continued from iii. 39–60.*

120–2.   Oroetes (Great Persians III): his rise.

123–5.   Death of Polycrates.

126–8.   Oroetes: his fall.

129–48.   The West:

133–4.   Democedes in Susa.

                        Atossa and Darius (Great Persians IV).

135–8.   Democedes in Italy.

139–48.   *Rise and Fall of Samos—III.*

THE SECOND CONQUEST OF BABYLON

III. 150–60.   *[Counterpart to Rise and Fall of Lydia.]*

153–8.   Zopyrus (Great Persians V)

DIAGRAMMATIC OUTLINE OF BOOKS I–III

A	Rise and Fall of Lydia.	Second Conquest of Babylon.	A′
B	Cyrus and the Persians.	Magian Revolt: Accession of Darius.	B′
C	Second Conquest of Ionia.	Rise and Fall of Samos I.	C′
D	First Conquest of Babylon.	Conquest of Egypt.	D′
E	The Massagetae and the Death of Cyrus.		

The Apparition of Darius.

IV. 1–144. SCYTHIA: PERSIAN EXPLORATION IN EUROPE

PROLOGUE

1–12.	Origin and History of the Scythians.
13–15.	[*Note on the travels of Aristeas.*
16–20.	Ethnology of the Scythians and their Neighbours.
21–31.	The Farthest East, beyond Tanais.
31–36.	The Farthest North: the Hyperboreans.
36–45.	The Three Continents.
46–58.	Geography of Scythia, with its rivers.
48–50.	Note on the Ister.
59–75.	Ethnology of the Scythians (continued).
76–82.	Greek contact with Scythians: Scyles.
81–82.	Wonders.

THE EXPEDITION OF DARIUS

A 83–93.	Darius advances by Bosporus and Thrace, to the Ister.	
83–84.	*Speeches*: Artabanus: Oeobazus.	
94–96.	[*Description of Scythian peoples.*	
B 97–98.	Darius crosses the Ister.	
	Speeches: Coes: Darius.	
99–101.	[*Map of Scythia.*	
C 102.	Scythian counter-measures I—to gain native allies.	
102–19.	[*The neighbours of the Scythians: 110–17 the Amazons.*	
D 120–3.	Scythian counter-measures II—to harass the invaders.	
124–5.	Darius reaches the Oarus.	
126–7.	*Speeches*: Darius: Idanthyrsus.	
128.	Further counter-measures.	
129.	Ruse of the asses.	
130.	of the sheep.	
E 131–2.	The Crisis: (1) the three symbolic gifts.	
	Speeches (reported): Darius: Gobryas.	
133.	(2) The Scythians at the Bridge.	
	Speech: Scythian leaders.	
134.	(3) The portent of the hare.	
	Speeches: Darius: Gobryas.	
135.	Ruse of the rearguard.	
135.	Darius withdraws from the Oarus.	
D′ 136.	Scythian counter-measures III [*continued from 123*].	
	[*No speech or digression.*]	
C′ 137.	Scythian counter-measures IV, to seduce Darius' allies: (cf. 102).	
138–9.	*Speeches*: Miltiades: Histiaeus.	
B′ 140–2.	Darius re-crosses the Ister: (cf. 97–98).	
	[*No speech or digression.*]	
A′ 143–4.	Darius retires through Thrace to the Hellespont: (cf. 83–99).	
	[*Speeches* (reported): Artabanus: Darius, introducing Megabazus, the central figure of the *Epilogue*, v. 1–27.	

EPILOGUE (*v.* p. 101), V. 1–27.   [*Libya interpolated, iv. 145–205, v. below.*]

IV. 145-205. LIBYA: PERSIAN EXPLORATION IN AFRICA

A. 145-67. GREEK INTERESTS IN CYRENAICA

145-9.   The foundation of Thera, the mother-city of Cyrene.
150-8.   The foundation of Cyrene.
159-65.   The history of Cyrene.
165-7.   Relations of Cyrene with Egypt.

B. 168-99. LIBYA AND THE LIBYANS

168-80. Ethnological survey, along the coast.
181-5.   Geographical survey, through the oases.
186-96.   Cultural survey: pastorals in eastern plains,
190-91.   as far as Lake Tritonis;
192-194.   cultivators in western mountains.
195.   Resources: gold-washing: pitch-well.
196.   silent trade on the Ocean-shore.
197-99. Cinyps River: Cyrenaica.

C. 200-5. CONQUEST OF LIBYA BY ARYANDES

200. Siege of Barca by Pheretima and Aryandes.
201.   Stratagem of Amasis.   202 Pheretima's vengeance.
203. Cyrene escapes.
204   Fate of prisoners from Barca.
205. Fate of Pheretima at Barca.

V. 1-27. EPILOGUE TO PERSIAN EXPLORATION IN EUROPE

1. Greeks and Paeonians at Perinthus.
2.   Megabazus in Thrace.
3-10.   [*Description of Thrace and its neighbours.*
11. Darius reaches Sardis.
          Histiaeus is rewarded by concession of Myrcinus.
12-13.   The Paeonian trap for Darius.
14-15.   Megabazus' success in Paeonia.
16.   [*The lake-dwellers of Paeonia.*
17-21.   Megabazus' failure in Macedon.
22.   [*The Greek Kings of Macedon.*
23.   Megabazus' warning.
23.   The trap of Darius for Histiaeus.
24. Histiaeus is withdrawn from the West.
25. Darius leaves Sardis for Susa.
26.   Otanes in Hellespont.
27. Greeks and Pelasgians in Lemnos.

V. 28–VI. 48. THE IONIAN REVOLT

A V. 28–35.   NEW CAUSES OF UNREST Miletus 28–29; Naxos 30–35.

35–36.   Personal grievances: Aristagoras 35; Histiaeus 36.
37.   Outbreak of the Revolt.

38.   Aristagoras seeks help from Sparta: 49–51 he fails.
38–48.   The situation in Sparta.
52–54.   [*The Royal Road.*

55–97.   Aristagoras seeks help from Athens: he succeeds.
[56–96.]   [*The situation in Athens: see separate analysis,* p. 124.

98.   Aristagoras seeks help from transplanted Paeonians.

B 99–126.   THE COURSE OF THE REVOLT

99–102.   The Athenian Raid on Sardis.
103–4.   Revolt in Hellespont, Caria, Cyprus [104; 108–15].
105–7.   The news in Susa: Histiaeus returns to Ionia.
108–15.   Collapse of revolt in Cyprus; 116 Ionia; 117 Hellespont;
118–23.   118–21 Caria; 122 Aeolis.
124–6.   Flight of Aristagoras.

VI. 1–5.   Histiaeus arrives in Ionia.

B′ 6–21.   THE BATTLE OF LADE, 6–16, AND FALL OF MILETUS, 18–21.

22–25.   Effect in the West, in Athens, and in Samos.
26–30.   Fate of Histiaeus.
31–32.   Persian reprisals: Chios, Lesbos, Tenedos.
33.   Chersonese
34–41.   [*Note on Miltiades.*

A′   42.   NEW FORWARD POLICY OF DARIUS

42–43.   Artaphernes and Mardonius.
44.   Advance in Europe: Mardonius fails at Mt. Athos.

45.   Mardonius succeeds in Macedonia.

46.   Revolt and Reduction of Thasos.
47.   [*Note on gold-mines in Thasos.*
48.   Heralds sent to demand homage from Greek cities.
[*See The Tragedy of Cleomenes,* vi. 49–94.

V. 55–96. RETROSPECT OF ATHENIAN HISTORY

The central figure is Cleomenes, using all means to defeat the new democracy.

A. THE FALL OF THE PEISISTRATIDAE: Cleomenes' first intervention.

V. 55–56. (*a*) Hipparchus assassinated by the Gephyraeans.
57.   [*Who were the Gephyraeans?*
58.   [*Note on the Cadmeans and the alphabet.*
59–61. (*b*) Hippias expelled by the Alcmaeonidae,
62.   [*Who were the Alcmaeonidae?*
63–64.   with Delphic and Spartan aid:
                by sea, Anchimolius; by land, Cleomenes.
65.   [*Who were the Peisistratidae?*

B. INTERNAL STRUGGLES IN ATHENS: Isagoras and Cleisthenes.

66–69.   The Democratic reforms of Cleisthenes.
68.   [*Who was Cleisthenes—on his father's side?*
71–72.   Isagoras and Cleomenes expel the Reformers.
                [*On his mother's side: the Curse of Cylon.*
73.   ·   The Reformers momentarily appeal to Persia.
              The Reformers are recalled, to replace Isagoras.

C. EXTERNAL ENEMIES OF ATHENS

74. (*a*) THEBES AND CHALCIS called in by Cleomenes;
              baulked by Corinth,
                    by Demaratus, the other King.
75.   [*Note on the Double Kingship.*
              Retrospect of Spartan invasions of Attica.
76–77.   Athenian reprisals on Chalcis and Thebes.
77–78.   The Double Battle and the Victory Monument.
                          [*Note in defence of Democracy.*

B′ 79–81. (*b*) AEGINA, brought in by Thebes against Athens;
82–87.   reviving the old feud between Athens and Aegina.
                          [*Note on Ionian and Dorian dress.*
89.   Shrine of Acacus.
90.   bringing in Cleomenes again.

A′   90. (*c*) CLEOMENES ATTEMPTS TO RESTORE HIPPIAS

              Debate at the Isthmus: Spartan proposition,
92.   Corinthian opposition.
                          [*The Tyranny of Periander.*
93.   Hippias' warning to Corinth, the friend of Athens.
94.   Hippias retires to Macedon, Sigeum, and Sardis.
95.   [*How Athens won Sigeum.*
96.   Persia takes up the cause of Hippias.

VI. 49–94. THE TRAGEDY OF CLEOMENES

A   49.   Persian envoys to Greece.

           Aegina medizes: Athens appeals to Sparta.

B   51.   The larger policy of Sparta: Cleomenes intervenes in Aegina.

C   52.   Cleomenes quarrels with Demaratus.

   52–60.   [*Second note on the Double Kingship.*

   61.   Cleomenes deposes Demaratus.

   61–64.   [*Who was Demaratus?*

   67–71.   Demaratus goes to Persia: Leotychides succeeds him.

   71–72.   [*Notes on Archidamus and Leotychides.*

D   73.   Cleomenes intervenes freely in Aegina.

C′   747–6.   Cleomenes loses his reason and dies.

   76–84.   [*Reasons for the fate of Cleomenes.*

   76–82.   The Argive War. 84 Spartan account of Cleomenes.

B′   85–86.   The smaller policy of Sparta: Leotychides in Athens.

   86.   [*The story of Glaucus.*

   87–93.   Consequent War between Athens and Aegina.

A   94.   Persian preparations for attack on Eretria and Athens.

VI. 94–139. MARATHON

PROLOGUE: THE EXPEDITION OF DATIS AND ARTAPHERNES

A   94–97.   The Advance to Delos.

   98.   [*Earthquake in Delos: the three reigns.*

   99–100.   Delos to Eretria.

   101.   Siege and capture of Eretria.

   102.   Persian landing at Marathon.   [*Hippias is their guide.*

B   103.   Athenian advance to Marathon.

   104.   [*The family of Miltiades.*

   105–7.   Appeal to Sparta: Pheidippides: Hippias' dream.

C   108.   Arrival of the Plataeans in time:

                 The Plataean alliance.

   109.   Council of War.   [*Note on the Polemarch.*

D 110–16.   The Battle and forced march to Athens.

   117.   [*Note on losses and prodigies.*

   118.   Return of the Persians: the Delian statue.

   119.   [*Note on Eretrian captives.*

C′   120.   Arrival of the Spartans, too late.

B′ 121–4.   The shield-signal: who was responsible?

   125–31.   [*Note on the Alcmaeonidae.*

EPILOGUE: THE FATE OF MILTIADES

A′ 132–5.   The Parian Expedition.

   136.   The disgrace and death of Miltiades.

   137–40.   His former success at Lemnos.

   138–9.   [*Pelasgians in Lemnos and Athens.*

GENERAL STRUCTURE OF BOOKS VII–IX

PROLOGUE, VII. 1–19.

VII. 1–7.	Persia at the accession of Xerxes.
1.	Egyptian Revolt.
2–3.	Disputed succession: Demaratus and Atossa.
4.	ACCESSION OF XERXES.
5–6.	Forward policy of Mardonius: Aleuadae and Peisistratidae.
7.	Egyptian Revolt suppressed, the last external obstacle.

THE DECISION OF XERXES, VII. 8–19.

8.	The First Council: Xerxes will fight.
9.	Mardonius encourages him.
10.	Artabanus opposes.
11.	Xerxes still intends to fight.
12.	*The First Dream.*
13.	Second Council: Xerxes will stay at home.
14.	*The Second Dream* threatens X. if he does so.
15.	Xerxes still intends to fight.
16.	Artabanus protests again.
17.	*The Third Dream* converts Artabanus to Mardonius'
18.	The Third Council: Xerxes will fight. [policy.
19.	*The Fourth Dream* removes last obstacle to loyal enthusiasm.
	[*This elaborate Prologue has its counterpart Epilogue, ix. 106–22.*

THE COURSE OF THE INVASION

VII. 20–137.	Persian Preparations and Advance to the Greek Frontier.
138–71.	Greek Preparations and Advance to Thermopylae.
175–VIII. 25.	Defeat at sea: Artemisium. 225–40. Xerxes advances.
VII. 196–239.	Defeat on land: Thermopylae.
VIII. 40–106.	CRISIS: Salamis.
IX. 19–89.	Victory on land: Plataea.
90–106.	Victory on land: Mycale.

EPILOGUE, IX. 106–22. A. CAPTURE OF SESTOS: B. PERSIAN DEMORALIZATION.

106.	Misconduct of Masistius, a Persian General.
108–14.	Misconduct of Xerxes.
115–16.	Misconduct of Artayctes, a Persian Governor and of Oeobazus.
117–18.	*Sestos.* 120. Reprisals of Xanthippus.
122.	*Finale: the warning of Cyrus.*

VII. 20–138. PERSIAN PREPARATIONS: ADVANCE TO THERMA

VII. 20–21.   PROLOGUE: Estimate of the Expedition.

22–23.   *Natural Obstacles.*
   Mount Athos: the canal.

24.   River Strymon: the bridge.
   [Hellespont, bridge of boats 33–36].

37.   Eclipse: (cf. 128–31).

26–32.   *From Critalla to Sardis.*

27–29. Story of Pythias I.

32.   Sardis: heralds sent to Greece [they return 131–7].

32–43.   *From Sardis to Abydus.*

33–36. Hellespont: bridges: eclipse 37.

38–43. Story of Pythias II.
   Speeches: Pythias, Xerxes 38. Xerxes 39.

44–104.   *From Abydus to Doriscus.*

44–45. Review at Abydus

45. *Speech* of Xerxes (reported).

46–47. Artabanus—Xerxes—Art: Xerxes:

47–49.   Artabanus—Xerxes—Artabanus:

50–52. Xerxes: Artabanus—Xerxes.

53. *Speech* of Xerxes to Persians.

54–55.   CROSSING OF THE HELLESPONT:

57. *Portent* of the Mule and the Hare.

58–60. Review at Doriscus: numbering of the army.

61–100.   [*Catalogue of the Army*]

101–2.   *Speeches*: Xerxes 101. Demaratus 102.

103.   Xerxes.

104–5.   Demaratus 104. Xerxes dismisses D. 105.

105–23.   *From Doriscus to Acanthus.*

107. Story of Boges at Eïon.

118.   Acanthus: distress of the natives.

119.   Persian supplies.

122–3.   The fleet: Athos to Therma.

124–7.   *From Acanthus to Therma.*

128–31.   *Natural Obstacles* again: (cf. 22–23).
   The passes into Thessaly: (cf. 22–24).

129.   Tempe.

132–3. *Therma*: the heralds return from Greece: (cf. 32).

134–7. The curse of Talthybius [balances story of Pythias 27–
   29: 38–43].

EPILOGUE: Estimate of the Expedition: Double Objective:

138.   against (*a*) Athens; (*b*) all Greece: (cf. 20–21).

VII. 138–74. GREEK PREPARATIONS AND ADVANCE TO THERMOPYLAE

VII. 196–239. THERMOPYLAE

PROLOGUE

VII. 196–7.   Xerxes' advance to Malis.
198–200.   Topography of Thermopylae.
201.   The armies in position.
202–3.   Greek loyal contingents.
204.   Leonidas: history.
205.   Greek disloyal contingents: Thebans.
206–8.   Carneia: Olympia.
209.   Demaratus warns Xerxes: (cf. 234–7).

THE BATTLE

210–12.   The First Three Days.
213.   Ephialtes: his history and fate.
214–17.   The Flank March.
218.   The Phocians escape: (cf. 222).
219.   The Warning of Megistias.
220.   Leonidas' decision: the ORACLE (*central*).
221.   The fate of Megistias.
222.   The Thespians remain: (cf. 218).
223–5.   The Fourth Day.
226–32.   Epitaphs: Exploits: Absentees.
233.   Fate of Thebans.

EPILOGUE

234–7.   Demaratus warns Xerxes.
238.   Xerxes' revenge on Leonidas.
239.   Demaratus warns Sparta.

N.B. *What is central and crucial is neither the flank-march nor the final combat, but the decision of Leonidas to fulfil the Oracle.*

VIII. 27-55. PROLOGUE TO SAMIS. *see p. 113.*

PROLOGUE A. PERSIAN MOVEMENTS AFTER THERMOPYLAE   A

VIII. 27-32.   Invasion of Phocis and Doris.

     33-34.   Alexander of Macedon protects Boeotia.

     35-39.   Persian raid on Delphi.

PROLOGUE B. GREEK MOVEMENTS AFTER ARTEMISIUM

     40.   Greek ships withdraw from Artemisium to Salamis.   *Snake portent.*

     41.   Evacuation of Attica.

     42.   Greek ships from Troezen to Salamis.

     43-48.   Greek naval catalogue.

     49-51.   Debate at Salamis begins.

     52-55.   Devastation of Attica: defence of the Acropolis.   *Olive portent.*

VIII. 56-83. SALAMIS: FINAL PREPARATIONS

DEBATE AT SALAMIS 56-57   B

     56.   Advice to Mnesiphilus to Themistocles.

     57-58.   Themistocles (privately to Eurybiades).

     59.   Adeimantus.

     60.   Themistocles.

     61.   Adeimantus.

     62.   Themistocles threatens to withdraw.

     63.   Eurybiades: decision to stay: debate continued 74.

     64.   Aeacidae summoned: (cf. 83).   *Earthquake portent.*

PERSIAN PREPARATIONS AND DECISION   C

     65.   Demaratus and Dicaeus: (cf. 11).   *Portent at Eleusis.*

     66.   Persian fleet from Trachis to Phalerum.

             Persian naval catalogue: reinforcements.

     67-68.   Council of War:

             Mardonius and Artemisia.

     69.   Xerxes decides to attack.

     70.   Preliminary advance, too late in the day.

     71.   Persian land force towards Peloponnese: (cf. 65).

GREEK PREPARATIONS AND DECISION   D

     72-73.   Land Catalogue.

     74-75.   Debate continued from 63: decision against Themistocles.

     75.   Themistocles' stratagem.

     76.   Persian reaction: Psyttaleia: three squadrons.

     77.   Oracles to the Greeks.

     78.   Debate continues.

     79-81.   Aristides arrives.

     82.   Ship from Tenos.

     83.   Themistocles' final speech. The Aeacidae arrive 83: (cf. 64).

             [*This is the centre-point.*

VIII. 83-96. SALAMIS

THE BATTLE: A. IN THE BAY   C′

     83-84.   The backwater manœuvre and the 'vision of a woman'.

     85.   Greek order of battle: Athenians: Spartans. 86 Aeginetans.

     86.   The melée: effects of Xerxes' presence.

             Greek losses.

     87-88.   Artemisia's prowess.

     89.   Persian losses.

     90.   Phoenicians and Ionians before Xerxes.

see p. 113.

THE BATTLE: B. OUTSIDE THE BAY   B'

91.   The Aeginetan rear-attack.
92.   Themistocles and Polycritus.
93.   Aeginetan and Athenian prowess.
94.   The Corinthians in the Bay of Eleusis.
95–96.   Aristides on Psyttaleia. Wreckage off Cape Colias 96.

THE RETREAT OF XERXES   A'

97.   The projected mole across the narrows.
98.   The news reaches Susa: (*a*) of victory.   [*Note on Persian posts.*
99.   (*b*) of defeat. (*c*) of Xerxes himself returning.
100.   The advice of Mardonius.
101.   Xerxes consults Artemisia.
102.   The advice of Artemisia.
103.   Artemisia is sent home with Xerxes' children.
104–6.   [*The story of Hermotimus.*
107.   Xerxes leaves Attica. The Persian fleet retires to the Hellespont.

VIII. 107–47. EPILOGUE TO SALAMIS.

108–12.   The Greek fleet among the Cyclades: autumn.
113–20.   Xerxes in Thrace: the loss of the Bridges 117.
121–5.   Sequel to Salamis: dedications and awards: Themistocles.

126–9.   Preparations for the next campaign (*a*) Artabazus in the North.
130.   The Persian fleet moves from Hellespont to Samos.
131.   The Greek fleet advances to Delos: spring.
                    Leotychides is in command: his pedigree.
132.   Mission from loyal Ionians.

133–5.   Preparations for the next campaign (*b*) Mardonius in the South.
136–44.   Mission of Alexander of Macedon to Athens.
137–9.   His pedigree.

IX. 1–18. PROLOGUE TO PLATAEA.

IX. 1.   Mardonius advances into Attica 479, spring: Thorex.   I
2–4.   Theban and Thessalian advice.
5.   Envoy sent to Athens: rejected.
6.   Athenians evacuated again to Salamis.
7–8.   Spartan delays at the Isthmus.
9.   Spartan decision to attack.
10–11.   More delays: eclipse earlier.
12.   Argos intrigues.
13.   Mardonius retreats from Attica.
15–16.   The banquet of Attaginus of Thebes.
17–18.   The testing of the Phocians.

IX. 99–106. MYCALE

PROLOGUE

90.	The Samians invite the Greek fleet to advance from Delos.
91–5.	The omen of the name Hegesistratus.
92–95.	The story of Evenius.
96.	The Greek fleet advances from Delos to Samos.
97.	The Persians send the Phoenicians home, withdraw from Samos to Mycale, and fortify a naval camp.
98.	Debate decision to attack, rather than retire or sail north.
	Leotychides addresses the Ionians (*cf. Themistocles viii. 22*).

THE BATTLE

99.	The Greeks land at Mycale, in the afternoon.
	The Persians disarm the Samians.
100.	*Portent of the Herald's Staff: news of Plataea.*
101.	Note on divine intervention.
102.	Athenians advance along beach: Spartans through hills.
103.	The Persians alone resist: disarmed Samians help.
104.	Milesians close the passes against the Persians.
105.	Consequent 'second revolt' of Ionia from Persia. Awards.

EPILOGUE TO THE AEGEAN CAMPAIGN

106.	Debate on liberation of Ionia.
	Peloponnesian proposal: transpose loyal with medizing Greeks.
	Samians, Chians, Lesbians, and others join the League.
	The Greek fleet moves north to Hellespont.

IX. 107–22. THE EPILOGUE TO THE WHOLE HISTORY

[Interposed between incidents in the Greeks' attack on the Hellespont are examples of Persian demoralization.]

	106.	*The Greeks discuss the liberation of Ionia, and sail north (above).*
A	107.	The misconduct of Masistes son of Darius towards Artayntes.
		Illustrating loss of nerve in the high command.
B	108–12.	The misconduct of Xerxes with Masistes' wife and daughter.
		Illustrating the levity and cruelty of Xerxes himself.
	113.	The fate of Masistes, after his misconduct.
	114.	*The Greeks arrive in Hellespont, and besiege Sestus.*
C	115–16.	The misconduct of Artayctes: against Elaius.
		Illustrating demoralization of provincial officers.
	117–18.	The punishment of Artayctes. *The Greeks take Sestus.*
		Oeobazus flees.
	119–21.	*The Greeks return to Greece,* and dedicate the Cables: (cf. vii. 36).
D	122.	The proposal of Artembares, grandfather of Artayctes.
		The will to inflict conquests was already present.
		Cyrus, founder of the empire, gave warning of consequences.

Refers back to i. 95, recounting 'who Cyrus was', and to i. 125–6.

Cf. Aeschylus' revival of the ghost of Darius in the *Persae*.

VI. HISTORICAL NOTES ON THE *HISTORIES*

Wbut a collection of notes on principal topics of the *Histories*, in relation to their historical context. For more detailed information and criticism, reference should be made to the lists of selected works under each head.

BOOK I
LYDIA AND PERSIA

The brief *Prologue* (i. 1) precisely describes the purpose of the work as we have it; and this purpose is kept in view by frequent reminders throughout. There are three linked objectives:

1. Great deeds have intrinsic value; they are the legacy of the past, and deserve to be immortalized.
2. Great deeds are no monopoly of Greeks; the Persians also have their distinctive virtues; this is indeed the tragic interest of the struggle.
3. Great deeds are not isolated events: they are connected as causes and effects, and it is the task of history to trace back the sequence of cause and effect as far as there is evidence.

This applies, no less, to the world of nature. The great rivers with their flood-seasons (ii. 17–27), the gorge of Tempe (vii. 129, 173), the threefold oil-well in Zacynthus (iv. 195), are memorable in themselves; memorable things occur in all regions alike, and they have their respective causes, which can be discovered. They may themselves be contributory causes of human events and characters. But the supreme cause in history is human choice and will.

Having stated the aim of his inquiry, Herodotus disposes of two current theories of history: we may call them the *cherchez la femme* theory, and the *east-and-west* theory; they attribute the course of events to causes either personal and romantic, or regional and racial. Who the 'learned Persians' were, to whom he ascribes them, he does not reveal; in Egypt he applies a similar phrase to the men of Heliopolis (ii. 3). He annotates their opinion from his own knowledge, quotes alternative versions, and reduces it to an absurdity. The severance between east and west he merely notes here; but it recurs in the Epilogue (ix. 116). For Herodotus' Persian informants see p. 149.

Not all past events, however, are historical causes. The heroic ages of Io, Medea, and Helen, like the sea-power of Minos (iii. 122), are separated by a great gulf from that of Croesus and Polycrates. There was no Egypt till the gift of the Nile was achieved; no Scythia till the Scythians came. Hence, too, the significance of the 'extremities' of the continents (iii. 106), or the sources of Nile and Ister; they are the frame of the historic land-scape; the Greek instinct for definition demands no less, but looks no farther, for causes. Accordingly, after recounting myths collected from 'learned' Persians and from Phoenicians, and exposing the futility of the *cherchez-la-femme* theory, Herodotus makes a clean break with the legendary past, and exhibits Croesus of Lydia as the first ruler in Asia to wrong his Greek neighbours.[1]

Lydia. The Greek world of Herodotus' time was bounded eastward by the peninsula of Asia Minor, essentially a high plateau, surrounded by still higher mountain-chains, with steep sea frontages to north and south, but wide valleys and large coast-regions opening westward on to the Aegean. The Cilician lowland to the south-east is isolated both eastward and westward.

For Herodotus, the Lydian Empire resulted from the domination by the Mermnad dynasty of Sardis over those western coast-lands, and the western half also of the plateau. It was bounded at its greatest extension, under Alyattes, by the lower northward

---

[1] It has been ingeniously argued by Powell (*The History of Herodotus*, 1939, 9–16, esp. 10) that this *Preface* was added to the Lydian story (i. 6–94) when that section was prefixed to the 'History of Persia' which now stands from i. 95 to v. 27, but had originally followed the account of Cyrus and Persia (i. 95–140). We are here concerned, however, with the text as Herodotus left it, and must look rather for reasons why he should have begun his *History* as he has.

course of the Halys, and what Herodotus calls the 'neck' of the whole country (i. 72), between the middle Halys and the southern sea. As long as this dominion held, no oriental dynasty could threaten Greek coast-cities. For this security they were ready to contribute from the wealth it brought them; and, for their own security, Greek states beyond the Aegean agreed to support Croesus in time of need. It was the failure of Croesus to give the covenanted protection that made him the 'first cause' of collision between East and West. Only when Sardis has become the capital of a western province of Persia has Herodotus any need to answer the question *Who Cyrus was?* (i. 95). For this catastrophe there were several causes: the rhythmic rise and fall of human fortunes; the initial treason of Gyges to his Heracleid master, and Apollo's penalty; the personal pride of Croesus, in spite of warnings; the failure of his oversea allies, bringing disaster upon them too, but tempting Persia to its fall. It is because none of these causes was sufficient that the 'Story of Croesus' has been found so difficult to explain, as Herodotus tells it.

The 'Lydian story' is drafted in episodes like a tragedy; (1) an historical prologue, beyond Gyges, whose treason his fifth descendant was to expiate; (2) repeated warnings, from Solon, from the domestic tragedy of Atys and Adrastus, and from the Delphic oracle, at the height of Croesus' prosperity. Between these scenes and (3) the rapid defeat by Cyrus, 'announcing himself' like a tragic messenger, followed by the rescue of Croesus through Apollo's rain-storm—another tragic episode—stands (4) like a dramatic chorus—prelude, strophe, and antistrophe—the presentation of the composite Greek nationality, Pelasgian and Hellene, the contemporary fortunes of Athens under Peisistratus and those of Sparta from Lycurgus to Chilon. The tragic outlay of this 'Lydian story'—a 'Capture of Sardis' like the 'Capture of Miletus' of Phrynichus (vi. 21), is enhanced by frequent dialogues and rapid sequence of self-contained episodes interspersed with anecdotes—the story of Candaules, and of Arion, the 'battle of the champions' between Sparta and Argos, and those final notes on Lydian archaeology, which, like the sketch-maps (i. 6, 28, 72) and the dedications of Gyges and Croesus, are all that remain of an original Lydian *logos* like the descriptions of Egypt and Scythia. The story of Candaules was already familiar in Attic tragedy.[1]

The inset retrospects of Athens and Sparta are even more formally composed. Each has not only 'a beginning, a middle, and an end', but culminates in the middle, pedimentally (pp. 84–85). The component episodes are restricted by the balanced rhythm, and cannot therefore be regarded as inclusive summaries of events, but as a selected sequence of crucial incidents, of causes and effects. These excursions into Greek history are best considered in connexion with similar passages in Books V–VI (p. 176).

EARLY LYDIA (i. 7–25)

Of the early history of Lydia, Herodotus gives a clear and intelligible account. From the fall of Sardis in 546 B.C., by dead-reckoning of reigns, he sets the accession of Gyges in 715 B.C., about a generation too early; for the earliest mention of Gyges in Assyrian annals, as a new-comer, is in 686 B.C. The discrepancy is probably due to neglect of co-regencies like those of Assyria and Egypt. From Candaules the Heracleid dynasty goes back twenty-two generations or 505 years—not mere lifetimes, therefore, but *reigns* derived from a list, such as Xanthus uses when he says that 'Spermos is not inscribed in the royal list'.[2] This sets the establishment of the Heracleids in 1191 B.C.; on the morrow, therefore, of the great Land-Raid of 1193 which wrecked the Hittite Empire and brought the Phrygians and the Bithynian Thracians from Europe into Asia Minor. In Priam's array (*Iliad* ii. 864) the place of Lydians is taken by Maeones, with the same ethnic as Paphlagones, Doliones, Cicones, Paeones, and Macedones, and probably of kindred origin. The 'Lydians' of Herodotus, then, should be a dynasty or régime like the Carians and Mysians who shared with them the cult of Zeus at Mylasa (i. 171). The affilia-

[1] E. Lobel, *Proc. Brit. Acad.* xxxv, 1950; D. L. Page, *A New Chapter in the History of Greek Tragedy* (Cambridge, 1951).
[2] *F.H.G.* i, fr. 49; *F.G.H.* 90. F 44: p. 347, vol. iiA.

tion of the Tyrrhenians at this point is developed later (i. 94: p. 141). Another aspect is the Lydian 'sea-power' in Eusebius' list, immediately following the Fall of Troy,[1] which permitted the Tyrrhenian migration to Italy. Herodotus, however, affiliates Agron, the first Heraclid, not to a Greek Heracles, but through Ninus and Belus to an oriental 'mighty hunter'—an echo of Nimrod in the 'Table of Nations' in Genesis x. Gyges therefore was leading a regional and national liberation of the western peoples from an oriental domination on the plateau. The Heracleid lion, however, kept its place on the coins of Mermnad Lydia.

The fuller account quoted by Nicolas of Damascus (fr. 49)[2] from the fifth-century Lydian, Xanthus, confirms this interpretation. Gyges is from Tyrrha in Maeonia; his father Dascylus from Dascyleum on the Propontis; the queen, Tudo, is a Mysian; Arselis, his chief accomplice, a Carian from Mylasa; his paymaster is Melas of Ephesus; the support of the Greek cities is acknowledged by the dedications at Delphi, second only to those of Midas. Thus installed, Gyges exploits the goldfields of Sardis, and the bazaar where the great eastern highway fed the roads to coast towns and principalities, from the Hellespont to Lycia. From wider knowledge, Herodotus selects typical or crucial struggles between Gyges and the Greek coast-cities, and supplements them from the chronicles of his successors.

By supporting Psammetichus in Egypt against Assyria, Gyges had already determined Lydia's place among the dynasties, though in the Cimmerian crisis his successor Ardys paid tribute to Assurbanipal. But the Cimmerian raids (i. 15–16)—whether they came through the Caucasus, or over the Bosphorus also as some suppose—damaged the western coastlands less than the plateau and the highlands overlooking Assyria. Alyattes' frontier was already on the Halys (i. 16, 72) and by Croesus' time the Phrygia of Adrastus was a vassal state (i. 35).

The Median and Babylonian conquerors of Assyria (606 B.C.) divided the spoil and the burden of empire. Babylon dominated

---

[1] p. 250: Myres, 'The Thalassocracies of Eusebius', *J.H.S.* xxvi. 1906, 84–150.
[2] *F.H.G.* i, fr. 49.; *F.G.H.* 90 F 44: p. 347, vol. iiA.

the Semitized lowland and the Syrian and Palestinian sea-board, with the reversion of Egypt, but was dead-locked at the Isthmus by 585 B.C. Media, pushing west through the highland, confronted Alyattes on the plateau. The 'six years war' (591–585 B.C.) was ended by the 'battle of the eclipse' (28 May 585 B.C.) between Halys and Taurus, on 'the neck of the whole country' (i. 72), followed by a Median débacle, the rumours of which reached Ezekiel by the waters of Babylon:[1] 'Gog' is Gyges in retrospect. But the Syennesis of Cilicia reconciled all four powers (i. 74); and the Dual Control of 606 B.C. became the League of Despots of 585 B.C., knit by marriage alliances and concerted exploitation.

Alyattes' other achievement was his treaty with Miletus (i. 17–22), which alone of Ionian cities lay south of the Maeander and enjoyed its own valley-route to the plateau, uncontrolled by Sardis. Thrasybulus' proof that, with sea-ways assured by Periander, he was independent of inland supplies, led to agreement to work the two land-routes in concert, but set Miletus in lonely opulence over against the rest of Ionia.

Croesus. The prosperity of Lydia culminates under Croesus, whose dual policy—domination over Greeks in Asia, friendly alliance with Greeks oversea, notably with Sparta and Athens—brought him into direct intercourse with Delphi, where his lavish dedications supplemented those of Gyges and the earlier Midas of Phrygia. To illustrate this material wealth, and contrast it with the real insecurity of Croesus, Herodotus introduces Solon as an organizer and economist from Athens (i. 29–33). Though Solon had been *archon* in 594, it was not impossible that he should have visited Sardis after 560; but this anecdote is one of a series of 'visiting sages' of which other examples are preserved (Diodorus ix. 26, 27); one such is assigned by Herodotus himself alternatively to Bias and to Pittacus (i. 27; cf. Diod. ix. 25).

Lydian Antiquities

Herodotus concludes his 'Lydian story' with excerpts from a geographical and ethnological account of Lydia like those of

---

[1] Ezekiel, ch. xxxviii; Myres, *Palestine Expl. Fund Q. S.* 1932, 213–19.

Egypt, Scythia, and other regions. The 'Pseudo-Sesostris' monument on the road between Ephesus and Sardis he describes elsewhere, inaccurately (ii. 106) : another Hittite sculpture, the 'Niobe' in Mount Sipylus, he does not mention at all. Sardis is briefly characterized in i. 84, v. 99–101 with its gold-workings and thatched shanties. Otherwise he found Lydia poor in 'wonders'.

The earliest coins of Lydia, bearing the Heracleid lion-badge, are often natural nuggets of varying weight and composition; the stamp guaranteed origin, not quantity or value. A series of barbaric copies probably represents the Cimmerian interlude. Coins of refined gold, of more uniform weight and maturer style, are attributed to Croesus. The double badge—lion and bull confronted—has been ascribed to agreement with Ephesus. What Herodotus meant by *kapêloi*, 'retail traders', is uncertain; he may refer either to travelling salesmen or to local agents of great firms. The whole passage illustrates his search for causes, and the debt of the Ionian cities to Sardis.

His account of the Tyrrhenians of Etruria is noteworthy both for its early date and for the confirmation which it has won in recent times. Tyrrhenian communities may be traced in Lydia, in Macedonia (with Pelasgians, Thuc. iv. 109), in Lemnos (where an alphabetic inscription is not in Greek), and at large as pirates in the Aegean. All these may be remnants of the Tyrsha sea-raiders who harried the Egyptian coast about 1225–1190 B.C. That the western 'Tyrrhenian' Sea and 'Tyrrhenia' between Arno and Tiber may be a refuge of the same folk is supported by other western names, 'Sicilia' and 'Sardinia', from sea-raiding Shakalsha and Shardana. Herodotus brings the Tyrrhenians among the Umbrians, and the later Etruria, too, may well have been peopled by Umbrian tribes. The peculiar Etruscan aristocracies, with their resemblances to the 'lords of the Philistines' recorded in Palestine after the Sea Raids, indicate invasion and settlement by small compact bands of adventurers, arriving apparently over a long period (*c.* 1200–900 B.C.), and loosely linked for mutual defence against populous native subjects. They were certainly established in Etruria before intercourse with

Greece began. Their language, corrupted and probably mixed, gives no clue to origin; but their essentially Greek alphabet has Phrygian elements. Their material culture combines the Villanovan tradition of north-western Italy, the last previous invasion from beyond the Alps, with a black polished (*bucchero*) fabric of pottery which has its nearest counterpart in Asiatic Aeolis. But arriving as refugees and adventurers, they brought little with them, and soon lost what they brought. Their cults, depicted in frescoed tombs of the sixth and fifth centuries, were mainly Greek, but barbarized like their bloodsports. The nearest parallels to their great chambered tumuli—the *Cucumella* at Vulci and the 'Tomb of Porsena' at Clusium described by Varro[1] also of uncertain age,[2] are those of Alyattes (i. 93) and his people round Sardis and southward into Caria.[3]

BIBLIOGRAPHY

RADET, G. *La Lydie et le Monde Grecque*. Paris, 1893.
HOGARTH, D. G. *Ionia and the East*. Oxford, 1909.
BILABEL, F. *Die Ionische Kolonisation*. Leipzig, 1920.
COOK, R. M. 'Ionia and Greece in the eighth and seventh centuries', *J.H.S.* lxvi (1946), 67–98.
MAZZARINO, S. *Fra Oriente ed Occidente*. Florence, 1947.

PELASGIAN AND HELLENE (i. 56–58)

When the Athenians refuse the Persian invitation to desert the Greek cause (viii. 144) they define 'that which is Greek' as 'of one blood, one language, similar gods and sacrifices, and customs of similar fashion'. But Herodotus does not apply this criterion absolutely. His presentation of the Greek people in the days of Croesus (i. 56) distinguishes the Dorian breed, originally Hellenic and 'very migratory', from the Ionian, indigenous and 'Pelasgian'. He gives no countenance to modern theories of immigration from central Europe, for his 'Hellenes' originate in Phthiotis, whence Hellenic ancestors of the Dorians moved northward to the foot-hills of Olympus and Ossa, and thence into the Pindus

---

[1] Pliny, *N.H.* xxxix. 91.   [2] Myres, *J.H.S.* lxxiii, forthcoming.
[3] Paton and Myres, *J.H.S.* xvi (1896), 188.

highland, where they were 'called Macedonians'; only later did they move south into Dryopis (cf. viii. 43), and so into Peloponnese under the name 'Dorian'. The Pelasgian ancestors of the Athenians spoke 'another language', of which vestiges survived in Hellespontine and East Macedonian communities: they 'became Hellenes' only when they learned to *speak* Greek (i. 57), like other Pelasgian and non-Greek-speaking peoples.

Stages, more in detail, in the transmutation of the Athenians (viii. 44) were the reign of Cecrops when they were 'Cranaan' Pelasgians, that of Erectheus when they became 'Athena's people', and the military rule of Ion (an immigrant of Hellenic lineage, vii. 94) when they came to rank as Ionians, and were tribally classified under Ion's four sons (v. 66, p. 177). Searching, as ever, for causes, Herodotus has more to say (ii. 52) about the Pelasgians as the aborigines of all Greece, with a sanctuary of a nameless god at Dodona, whither dove-priestesses from Egypt brought divine names and a ritual which Greeks adopted later. Other Pelasgians, un-Hellenized, lived on in Attica till they were expelled to Lemnos and Imbros (vi. 138) and to Samothrace (v. 51); others in north Peloponnese (v. 68; vii. 94); others again in Arcadia (i. 146), whence some migrated into Ionia: the people of Cynouria (viii. 73), between Argolis and Laconia, were aboriginal but already spoke Ionic before they learned Argive Doric (viii. 73).

This is all in accord with our fragmentary knowledge of Greek ethnography. Even in Homer, alongside actual Pelasgian allies of Priam (*Il.* x. 429), located between the Hellespont cities and Thrace (*Il.* ii. 840), and other contemporary Pelasgians in Crete (*Od.* xix. 177), there is a 'Pelasgic Argos' in Thessaly (*Il.* ii. 681), inhabited, however, actually by Hellenes and Achaeans, and a 'Pelasgic Zeus' at Dodona, worshipped by Achilles (*Il.* xvi. 233); but Dodona is inhabited by Aenianes and Perrhaebi, not by Pelasgians (*Il.* ii. 750). The name 'Pelasgic' therefore had already a secondary connotative sense, perhaps 'aboriginal' or 'immemorial'. The Hellespontine 'Pelasgians' reappear in Apollonius (*Argonautica* i. 1024) and in the 'Pelasgian' Antandrus (vii. 42) of Herodotus. The 'aboriginal' notion becomes canonical in Hesiod (fr. 68 Kinkel, 411 Rzach) and Asius (Paus. iii. 1. 4, 'earthborn, that the human race might be'). Acusilaus (fr. 25)[1] apportioned mankind between Pelasgus and Argos, and confused or identified the 'Pelasgian' Argos with the Peloponnesian. Pherecydes (156)[2] made Pelasgus to be father of Lycaon in Arcadia. Hecataeus has Pelasgus as King of (Argos in) Thessaly (fr. 334–75));[3] Aeschylus, king in Argolis (*Suppl.* 246) but with frontiers on the Strymon, in Pindus, and on the sea beyond Dodona: and in *Prom.* 879 Argos itself is 'Pelasgian'. The coincidence with Herodotus' outliers is noteworthy (compare Soph. fr. 249 Nauck and Schol. Ap. Rh. i. 580).

This 'Pelasgian Theory' continued to grow; Thucydides (iv. 109) confirms Herodotus' record of 'Tyrrhenian' Pelasgians in eastern Macedonia, not speaking Greek. He regards the aborigines of Greece as generically Pelasgian, and says that Hellen and his sons 'grew strong' in south Thessaly and spread their language by intercourse; whereas Herodotus had only supposed that Pelasgians somehow 'changed their speech' to Greek. The Arcadian theory of Ephorus, and the etymologies of Philochorus (Pelasgos = *pelargos*, 'stork' because migratory) and Apollodorus (Steph. s.v. *Dodona*, p. 249 Mein. = *pelas*, 'neighbours') are wholly later.

Herodotus' account of the Hellenes, and especially of the Dorians, is also in accord with popular beliefs. In Homer, alongside the actual and topical Hellenes—a people in Phthiotid Achaia, including the Myrmidons of Achilles—there are generically Hellenes and pan-Hellenes (*Il.* ii. 530), including Oileus from Locris: and Menelaus proposes to conduct Telemachus from Sparta to Ithaca 'through Hellas and midmost Argos', which can only refer to the Peloponnesian Argos and the later 'Achaea' along the Gulf of Corinth where Odysseus is renowned (*Od.* i. 344).[4] But Hesiod has already Hellen as common ancestor (p. 7 Rzach), and Pan-hellenes as an inclusive term. Hellanicus ex-

---

[1] *F.G.H.* 2. F 25, vol. i.
[2] *F.G.H.* 3. F 156, vol. i; Natal. Com. ix. 9 (not in Jacoby).
[3] *F.G.H.* i. F 14; F 3, vol. i.
[4] *Od.* xv. 15–80.

panded the Hellenic family to include Achaeans as children of
Xuthus and cousins of the Ionians; and this is implicit in Hero-
dotus' phrase 'Ion son of Xuthus' (v. 66; vii. 94; viii. 44: cf.
Achaeus ii. 98). But the Greek adventurers in Egypt are always
'Ionians and Carians', not Hellenes or Dorians; and there is no
hint yet of *Megale-Hellas* in the West—as suggested by Bury[1]—the
Magna Graecia of the Roman geographers. Thucydides (i. 3)
restricts the original Hellenes to a tribe in Phthia who dominated
their neighbours and spread the Hellenic name as symbol of
Hellenic culture.

For the digressions on early Athens and Sparta (i. 59–68), see
pp. 177, 184 below.

BIBLIOGRAPHY

MEYER, E. *Forschungen zur alten Geschichte*, i. 1. 1892.
PARETI, L. *Studi Italiani di Filologia Classica*, xxi.

CYRUS THE PERSIAN (i. 96–140)

As with Lydia, so with the Medes and Persians, Herodotus
traces the main line of history back to a traditional crisis and has
little to say of what preceded it. His chronological perspective is
approximately correct. The five hundred and twenty years of
Assyrian rule, reckoned back from the capture of Nineveh
(612 B.C.+520: 1132 B.C.), lead straight to the victory of Ashur-
rish-ishi I over Nebuchadrazzer I of Babylon (1127 B.C.) followed
by that of Tiglath-pileser I in Phoenicia (1115 B.C.). The historical Deioces (Dayakku) whom Herodotus mentions in i. 96 was
conquered by Sargon (715 B.C.),[2] and 520 years from that event
(1233 B.C.) outranges the historical Assyria; though it would set
'Ninus' as its founder in the right relation to Agron the founder of
the Lydian kingdom (i. 7). Herodotus, however, does not make
Median revolt *terminate* Assyrian dominion, but mark the 'beginning of the end'; and the irruptions of the northern Umma-
Manda, of whom the Medes were a people, were the chief 'cause'
of Assyrian decline.

Similarly, it was during the disruption of the old Elamite

[1] Bury, *J.H.S.* xv (1895), 217.   [2] H. R. Hall, *Anc. Hist. of the Near East*, 475.

kingdom by Assurbanipal (650–640 B.C.) that there was contact
with an early Cyrus, of the vassal state of Parsumash which had
now become independent under the Achaemenid house, though
later a Median tributary.[1]

Even more significant than the political development was the
religious teaching of Zoroaster, and its adoption by the Achaemenid princes—by Darius certainly, and probably by Cyrus the
conqueror. It is a commonplace to contrast both the Medes and
the Persians with Babylonians and Assyrians as peoples of Iranian
speech and antecedents, intruded into a region, the higher culture
of which had long˙been Semitic, and Sumerian before that. It is
more significant to distinguish between the Medes and the Persians; for while the Medes had suffered more—and perhaps
learned more—from the Scythian and Cimmerian raids, the
Persians, in secluded dependence on the old highland Elam, had
been far more profoundly influenced by a religious and moral
revolution, the historical significance of which is unaffected by
controversies as to its date; its rapid spread followed its adoption
by the Achaemenid kings. Hence the value of Herodotus' summary of Persian religion and morals, confirmed in essentials by
Achaemenid inscriptions and the earliest Zoroastrian hymns.

All earlier empires had rested on the same 'rule of force', which
the Greeks called 'dynastic' or 'despotic'. It was justified, among
those who exercised it, by appeal to the same rule of force in
Nature and in Heaven. Early Hebrew theology has made this
rule familiar in its crudest form. The king on earth is absolute
viceregent of a God in heaven, who is a 'Lord of Hosts'. The God
of Armies is on the side of the big battalions, and they are on His.
He is a zealous ('jealous') God, capricious, petulant, venal,
oblivious, self-expressed in whirlwind, earthquake, and fire as
well as in the 'still small voice' within his votary. On earth, the
only restraint on despotism was the balance of power, the existence of other despots, to whom overtaxed and underfed subjects

---

[1] Dr. Oliver Gurney refers me to a cylinder from Babylon (Weidner, *Archiv. f.
Orient forschungen*, vii. 1931, 1–7) and an inscription from Nineveh (Campbell
Thompson, *Liverpool Annals*, xx (1933), 79 ff.).

might revolt. Then there would be 'war in heaven' too, for gods defended despotically their own viceroys and worshippers. Usually this balance of power made existence tolerable for little people. But a League of Despots, such as was contrived between Media and Babylonia after the fall of Nineveh, and became inclusive after the Lydian war of 585 B.C., meant hell-upon-earth for the subjects of each. Only some quite fresh 'deliverer' from outside the dynastic 'ring' could break the spell and 'liberate the nations'. It is at this point that Herodotus asks, and answers, the twin questions *Who was Cyrus?* and *How did the Persians become lords of Asia?*

Herodotus describes his own authorities for Cyrus as 'those who do not wish to glorify', and alludes to three other versions. Of these one must be that which *did* 'wish to glorify', the story of animal nurture (Justin i. 4: cf. Hdt. i. 110, the name *Spako*); one, presumed by Ctesias, of a peasant origin; one, more favourable to Astyages, of Median birth and palace training, followed in the main by Xenophon. For Herodotus, a leading part is given to Harpagus, the Mede with a grievance, chief minister of Cyrus, whose family settled in Lycia: in him Herodotus has a personal cause for the emergence of a national leader.

Cyrus was confronted with the same array of western powers as Assyria had been, behind the immediate enemy. His initial reconciliation of the Medes put the whole highland region in his power, but exposed him to counter-attack from Lydia. Babylon was in disorder and could wait; against Egypt, the 'bruised reed' as ever, his gracious revival of Jerusalem and the Phoenician cities established the traditional outer-guard west of Euphrates. His highland forces could have outstayed the Lydians on the plateau if he had not driven them off it by surprise, using the northern route across the Halys, whereas the Medes in 585 B.C. had gone southabout along the 'neck of the whole country'. Xenophon (*Cyrus* vi. 2. 10) (i. 72) reveals a very large 'Egyptian' contingent in Croesus' army, who came in their own ships, fought well, and at last only asked leave to remain where they had come; clearly they were the sole efficient troops of Egypt, the

Greek mercenaries; conversely, long before, Gyges with Greek adventurers had helped Psammetichus against Assurbanipal, and Polycrates had once planned to support Amasis against Cambyses.

With the fall of Sardis, success seemed to be complete in the west. For Herodotus, the cause of fresh trouble was Cyrus' misreading of Greek character (i. 153) and of the relations between the Greek cities and Sardis, which permitted the revolt of Pactyas.

Cyrus represents his own acts, not as conquests, but as a remedial replacement of bad rulers on earth by a good one. The gods, like the nations, were released from captivity and 'returned to their places'. In Babylon he claims to be the legal successor of Nabunahid 'King of Babylon', 'King of the lands', 'servant of Merodach', and patron of Merodach's priests with whom Nabunahid had quarrelled. In Phoenicia he installs what he calls 'kings and judges'; to exiles 'by the waters of Babylon' he is the 'servant of Jehovah'. So, too, Darius in Egypt assumes Pharaoh's titles and is 'servant of Amon-Ra'. To be 'servant' of the god of each of his vassals was the surest way to be accepted as their master; and the same tolerance and respect for local gods, their sanctuaries, and their priesthoods, were characteristic of Persian administration. Xerxes sacrifices to Athena at Ilium (vii. 43) and to Athamas at Halos (vii. 197); Tissaphernes, later, to Artemis of Ephesus (Thuc. viii. 109). Only if a local god or his worshippers, once surrendered, broke their covenant—as Athens had done— was Persian 'righteousness' implacable; for what was broken was the 'law of the Medes and Persians which altereth not'.

The reason for this difference between Persian over-lordship and all earlier despotisms does not become obvious till the proclamations of Darius supplement those of Cyrus; and the description of Persian religion and manners (i. 131-40) shows us the simple faith of the ordinary householder, on which were founded the philosophy of Zoroaster and the state-religion of Achaemenid kings. It reads like eyewitness, and there were certainly Persian households in the coast provinces.

'Images and temples and altars it is not their custom to set up, and they impute foolishness to those who do so; I suppose because they do not think the gods to be of human nature, as the Greeks do. . . . It is not proper for him who is sacrificing to pray for blessings for himself privately, but he prays "that it may be well with all the Persians, and with the King": and among "all the Persians" he himself is included' (i. 131–2).

Though a Magian chaplain stands by, and chants, it does not much matter what he sings: a Persian is priest in his own house.

Here is a simple nature-worship, like that of Aryan India; more primitive and 'numinous' than that of Homeric Greece or early Israel, in that the gods are not conceived in human form. Iranians and Aryans, like the Indo-European elements in Greece, inherited the same anthropomorphic nature-powers; but under different external conditions, these beliefs diverged. In Greece, 'Homer and Hesiod made for the Greeks their gods' (ii. 53) in a loose patriarchal polytheism, almost dissociated from nature-cults: in that climate there was little to fear except thunderstorms (Zeus), crop-failure (Demeter), or plagues of mice and locusts (Apollo). Moreover, the migrations had wrecked the old southern nature-gods as they wrecked the priest-kings; only hero-worship survived. A god can offer help and punish excess, but man is free.

In India, a climate of extremes and jungle-dangers make the gods terrible, and obscure the high-god Brahma. Life is so precarious and evil that the best hope is to quit it, and meanwhile, to withdraw from the world of sense.

In Persia, a great teacher made a fresh interpretation of traditional beliefs. In nature, and in man, there is good, and there is evil; the Good is manifested in Truth, and the Truth is revealed by Light: the sun, Mithra, maintains all contracts. Hence the observance rendered to sky, sun, and moon, and to fire which is artificial light: light in the service of Man. All good things, earth, fire, water, and winds—we recognize at once the 'four elements' of Ionian physicists—work together for good in the brisk mountain air of Farsistan, to fulfil the ends of the Lord of all Good, who *will* assuredly conquer evil, but only if all good things, and all good men, strive their utmost in his service. So, too, all evil things, including the *daevas*—the Greek *daimones*, who 'infested the world of men'—work together for the evil ends of a Lord of all Evil, the 'Lie' that infested each enemy of Darius. On earth, then—and above all in Persia—the good man is he who leaves the world better than he found it; he irrigates, plants and grafts trees (like Gadatas, Tod, *G.H.I.* 10), breeds horses, cattle, and hounds, administers the affairs of men who have not the Truth.

As an inquiry into causes, this description of the Persian people is mainly concerned with their origin and indigenous culture, and the theme is echoed in the closing words of Book IX. But their virtues do not disguise their faults. Atrocities are described as they occur in the story, normally without censure:[1] they are incidental to unbridled power (iii. 80), to *hybris* and *phthonos*, and to the failure of nerve after defeat (ix. 107 ff.) like the final chorus in the *Persae*. The portraits of great Persians, on the other hand, maintain Herodotus' claim to record the 'great and admirable deeds' of foreigners as well as of Greeks (i. 1). But he insists on the facility with which Persians assimilated the manners of the subject-peoples, and the demoralization which ensued (i. 135, ix. 122).

BIBLIOGRAPHY

OLMSTEAD, A. T. *History of the Persian Empire.* Chicago, 1948.

THE SECOND CONQUEST OF IONIA (i. 141–76)

Continuing the 'former story' of the conquest of Lydia, this section likewise includes three main episodes: the negotiations with Cyrus and with Sparta (i. 141–53); the revolt of Pactyas, after Cyrus had withdrawn to deal with troubles elsewhere (i. 154–61); the consequent reconquest by Harpagus, with severer repression, and diverse fates for Phocaea, Teos, and Miletus (i. 161–70).

Of these the second is central, and the 'cause' of the subsequent troubles. In the first are inlaid the history and description of Ionia and Aeolis; at the end of the third, those of Caria and Lycia, on

---

[1] iii. 3, 35–38, 48, 125–6; iv. 84, 85; v. 25; vi. 23; vii. 22, 39, 103, 114, 135; viii. 90; ix. 112–13, 120.

the annexation of those districts. It is a well-wrought pedimental composition (*a b c b a*), not a military history.

From this narrative three matters emerge, of later significance.

(i) The divergence of policy between the other Greek cities, which had remained loyal to Lydia, and Miletus, which transferred to Cyrus its former alliance with the Mermnad kings and remained loyal to Persia till the Ionian Revolt of 500 B.C.

(ii) The organization of the Panionian League, supported by the Aeolian cities farther north. Four meetings of this league can be traced: (*a*) before the fall of Sardis, when the cities (except Miletus) rejected Cyrus' offer of alliance; (*b*) after that event, when they repented and were rebuffed (i. 141); (*c*) when thereupon they appealed to Sparta and supported Pactyas' assault on Sardis (i. 152–4); (*d*) when they discussed and rejected the advice both of Bias, to evacuate Ionia and follow the Phocaeans to the west, and that attributed to Thales (surely dead by 540 B.C.) to form a single federal state, with Teos as capital and the other cities 'as if they were *demes*'—a clear allusion to the constitution which had saved Athens long ago, and might have saved also the Delian League of Herodotus' own day.

(iii) The third significant point is the combination of a federal council at the Panionion with the executive leadership of Phocaea, anticipating eventual relations between the Delian League and Athens. The same fundamental structure reappears in the 'seapowers' of Samos (iii. 39), Naxos (v. 31), and Eretria (v. 99) and in the leadership of Miletus in the Ionian Revolt. Without such acknowledged executive, no Hellenic alliance could be effective; and the Delian League and Athenian 'hegemony' had thus historical precedents, if not a political 'cause'.

The First Conquest of Babylon (i. 177–200) is chiefly of interest in relation to the general structure of the *Histories*, and to the lost *Assyrian Stories*, and has been discussed already in that connexion (p. 94).

From the west, Cyrus turns to the south and the east. It was the *nemesis* of his good fortune, already passing human limits, that he attacked the Massagetae on the advice of his own first victim,

Croesus (i. 207); and that inadvertently he preserved his pre-
destined successor, Darius, whose later reconquest of Babylon and
perilous reconnaissance of Scythia so closely resembled his own
achievements, but with happier issue. All this romantic construction is central in the design of Herodotus, but its position is
disguised by the loss of the *Assyrian Stories* (p. 94).

BOOK II

EGYPT (ii. 1–182)

The description of Egypt is a test-piece for Herodotus as
observer and historian. After severe and perverse criticism in the
last century (pp. 20–25) it has been rehabilitated as an honest,
industrious, intelligent account.[1] It consists of a geographical
account of the Nile valley (2–34) with its manners and customs
(35–98), and an historical outline partly from native sources
(99–141), partly, for recent times, from Greek (148–52). It is
prefixed to the story of Cambyses' conquest (iii. 1–38) and is the
counterpart of the lost *Assyrian Stories* (i. 106, 184–92). Its
materials were collected during a visit, later than the restoration
of Persian rule about 454 B.C. (ii. 30, 98, 99) and probably after
449 B.C. (iii. 12, 15); but certainly some while before the ninth
centenary of Moeris (ii. 13). It was between August and Novem-
ber—for the Nile was in flood (ii. 92) and Herodotus reached the
Pyramids by boat—and included an excursion to Elephantine on
the southern frontier (ii. 29); but most of his time was spent in
and about the Delta. For the places which he visited, in detail,
see p. 7. Powell[2] thinks there may have been two visits, one
before the Athenian adventure, the other after it.

Egypt, after long foreign oppression and the false-dawn of the
XXVIth Dynasty, was in decline again since the Persian Conquest (525 B.C.) and subsequent revolt (vii. 1, 3, 7), and recalled

---

[1] By Wiedemann (1890), Sourdille (1910), Jacoby (1913), and Spiegelberg
(1936).
[2] *The History of Herodotus*, 1937, p. 29.

its great past through folk-tale and legend attached to monuments. Herodotus shows no knowledge of Egyptian speech or writing, beyond the difference between hieroglyphic and demotic characters (ii. 36). He relied on temple-attendants and the guides who were organized by Psammetichus (ii. 154–64). One of them showed him a written list of kings, another, at Sais, he thought he caught trying to fool him (ii. 28) with an old folk-tale about the sources of the Nile; but the man may have been serious and well informed.[1] He took no notes, but relied on his memory (ii. 125). His sources were thus hearsay and monuments.

For the country itself and the life of the people he had his own acute but imperfect observation; but he had not (for instance) visited the vine-growing districts (ii. 77), and he thought all Egyptian wine was imported (iii. 6). He also thought the *fellahin* were not overworked (ii. 14). Allowing for the displacement of the Pyramid-builders (ii. 124–36: p. 4), his historical outline is remarkable, for its period, but he had no appreciation of Egyptian art except its scale and crowded decoration; and he was thus unwittingly responsible for the presentation of Egypt as a land of the 'unchanging East'. Souvenirs of his visit to Naucratis may be two small votive bowls of about this time and inscribed with his name.[2] He was a keen observer, but he mistook a divine figure for a votive statue (ii. 141) and tells a folk-tale about a victory monument of Sesostris (ii. 107), while he rejects a guide's tale about old statues which had lost their hands (ii. 135). When he tries to equate Egyptian divine names with Greek, he fails (ii. 50–156). About other temple-stories he believed himself bound to secrecy (ii. 46, 48, 51, 81, 123), but Egypt knew no mystery-religions. In any case it is unlikely that a Greek traveller, with little knowledge of the language, could enter Egyptian society in a few months. What is remarkable is that he should have combined his observations and hearsay into a picture of the country and people so vivid and true in its

[1] Wainwright, *Sudan Notes and Records*, xxiii (1947), 11 ff.; *J.H.S.* (forthcoming).
[2] J. G. Milne, *Journ. Eg. Arch.* iii (1916); D. G. Hogarth and others, *J.H.S.* xxv (1905), 116.

outlines. In one passage he seems to expect local readers (ii. 14), but most of his controversies are with Ionian predecessors (ii. 15–27).

The clue to his choice of topics, as usual, is his interest in causes. Human progress begins with language: who then were the first to use words? The Egyptian claim was refuted by the experiment of Psammetichus (ii. 2), the first king who had Greek advisers. How was Egypt itself formed, and when? (ii. 5–14): from former marshes, with Nile-silt, in the days of King Menes. The process may be observed in flood-time and in soundings off shore. But what causes the Nile flood (ii. 19–27)? Where does the Nile rise? (ii. 28), and so forth. Was Egypt in Asia or in Africa? Between the 'continents' of formal geography (ii. 16) the boundary is the Nile: but this bisects Egypt, which he therefore defines, in defiance of 'continents', as the region watered by the Nile. Of the Nile flood he had heard three theories: (i) that the current is held up by the northerly winds of summer: but this he finds is inadequate, as other north-flowing rivers show; (ii) that the Nile rises in a circumambient ocean—perhaps a travel-tale of the equatorial lakes—but of this stream he has no knowledge; (iii) that the summer flood comes from melting snow: but the climate becomes hotter southward. His own view (ii. 24–27) is that the sun is driven by winter north-winds out of its normal ('original') course and nearer to the earth, and evaporates water from the Nile in winter, as it does in summer from northern streams. This leads to geographical comparison of Nile and Ister (ii. 26–34), both described as rising in the far west, and the Nile as turning north at Syene (ii. 28).

In his account of Egyptian religion (ii. 37) the long digressions about Heracles (ii. 42–46) and Pan (ii. 46) are notes to the account of the sacred animals, oxen, goats, and swine (ii. 38–49), and lead to further comparison between Egyptian and Greek gods (ii. 50–53), the latter transmitted through Dodona in 'Pelasgian' times (ii. 53–58). Other sacred animals include the crocodile (ii. 68), the phoenix (ii. 73), certain snakes (ii. 74), the ibis (ii. 75–77); followed by notes on embalming (ii. 86) and other customs, and on food-plants, fishes, and boats (ii. 92–98). This ends the summary of his own observations and inquiries.

His presentation of Egyptian history is what was current in the country in his time. The 'Old Kingdom' from Menes to the Pyramid-builders (about 3200 B.C. to 2800 B.C.) had fallen to pieces about 2500 B.C.; the 'Middle Kingdom' culminating under Dynasties XI and XII (2400–1700 B.C.) had been destroyed by the Hyksos invaders (1700–1600 B.C.); the 'New Kingdom' of Dynasties XVIII–XIX, nationalist and aggressive as far as the Euphrates, had been repelled by the Hittites and the Land- and Sea-raiders, and conquered in turn by Libyans, Ethiopians, and Assyrians (664 B.C.); and a fresh nationalist revival under Dynasty XXVI had been checked by Babylon (583 B.C.) and crushed by Cambyses (525 B.C.), in spite of interested support from Greek adventurers and traders. In this last cosmopolitan phase (iii. 139) native pride in half-forgotten glories, attested by time-worn monuments, of which the age was exaggerated (ii. 143), kept the Egyptians, like many modern Orientals, aloof from 'foreign devils' whom even the 'Greek-loving' Amasis had to restrict to mercenary camps and the 'treaty-port' of Naucratis (ii. 178–9).

Herodotus says that the first human being of Egypt was Min: also that Min, first king of Egypt, drained and entrenched the site of Memphis and founded the city (ii. 99). There is no reason to doubt that he means the same person, the *Menes* of Manetho's list. Of this first king neither tomb nor inscriptions are known: he appears first in the Abydos list and the Turin papyrus. But his name was a royal title in the First Dynasty and in the Pyramid texts. Of the god Min, a pastoral deity whom later Greeks called Pan, Herodotus says nothing: his 'Egyptian Pan' was called Mendes (ii. 45–46) and was a goat-god, whereas Min had attributes of a bull. Though Min was a god of Upper Egypt, he was the only one in close association with Memphis; Herodotus may have heard of him as founder, and confused him with the first human king.[1]

---

[1] Elise Baumgartel, *Antiquity*, xxi (1947), 145–50.

When the account of the Pyramid Kings is replaced in its original context (p. 4), the leading passages and episodes are as follows:

II.	99.	Menes: foundation of Memphis: the valley drained.	Dyn. I
	124.	Cheops: oppression and Pyramid building.	„ IV
	127.	Cephren: 106 years in all.	„ „
	129.	Mycerinus: perhaps confused with Bocchoris; cf. Diod. i. 64–5, 94.	„ „
	134–5.	Story of Rhodopis.	
	136–7.	Asychis: perhaps Sasyches (II); cf. Diod. i. 94.	
	100.	330 kings: 18 Ethiopians: 1 woman, Nitocris (VI).	
	101.	Moeris: last of 330 kings; cf. 149.	
	102–10.	Sesostris: (Usertesen) Red Sea expedition: Asiatic conquest: Colchis and Thrace.	„ XII
	111.	Phero: blind.	
	112.	Proteus: story of Helen 112–120, c. 1200 Greek reckoning.	
	121.	Rhampsinitus: story of the treasury.	„ XIX–XX
	137.	Anysis: Ethiopian conquest.	
	137–9.	Sabaco.	„ XXV
			725–667 B.C.
	140.	Anysis restored.	
	141.	Sethos: priest (*Setne*) of Hephaestus. Sanacharibos (Assyrian invader Sennacherib).	701–667 B.C.
	142.	341 generations from Menes. (1,340 years.)	
	147.	[*Egyptian history from foreign sources.*]	
	148.	The Twelve Kings: the Labyrinth: Lake Moeris. Moeris. 149–50.	663 B.C.
	151.	Psammetichus: invasion of Palestine.	Dyn. XXVI
	158.	Necho: reopened the canal of Seti I. (1326–1300) to Red Sea: invaded Syria, 159.	„ „
	160.	Psammis: Ethiopian expedition.	„ „
	161.	Apries.	589–570 B.C.
169–82.		Amasis. Foundation of Naucratis (178–80).	Dyn. XXVI
			526 B.C.
III.	1.	Cambyses: Persian Conquest.	Dyn. XXVII
			525 B.C.

Very few monuments are described in detail. The Pyramids are carefully studied and correctly attributed: but there is no mention of the Sphinx. Was it covered with sand-dune then, or regarded as a freak of nature? The 'Labyrinth', on the other hand, so vividly

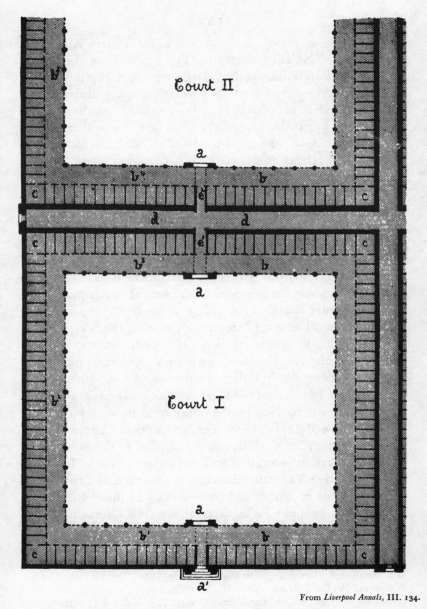

Court II

Court I

FIG. 11. THE EGYPTIAN LABYRINTH ACCORDING TO HERODOTUS.

a. entrances.   b b¹. cloisters.   c. closed rooms.   d. corridors.

and precisely described, and assigned to the Twelve Kings who precede the XXVIth Dynasty (ii. 147–8), does not correspond with any known building: the XIIth-Dynasty 'Labyrinth' in the Fayum, described by later Greek writers, is quite different.[1] Of the immense hall at Karnak he only says that it was 'large'; but the Temple ascribed to 'Athena' at Sais he notes with care, with its two obelisks and the royal tombs (ii. 169). Lake Moeris and the canal of Necho interested him as engineers' work, like the Pyramids. Frescoes and mural reliefs did not detain him (ii. 148), but portrait statues had historical interest.

Naucratis. Greek intercourse with Egypt, after long isolation, became active with the assistance of the 'bronze men from the sea' to Psammetichus of Sais, the founder of the XXVIth Dynasty in 664 B.C. At first unrestricted, it was limited about 570 B.C. by Amasis to the 'treaty port' of Naucratis on the Canopic branch of the Nile. Its principal establishment, the *Hellenion*, was governed under charter by a college of 'protector' cities, Ionian (Chios, Teos, Phocaea, Clazomenae), Dorian (Rhodes, Cnidus, Halicarnassus, Phaselis), Aeolian (Mytilene). Samos, Miletus, and Aegina the sole European corporator, had their own sanctuaries and compounds. Other sanctuaries, of Aphrodite and the Dioscuri, are known, but not identified with any city-state. After great prosperity, testified by the offerings in these shrines, Naucratis fell on evil days after the Persian Conquest, but revived in the fifth century for a while, always exposed to Greek attempts to subvert Persian suzerainty and to Persian reprisals. In Herodotus' narrative Naucratis illustrates the extent and character of Greek interests in Egypt, and consequently in the Persian Conquest, which brought Persia face to face with Greeks in Africa as in Asia Minor.

BIBLIOGRAPHY

WIEDEMANN, A. *Herodots zweites Buch.* Leipzig, 1890.
WADDELL, W. G. *Herodotus, Book II.* London, 1939.
COOK, R. M. 'Amasis and the Greeks in Egypt', *J.H.S.* lvii (1937), 229.
ROEBUCK, C. 'The Organization of Naucratis', *Class. Phil.* xlvi (1951), 212.

[1] Myres, *Liverpool Annals,* iii. 134.

BOOK III
HERODOTUS' SOURCES FOR PERSIAN HISTORY

The descriptions of Persian affairs are remarkable for their variety and definition. Herodotus had information, which he believed to be trustworthy, about the Persian mode of life and social organization, about the provincial and military administration, the rise of the Achaemenid dynasty, the establishment of Darius on the throne, the inner court-circle under Darius and Xerxes. Unlike Ctesias a generation later, who made far less use of better opportunities, Herodotus neither spoke Persian nor travelled much, if at all, in Persia; his etymologies of Persian names are fanciful (i. 131, 139; vi. 98). He must therefore have had acquaintances who knew Persia intimately but were accessible somewhere in the West. It has been suggested[1] that these conditions are fulfilled in the younger Zopyrus, a grandson of the captor of Babylon (iii. 92, 153–60; vii. 61) and son of Megabyzus, one of Xerxes' generals (vii. 82–121). Of this younger Zopyrus Herodotus only says that after his father had fought the Athenians in Egypt (456–454 B.C.: cf. Thuc. i. 109) he deserted to Athens (iii. 160) : Ctesias gives more details. After his death his son Zopyrus deserted, as Herodotus says, and was killed in an Athenian attack on the Caunians, probably about the time of the Samian War.[2] At Athens, then, Zopyrus may have met Herodotus, shortly before he migrated to Thurii.

Another Persian 'friend' is Artabazus, of whom personal and intimate stories are told (viii. 126; ix. 41, 89). But there must have been many Persian officials domiciled on estates granted by the King in the western provinces. An example is the family of Harpagus in Lycia. There were also renegade Greek families, like those of Democedes, Themistocles, and Metiochus son of Miltiades (vi. 41).

[1] Joseph Wells, 'The Persian Friends of Herodotus', *J.H.S.* xxvii (1907), 37–47; cf. *Studies in Herodotus*, Oxford, 1923.
[2] 440 B.C.; Thuc. i. 116.

THE MAGIAN REVOLT AND THE ACCESSION OF DARIUS (iii. 61–119)

The vivid account of the Magian Revolt and the Accession of Darius is carefully selected, like the story of Cyrus, from variant sources. The portraits not only of Darius but of his associates are especially notable, but leave it an open question between very high authority and exceptional literary skill. The insistence of Herodotus that the 'Debate of the Conspirators' really occurred —reaffirmed as it is in vi. 43 in reply to sceptics—is a crucial instance of his confidence in his sources; and here he offers no alternative such as he mentions elsewhere (i. 95, 204).

The Survey of the Satrapies (iii. 89–94), like the *Catalogue* of the forces of Xerxes (vii. 61–99), must be derived from Persian documents, accessible doubtless at Sardis. The geographical provinces and the national contingents do not exactly fit, which supports the authenticity of both. The satrapy-list was an old one, before there were dependencies in Europe (vii. 86).

It is the peculiar dependence of the Persian Empire on the gold of India (iii. 98 ff.)—the pendant to Croesus with the gold of Sardis—that gives significance to the long disquisition on the theme that the most precious things come from farthest off; an inverted economic fact, for only objects of high intrinsic value are worth bringing so far. But Indian gold was only one instance of the general inference that the Empire was so powerful because it extended so widely, and so nearly included all possible sources of wealth. Once again, Herodotus is tracing things to their causes, to the very edge of the map, as into the far past; insisting both on the overwhelming might of Persia and on the impossibility of controlling the forward policy imposed by an ever-advancing frontier.

Darius and his Helpers. Throughout the story of Darius, Herodotus recalls attention to contrasted portraits of his principal grandees and contemporaries, using them to illustrate various problems of administration and policy: the Seven, characterized by their shares in the 'Debate on Government', and especially

Otanes absolutely loyal to his chief (iii. 80, 83); Zopyrus son of Megabyzus (iii. 153–60); Intaphernes, unfit for high office (iii. 118–19); Oroetes, the disloyal satrap (iii. 120–28); Bagaeus, the trusty agent (iii. 128); and, on the Greek side, Polycrates and other Samians (iii. 39–47, 123–5, 139–48), and Democedes (iii. 129–38). Intaphernes shows the King's intimate counsellors, highly privileged, but bound by a political code: *noblesse oblige*. It is a Persian anecdote originally: Herodotus could not foresee the new turn which Sophocles was to give it (*Ant.* 909 ff.). Oroetes, an ambitious administrator in a frontier satrapy, like Aryandes in Egypt (iv. 165–7, 200–3), combined intrigue with premature and unauthorized aggression against a dangerous neighbour, and was only brought to book by the tact and firmness of Darius. Democedes shows Darius himself about to probe the West from front to rear, by any competent agent; the tale also reveals a power behind the throne, that 'man-counselling heart' who was the mother of Xerxes (vii. 2, 3) and of Masistes (vii. 82; ix. 110); the Atossa of the *Persae*.

BIBLIOGRAPHY

OLMSTEAD, A. T. *History of the Persian Empire*. Chicago, 1948.

SAMOS (iii. 39–60, 120–8, 139–49)

The significance of the Samian story is not at first sight obvious, especially as an important aspect of it is buried in the Libyan story in Book IV. That Sparta should now at last have intervened in eastern affairs is a turning-point in the great struggle. Another landmark is the association of Sparta with Corinth, which becomes relevant again in v. 92, with another excerpt from the romance of Periander (cf. i. 22–24). But what is more notable is that Corinth, a traditional friend of Samos under its hereditary aristocracy, is at enmity with Samian tyranny. Sparta's hostility expresses its new role of defender of traditional régimes against popular and personal. This hostility goes so far as to harass the only state east of the Aegean which still maintained its independence; and the same policy threatened the democratic government of Maeandrius (iii. 148) and put an end to Samian sea-power.

So much of Polycrates' constructive work perished with him that it needs to be insisted how important a phase his 'sea-power' was. With the fall of the Panionian League under the leadership of Phocaea the only hope for Greek freedom was in oversea resistance under island leadership. Lesbos had surrendered; Chios, an old friend of Miletus, was lukewarm; the Dorian states in the south do not come into the picture at all. Only Samos remained; and oligarchic Samos probably looked for safety as much to Persia as to Sparta or Corinth.

After the Fourth Congress (p. 151) Herodotus has a long silence about Ionian affairs. Harpagus had 'turned Hither Asia upside down', but the conquests of Cyrus and Cambyses, and the reforms of Darius, only touched Greek interests indirectly. Cambyses' agreement with the Phoenicians gave him their fleets on condition that they were not used against Phoenicians in the West (iii. 19). If the Cypriots in the same context made the same bargain, they were exempt from service against other Greeks, until they took part in the Ionian Revolt. After that, they served Xerxes at Salamis. Both took their share in the invasion of Egypt, though the project included oversea attack on Carthage (iii. 17) and though Cyrene surrendered forthwith. Moreover, Herodotus notes (and repeats ii. 1; iii. 1) that Cambyses had contingents from Ionia and from Aeolis, and his envoy reached Memphis on a ship of Mytilene (iii. 13).

This Egyptian expedition, though left for Cambyses by the untimely death of Cyrus, was the necessary complement to the conquest of Lydia, Media, and Babylon. Egypt was the last remnant of the old Four-Power régime; the last refuge of malcontents from elsewhere, and especially from Ionia. The influx of Greek adventurers and traders, especially after the 'second conquest', had indeed embarrassed Apries, and had to be strictly controlled by Amasis in view of Egyptian repugnance to 'foreign devils'. This is the political stage on which the next act of the Ionian tragedy was to be played. That adventure is presented by

Herodotus, not merely as a typical collision of a Greek city with fresh Persian aggression, but as a pendant to the reorganization of the Persian Empire itself by Darius, interwoven in alternate sections of the history.

To reconstruct the background of these events is not easy; but there is one priceless document for this period, too little regarded, the *List of Sea Powers*, preserved by Eusebius,[1] from the 'Fall of Troy' to the 'Crossing of Xerxes'. It is in tabular form: peoples and cities are listed in numerical order, with the number of years when they 'ruled the waves'. Its statements are supported by isolated facts in Eusebius' *Chronicon*, and by almost everything in other historians. As the list closes in 480 B.C., it must have been composed under the Delian League as an historical prologue to it; but neither Herodotus nor Thucydides makes explicit use of it. Thucydides, indeed, notes the historical significance of sea-power and the Phocaean exploits in the West: for Herodotus there was no sea-power before Polycrates, except legendary Minos (iii. 122). With the earlier part of this list, filled with mainland peoples of the Near East, we are not concerned. But the late 'sea-powers' are Greek—Miletus, Lesbos, Phocea, Samos, Sparta (2), Naxos (10), Eretria (15), Aegina (10). The last four date-numerals are preserved, but the Samian is missing and the Lesbian uncertain.

In the *List of Sea Powers* above, Phocaea is succeeded by Samos. The date of the change is missing, but the fall of Phocaea immediately followed Cyrus' capture of Babylon (539 B.C.), and the fall of Polycrates was early in the reign of Darius and close to his siege of Babylon. Eusebius makes Polycrates 'flourish' in 528 B.C. If the statue of Aeaces dedicated by Polycrates represented his father (Athenaeus 540 *d*), the family was of good standing; but late gossip made Polycrates himself a tradesman and popular leader against the landed aristocracy who had submitted to Cyrus (i. 169). The occasion was during a war with the Aeolians, and an early achievement of Polycrates was the interception of the whole force of Lesbos on its way to help Miletus (iii. 39; Polyaenus i. 23): this success provided labour for his fortifications (iii. 39).

[1] Eusebius, ed. Schoene, ii, p. 226.

In partnership at first with two brothers, he murdered Pantag-
notus and expelled Syloson, who made friends with the young
Darius in Egypt. The expelled 'landlords' (*geomoroi*) intrigued
in Corinth and Sparta, but for a while Polycrates prospered.
Herodotus notes his hundred war-ships, his thousand archers, his
mercenaries, his fortifications, his tunnelled aqueduct, the first
deep-sea harbour, and the vast temple of Hera, one of the
'wonders of the world'. From this island-fortress he dominated
'many islands' (iii. 39) such as Thera (iv. 152) and Amorgos
which only entered the Delian League after the defeat of Samos
in 440 B.C.—and 'many towns of the mainland', and blockaded
the Great King's frontage against friends and foes alike. Corinth
had kept the seas open for Miletus when both cities were under
tyrannies (i. 20) : under restored oligarchy, Spartan protectorate,
and 'landlord' intrigue, Corinth had instant as well as historic
grievances against the Samos of Polycrates. The 'causes' collected
by Herodotus (iii. 48–53) are not the whole story, but probably
Athenian gossip from the years between 445 and 440 B.C., like
the references to the stolen bowl (i. 69–70) and the Messenian
Wars (iii. 47).

The adventures of the Samian exiles (iii. 57–59) illuminate for
a moment the dark background of the sixth century; of Siphnos,
Troezen, and Hermione; Aegina and Cydonia; Zacynthus and
Campanian Dicaearchia, which its slogan-name 'the Rule of
Right' reminds us of Concord, Providence, and Philadelphia.
Full commentary would be a volume of Greek history. As ancient
friends of Phocaea, Samians had the entry to western waters, to
which Cydonia and Zacynthus were stepping-stones.

The relations between Samos and Egypt are in accord with
their historical interests, but with a difference. Gyges had supported Psammetichus against Assyrian aggression. Egypt and
Babylon had supported Croesus against Cyrus. On both occasions
Babylon had moved too late. Samos had its own depot at Naucratis; Polycrates, now the dominant power west of the Persian
Empire, had been allied with Amasis; and when Egypt fell, and
then Samos, Babylon was 'very well prepared' to revolt against

Darius; but again too late. But why did Amasis repudiate Polycrates, whose gesture of help to Cambyses was a device to dispose
of disloyal Samians? Once again, what Herodotus has selected
for record is the ulterior 'cause', as he detected it, of the collapse
of Persia's enemies in the West, leaving the way open for invasion of Europe by Darius himself (iv. 1). The Samos of Polycrates was the keystone of the arch.

Farther afield, Samian support of Arcesilaus III revived older
associations with Cyrene (iv. 152, 163–4); there was even a
Samian settlement seven days on the road from Egypt to the
Oasis of Ammon (iii. 26). Battus II had annoyed the Libyans by
enlarging Cyrene; the Libyan chief Adikran had become a vassal
of Apries; and Apries' ill-fated attack on Cyrene had provoked
the native resentment which put Amasis on the throne. Under
Battus III the reforms of Demonax (iv. 163) reconciled 'old
burghers', Libyan neighbours, and immigrant Greeks, including
many islanders. Arcesilaus III, who created 'much disturbance
about privileges' withdrawn by Demonax, was expelled, but
returned with help from Samos and an extreme, popular programme; and after excesses which fulfilled a Delphic warning,
both he and his Libyan father-in-law Alazeir retired to Barca,
and were killed by Cyrenean exiles 'for medism'.

In all these events we may trace Samian intrigues. The surrender to Cambyses gives a date, and connects with the medism
of Polycrates. Pheretima, the mother of Arcesilaus, had re-
established herself peacably in Cyrene; but after his death she
withdrew to Egypt and gave to Aryandes, Cambyses' governor,
the pretext for an invasion of Libya which ended badly. These
Libyan affairs, which Herodotus recounts in Book IV (161–7),
must be taken into account in connexion both with Samian
events and with Persian; for Aryandes (iv. 166), as we shall see,
is the southern counterpart of Oroetes at Sardis.

The career of Polycrates thus falls into four phases: (1) his
Samian sea-power, with outposts in Campania and Corcyra,
Zacynthus, Cydonia, and Cyrene, but a quarrel with Corinth and
Sparta; (2) his alliance with Amasis, renewing the Western

League but flawed by Egypt's designs on Libya, and Egyptian friendship with Sparta and Rhodes; with so large a mercenary force, Amasis may have had to choose among his Greek friends; (3) his overt transfer of allegiance to Cambyses, anticipating the defeat of Amasis, and Aryandes' designs on Libya; (4) his renewed project for a Western League with Oroetes, governor of Lydia.

The resemblance between the doings of Aryandes and of Oroetes is significant. Aryandes attempted the conquest of all Libya (iv. 167), as contemplated already by Cambyses, and it is in this connexion that Herodotus surveys Libyan geography and ethnology as far as Lake Tritonis (iv. 188–91). Having large operations in mind, he also took the perilous step of coining silver, of exceptional fineness, probably from the self-assessed tribute of Cyrene (iv. 165), a challenge to royal prerogative which Darius rightly treated as rebellion. It is noteworthy that in Darius' inventory of the materials for his great temple the silver comes only from Egypt—not a silver country; it was probably the famous 'Aryandic' windfall (iv. 166).[1] Here was a Persian satrap, under an impetuous but erratic king, preparing to recreate the Egypt of the XXVIth Dynasty with its Libyan ambitions; and, on Cambyses' death, to revive a Western League. Babylon, too, as we have seen, was 'very well prepared' when Darius unmasked it (iii. 150).

Turn now to Oroetes. Of him, too, there was gossip and guess-work (iii. 120), but Herodotus sketches a character and an adventure. Appointed by Cyrus as viceroy of Lydia, he had a check and a rival in Mitrabates of Phrygia, the other great governor west of the Halys, with a similar Greek frontage on Propontis around his capital Dascyleium. Mitrabates' reproach

[1] A. T. Olmstead, *Hist. Pers. Empire* (1948), 168, objects that no Aryandic coins have been found (p. 225). But how could they be identified, since Persian coins bore neither portraits nor inscriptions: see J. G. Milne, *Journ. Eg. Arch.* xxiv (1938), 245–6. Dr. Milne tells me that the American Numismatic Society has a hoard of silver from Egypt containing 102 Persian *sigloi* with punch-mark A. Herzfeld, *Trans. Int. Num. Congress*, 1936, p. 413.

The Curator, Dr. S. Noe, doubts whether this can be Aryandes, but Dr. Milne thinks it possible: cf. Robinson, *Iraq*, xii. 1950. The same mark occurs in *B.M. Cat. Arabia*, pl. xxix. 18.

to Oroetes, that 'he had not taken Samos', was said to have been provocative, but may have been a hint that he was watched: and his own envoy to Polycrates was affronted by Oroetes. The latter, professing to be in disgrace with Cambyses—which may well have been true—offered Polycrates gold for his enterprises in return for escape. But during the anarchy Oroetes murdered Mitrabates and also a messenger from Darius. He had thus 'set his cap erect', as Persians said (iii. 127), and Darius had to act warily; for Oroetes now held the Phrygian command as well as the Lydian, restoring, like Pactyas, the dominion of Sardis from the Halys to the coasts. All that he needed was control of the coast cities which were in Polycrates' hands, and control of the seaways against either a Spartan or a Phoenician fleet. Samos only needed the gold of Oroetes to 'rule over all Greece' (iii. 122); Oroetes, only Polycrates' fleet, to be secure against the king of Persia. Between Oroetes, Polycrates, and Aryandes, the Western League waited for Babylon and an occasion. The dates, it is true, are not quite certain. Herodotus puts the murder of Polycrates 'not long before the death of Cambyses', probably therefore when Cambyses was in Ethiopia; that of Mitrabates 'before the accession of Darius'; but they are clearly in the same course of events. Darius had to deal with Oroetes without encumbrances.

A small detail enhances the situation. When Oroetes was negotiating with Polycrates he was not at Sardis but 'sitting at Magnesia-on-Maeander' (iii. 122). As in Alyattes' time, the lord of Sardis had to be sure of Miletus before dealing with confederates or adversaries elsewhere. It was difficult at all times to be friends both with Samos and with Miletus. To prevent trouble Oroetes must be prepared to deal with it; and Magnesia is the strategical rendezvous for coercion of Miletus as well as for collusion with Samos.

What spoiled all was the rapid establishment of Darius, his prompt suppression of Aryandes, and his skilful handling of Oroetes. It was an accident—but, for Herodotus, a 'cause'—that he owed a favour to Syloson, which wrecked also the free democracy in Samos (iii. 139).

From this tangled tale Polycrates emerges not as the betrayer of Greek interests to Persia but as a statesman who saw that only by Aegean sea-power could aggression be stayed at the seaboard. What ruined his project was failure to conciliate the other League states and the refusal of leading cities in mainland Greece, through internal differences and grievances, to collaborate with a strong man in Ionia. Against Cyrus a league had failed for want of efficient executive; now an efficient sea-lord was betrayed by his compatriots, and democracy by the *ancien régime*. Herodotus did not live to see the cooperation of Lysander with Tissaphernes after 412 B.C.; perhaps not even the mission of Alcidas to Ionia in 427 B.C. which 'hoped that Pissuthnes would join in the war' (Thuc. iii. 31).

Having traced to its causes the collapse of the Samian defence, Herodotus, after his manner, lets the curtain fall. What happened in the Aegean, after the rejection of Maeandrius by Sparta, has to be pieced together in Book V from the affairs of Naxos and Miletus, nearly twenty years later.

BIBLIOGRAPHY

COLE, E. S. *The Samos of Herodotus.* Yale (thesis), 1912.
URE, P. N. *The Origin of Tyranny.* Cambridge, 1922, ch. iii.
BILABEL, F. 'Polykrates von Samos und Amasis von Aegypten, *N. Heidelberg. Jahrbb.* 1934, 129.

BOOK IV
THE SCYTHIAN AND LIBYAN STORIES

In Book III the Persian Empire had been established and reorganized in Asia. Babylon had been finally disarmed, Asia Minor had been secured against revolt, Samos had been annexed, and Democedes had traversed the Greek world from front to rear. But on the map (p. 39), as well as in political and strategic fact, the Midland Sea lay between two continental land-masses, and one of these extended also along the northern frontier of the Empire. 'Beyond Caucasus no account was taken of Persia' (i. 97)'; it was hence that the last external shock had assailed the

civilized world, more than a century before, and it was in the
north-east that Cyrus had failed and perished.

Thus the reconnaissances into Libya and Europe are counterparts, if only in this, that in both regions the foreshores were
already infested with Greeks; and if the Empire was to include
the Greek world, it must embrace both these outlands. Though
Olbia does not figure in the northern campaign, the story of
Scyles (iv. 76–80) is a pendant to that of Alazeir (iv. 78–80, 164).

Much of the material of the Scythian story is a conventional
logos, geographical and ethnological, but it has been re-modelled
as the background of a military narrative. Its political significance
is enhanced by the frequent speeches—set in pairs as in a tragedy,
and in a group of four at the crisis—illustrating the characters and
doings of Darius and the men about him; Miltiades, Histiaeus,
and Coes, as well as Artabanus and Megabazus: for with them
must be compared the words of Darius and Megabazus in the
sequel (v. 23, 24).

As an independent episode, indeed, the story has a tragic
tension and coherence, like the plot of the *Philoctetes*: like Neo-
ptolemus, Darius 'comes through', after uttermost peril to himself and his cause.

It is this breadth of construction that makes tolerable the geographical and ethnographical passages, the former illustrating
the vastness of the region and its emplacement in the world; the
latter the dependence of its inhabitants on its river-system, which
at the same time defines its regions and its economy—woodland,
nomadism, 'corn for food', 'corn for sale'—and through-trade
with the lands beyond. It was not only a region in itself but the
forecourt to a continent more varied still.

While the Second Capture of Babylon established the rule of
Darius in Asia, the conquest of Samos, consequent on the fall of
Polycrates, as expressly noted (iii. 139), was his first intervention
in a Greek state beyond the sea-front of Asia Minor. It also
broke down the defensive sea-power of Polycrates in the Aegean,
and the death of Oroetes had checked the threatened revival of a
new land-power beyond the Halys.

The African conquests of Cambyses had left undecided the fate of Greek interests in Libya, already involved in those of Egypt since the days of Apries (iv. 159). The intervention of Cambyses' governor, from Egypt, failed; Aryandes himself fell, like Oroetes, under the displeasure of Darius (iv. 166); and there was no further Persian advance beyond the natural barrier of the Libyan desert.

In the north-west the geographical position was different. The mountain ranges of northern and western Asia Minor, converging on the Marmara lake-land, are continuous beyond it into the chains which form the eastern half of the Balkan Peninsula and touch the Dinaric folds which extend out of Alpine Europe into peninsular Greece. Then sweeping north-eastwards, they are divided only by the gorge of the Danube from the Carpathian bastion of central Europe, overlooking the steppe. Thanks to the great valley-route of the Hebrus, this hinterland of the Marmara was fairly well known to the Greek cities from Byzantium to Abdera.

Thus far there is no natural frontier towards Danubian Europe. But from the Danube gorge to the Black Sea these 'Balkan' highlands have a straight steep escarpment, with the great river at its foot, and beyond it a wholly different régime, the northern steppe. Here is a natural frontier, of race and culture as well as physical.

Continuity here was not geographical only. The Bithynians were 'Thracians in Asia' (i. 28; vii. 75); the Phrygians as far east as Armenia were of Thracian origin (vii. 73); and Herodotus knows of a backwash of Mysians and Teucrians into Europe (v. 14; vii. 20). Croesus had mercenaries, and perhaps tributaries, from Thrace (Xen. *Cyrus*. vi. 2. 10). Paeonians raided as far east as Perinthus (v. 1); it was a reasonable precaution later for Darius to transport these sturdy tribesmen into Asia (v. 14). Moreover, like the coast of Asia Minor, the foreshore was occupied by Greek cities of various origin; but from the Danube mouth northward (except Heraclea) by Milesian colonies only. Since the 'Trojan Catalogue' (*Iliad*, ii. 849–50) where Priam's writ ran as far as the Axius river, Hellespontine Pelasgians, and the

Cicones west of the Hebrus, had been overlaid by Thracians, and the Paeonians had been pressed back to the Strymon valley by Macedonians, closely related to the peninsular Greeks (i. 56).

All this complexity ceased at the Lower Danube. Beyond lay Scythia, of which Herodotus has much to say, as far as the Tanais. The Scythians, still mostly nomad-pastorals—though some grew corn 'for sale' (iv. 17) or merely 'for food' (iv. 18)—had come from the east (iv. 11) and supplanted the Cimmerians, and were now threatened along the Tanais by Sarmatians (iv. 21) who flowed westward later. Darius apparently connected them with the trans-Caspian Massagetae, who had killed Cyrus (i. 201–15), and with the nomad invaders of western Asia in the seventh century (iv. 1; cf. iii. 134). Herodotus even says that the Massagetae were Scythians.

Here were two major objectives; to protect the Marmara frontage of the Empire, and to prevent incursions of the steppe-nomads either east or west of the Black Sea. And there was a third consideration. The Black Sea foreshore of the steppe was occupied by many colonies and factories from Miletus, trading Aegean produce and manufactures for corn, furs, and gold from the interior. The Libyan expeditions had ascertained the extent of the Greek hinterland southward; the mission of Democedes had probed the western depths of the Greek world; what was still lacking was similar knowledge of Greek enterprises in the north.

The dependence of Darius on Greek, and specifically on Milesian, sources for information about these northern regions explains both the scope and the miscalculations of the 'Scythian Expedition'. On the Greek map outlined by Herodotus (iv. 100: p. 33) the 'Scythian Square' had two sea-faces, from the Danube mouth to Panticapaeum and thence to the Tanais, and two 'transverse' faces, drawn inland from the Danube and the Tanais; and as the sea-faces were at right angles to each other on the map these land-faces also met at a right angle in the north-west. But in fact the two sea-faces lay almost in the same straight line, so that the land-faces ran parallel into the interior indefinitely; and the 'diagonal', the route from Danube to Tanais, was actually about as long as the two sea-faces together: Rustchuk–Odessa *c.* 350 miles; Odessa–Rostov 400 miles: 30 days at 25 miles a day. Moreover, beyond the Tanais the direct route to the northern boundary of the Persian Empire would be only the diagonal of a similar 'square' bounded by the Sea of Azov and the Caucasus— equal, that is, to the Scythian diagonal—not (as in fact) nearly as long as those two boundaries together. The estimate attributed to Darius—and translated, round the camp-fires, into sixty knots on a cord—was therefore ample for an outward march of thirty days to Tanais and beyond, plotted on the Milesian map. If anything went wrong, thirty days, at most, would bring the force back to the Danube Bridge; if all went well and the King did not return, the bridge might be destroyed, for the next news of Darius would be south of the Caucasus and half-way to Susa. How far Darius penetrated into Scythia or beyond the Tanais is suggested, at most, by the reference to his 'forts' on the Oarus river (iv. 123–4) —seen unfinished in Herodotus' time—perhaps block-houses on the old route from the Caucasus into the far north. Wanderings and Scythian opposition prolonged the march beyond the estimate of Darius, and his retreating remnant was saved—we are not told how many days later—by the self-interested loyalty of Histiaeus and other Ionian vassals.

On this outline of circumstances and probabilities the narrative of Herodotus is displayed, a final episode in the expansion of the Empire.

BIBLIOGRAPHY

MINNS, E. H. *Scythians and Greeks*. Cambridge, 1913.
ROSTOVTZEFF, M. *Iranians and Greeks in South Russia*. Oxford, 1922.
—— *Skythen und der Bosporus*, i. Berlin, 1931.

LIBYA (iv. 145–205)

The Libyan story is a counterpart to the Scythian, describing Persian aggression into Africa and an attempt to outflank the Greek World southward, like the conquest of Thrace to the north. But its connexion with the main narrative is looser, its achievements less significant, and its structure much simpler. Essentially it is a conventional *logos* (iv. 168–99), set between the retrospect of Greek colonization and the attempted conquest of Cyrene by Aryandes. The history of Cyrene is taken right back to its 'cause', the foundation of its mother-city Thera (148–58), and brought down to the reign of Cambyses (165–7). The failure of Aryandes balances that of Darius in Scythia, and his agent Pheretima comes like himself (166) to a bad end (200–5). The description of Libya, ethnological along the coast-land (168–80) and through the interior (181–97)—with a note on the colonizable regions, the Cinyps basin and Cyrenaica (198–9)—is commentary on a schematic map, in parallel zones, quite remote from the political narrative, and the futile adventure of Dorieus (v. 42) is nowhere brought into connexion with it. The political history of the Libyan story has been brought already into its historical connexion with that of Polycrates in Book III (p. 173 above).

THE EPILOGUE: THRACE, PAEONIA, AND MACEDON
(v. 1–27)

Darius' conquest of Thrace sets Persian rule firmly on European soil and closes the long rhythmical sequence of conquests: Lydia and Ionia, Media and Babylon, Egypt and Ethiopia, followed by Scythia and Libya. The pause which follows (v. 28) divides these almost unbroken advances from the new period of 'troubles', no less for Persia than for Ionia; and the Persian miscalculations, both in Scythia and in Libya, are tragic 'warnings'. What Herodotus has not done is to fill the void between the annexation of Samos and the attack on Naxos; and it is here that it is least easy to supply the historical background to his episodic story (p. 194).

BOOKS V AND VI
THE TRAGEDY OF CLEOMENES

In the fifth and sixth books Herodotus had a difficult task. There was nothing more for Darius to do in the West. Faithful friends were rewarded, Histiaeus so well that Darius could only retrieve his mistake if he offered him a seat at his own table—and saw that he took it. And the loyal officer who exposed that mistake had his reward too; at all events we hear no more of Megabazus; he knew too much about the West, and was not a safe person to leave where the Great King's Eye could not see him. Old Otanes, rheumatic and incorruptible, audibly 'mindful in what seat he sat when he gave justice', was a better yoke-fellow for the fainèant viceroy, Darius' own brother, who lets nothing happen without first 'asking the King'. So there was 'remission of troubles' in the West.

When 'troubles began for the second time to arise from Naxos and Miletus' (v. 58), the story would have been a simpler one had not Athens intervened (v. 99). That single act put a whole world of complex stresses to the test of a 'cause' and an initiative, a 'beginning of troubles'. That it was the initiative of thirty thousand fools, or sentimentalists, or loyal friends of Miletus, does not make it less momentous, nor Aristagoras less responsible.

But how different, had the Ionian's unfinished lecture (v. 49–50) launched Cleomenes on the task which dazzled Pausanias, fascinated Agesilaus, and inspired Philip, so that all might be 'ready on the day' for Alexander, the heir of Perdiccas, to inherit 'what the sun shone on' (viii. 137).

Here was a double tragedy. Athens, full of exuberant optimism after expelling the Peisistratids, and launching out under Cleisthenes' leadership to a Utopia of equality and fraternity, was caught, hardly clear of harbour, in the cross-currents of inter-state politics. Like the knight in the ballad

> . . . who blew the horn
> Before he drew the sword.

Athens burned Sardis before she built a fleet.

But all that is underplot, however necessary it was to find 'causes' for Athenian heroism. What makes Books V and VI so difficult is not Athenian knight-errantry but the recurrent personality of Cleomenes. In him, as in Croesus, in Polycrates, in Mardonius, Herodotus finds a hero, and a tragic one. His entry is prefaced by elaborate retrospect of his personal and dynastic position (v. 39–41), and his rivalry with the brilliant half-brother who 'might have been king' (v. 42–48). Later, to explain his difficulties at home, comes the careful description of the double kingship (vi. 56–60) and the disastrous outcome (v. 61–72) when both of the kings had ability and one of them genius—for Demaratus was able, though misguided. Later again (vi. 75–84) there is a sequence of myths from victims of the Spartan policy which had become his personal policy; and a vivid glimpse of 'Hamlet without the Prince' when Sparta had to do without him. Here is a 'myth' in Aristotle's sense; and the title-part in this tragedy is 'Cleomenes losing his Wits'.

Thus, between the highly schematic epilogue of the 'Rise of Persia (v. 1–27), and the no less elaborate prologue of the 'Expedition of Xerxes' (viii. 1–19), the structure of Books V and VI is looser, and the subject-matter more complex. But in addition to frequent cross-references and recapitulations, Herodotus has worked here, too, on a formal construction, though he has not always imposed it fully on his narrative.

As in Book III, he is telling two stories concurrently; that of the Ionian Revolt (v. 28–38, 98–126; and its sequel vi. 1–50, 94–140) and that of contemporary Athens and Sparta (v. 49–97; vi. 51–93), both illuminated by explanatory notes. In some sections there is symmetrical arrangement. At Sparta, Aristogoras' appeal to Cleomenes is preceded by an account of the position of the kings in Sparta, and followed by a commentary on his famous map; all enframed between his arrival and his departure (v. 40–54).

The story of Cleisthenes is similarly displayed (v. 66–73: p. 180). In this tragedy, the centre-piece, from the deposition of Demaratus to the death of Cleomenes himself, culminating in his triumphant return to Aegina with Leotychides (vi. 51–73), is preceded by another dissertation on Spartan customs and followed by inquiry into the causes of the hero's end (vi. 75–84) and in particular into his disarming of Argos, the significance of which is revealed when disarmed Argos takes the Persian side in 479 B.C. All this is enframed in Aegina's medism, the consequence of which was that, though Cleomenes had foreseen the expansion of Athens and used all means to repress it, his instruments—Hippias, Aegina, perhaps also Thebes, as the event showed—sold themselves to Persia, and left him in the dilemma that if he repressed Athens now, it must be hand-in-hand with Persia; if he repelled Persia, it must be hand-in-hand with Athens. He adopted the larger policy. He even momentarily closed the breach between the two Royal Houses in Sparta. But when the other King took the other side, and Cleomenes himself broke down, his own tool, Leotychides, reverted to the smaller. So there was war between Athens and Aegina, tension between Athens and Sparta, providential occasion for the Persian 'to do his own business' (vi. 94).

Thus composed, and thus analysed, history has causes and a purpose. As Herodotus says on another occasion, 'if things happened so or not, I know not, but I write what men say'. Difficult and complex as is his telling of the story, this counter-narrative to the Ionian Revolt is the revelation, through the failures of Cleomenes, of Athens as the sole champion of Greek freedom. The real break between the prefatory books and the Persian Wars is not at the end of Book IV but at the beginning of the story of Marathon (vi. 94).

ATHENS, SPARTA, AND AEGINA

This is perhaps the most convenient point at which to collect the occasional references of Herodotus to Athens, Sparta, and Aegina. The references to Corinth, Argos, and Thebes are less difficult to explain in their contexts, but more easily displayed against the general current of events.

Both Athens and Sparta attracted the attention of Greek historians, not as typical Greek states, but by reason of abnormalities which called for explanation. Aegina, the only great Greek city which did not survive the fifth century, perished in disgrace and without memorial. Of all three, much that has been transmitted is late, speculative, even allegorical. The more precious, then, are the rare statements of fifth-century writers. But neither Herodotus nor Thucydides was writing political or constitutional history. Nevertheless, in his search for causes Herodotus has happened to refer to most of the principal turning-points in the growth of all three cities.

ATHENS

Herodotus knows of all the principal crises in the long early history:

i. The prehistoric change which established the four Ionic tribes, with tribal chiefs, reorganizing the old family groups for regional defence; genealogically dated about 1330 B.C. (i. 65; viii. 44).

ii. The centralization of Attic government in Athens by Theseus; the background to the treachery of the namesake of Deceleia; and the privileged position of that deme in Sparta, about 1230 B.C. (ix. 73).

iii. The immigration, during the Dorian Conquest, of the family of Peisistratus from Pylos (v. 65), of the Gephyraeans from Tanagra (v. 37), of the family of Isagoras perhaps from Caria (v. 66), and the outflow of similarly displaced persons to the Ionian cities (i. 146–7, ix. 97).

iv. The resistance of Codrus to the Dorian invaders about 1066 B.C. (i. 176, v. 76).

v. The abortive tyranny of Cylon (v. 71) suppressed by the 'head-men of the *naucraries*'. The name probably describes the members of the pre-Solonian Council. Thucydides (i. 126) tacitly corrects to 'the nine archons', an anachronism, for the college of archons was a creation of Solon (Plut. *Sol.* 8. 3; 21. 5; Arist. *Pol.* ii. 12 (1273b40), iii. 7 (1281b32).

vi. The exceptional position of the Alcmaeonidae, highly placed, but 'under a curse', with wealth derived from Sardis (vi. 125) and a marriage connexion with the Orthagorid tyrants of Sicyon (vi. 130).

vii. The legislation of Solon, only mentioned briefly (i. 29; ii. 177). For Herodotus, Solon is a wandering philosopher and economist (i. 29–33; v. 113), not an administrator.

viii. With the tyranny of Peisistratus the narrative becomes
continuous (i. 59–64), and is resumed after his death (v. 55) with
the intervention of Sparta, the expulsion of Hippias (v. 65), and
the reforms of Cleisthenes (v. 66–69). For the details of these
narratives see below (p. 180).

This account is set where it is (i. 59–64) to explain why Athens
failed to help Croesus. But the reason why Croesus expected Athenian help is given elsewhere (v. 125). Croesus had not enriched
either the Alcmaeonidae or Apollo of Thornax without hope of
return. When the Spartans found that they could not respond to
Croesus' appeal, they recompensed his gift of gold with that
golden bowl which only did not reach Sardis because it was sent
too late (i. 69–70; iii. 47). When Croesus summoned the Athenians the Alcmaeonidae were in exile and Peisistratus in power;
Croesus had backed the wrong party. These gifts between states
and individuals or sanctuaries were political expression of the
maxim *do ut des*. Athena's golden robe, even, was made to be
taken off. (Thuc. ii. 13. 5.)

When the story of Peisistratus has been analysed (p. 84), it
becomes clear that it is not intended to be either a mere chronicle
of events or inclusive in its contents. It is told in three episodes.
Peisistratus is presented in turn as a party leader, as the chosen
of Athena in coalition with Megacles, and as the founder not
only of a greater Athens but of an Athenian Empire. All the
corner-stones of fifth-century leadership are there: the mineral
wealth of Laureium and the Strymon, a subservient Naxos, a
benevolent Delos, and a friendly seer from Acarnania: we may
add, from other passages, Athenian interests in Sigeum and the
Chersonese (vi. 37–38), allies in Thessaly (v. 63) and Argos, and
'very friendly' relations with Sparta (v. 5, 63).

Who were the *Hyperakrioi* (or *Diakrioi* as they are called elsewhere), the original supporters of Peisistratus? The name has
been applied to the people '*among* the peaks', pastorals above the
farm-lands of the 'plain'; to those of the midland region '*beyond*
the peaks' of the Hymettus watershed; and to the mining settlements of the rugged Laureium promontory, where Peisistratus

certainly had large interests (i. 64). A story in *Ath. Pol.* 16. 6
shows Peisistratus exempting from land-tax a squatter on the
waste, 'hoeing among the rocks' on Hymettus and enlarging the
cultivated area by his own labour. The word *akra* means 'edge'
as well as 'peak', and *akris* is the name of the predatory locust which
breeds in the waste and thence invades the cornland. Such
squatters were small freeholders, under no vassalage to old landowners in the 'plain': we may compare the refugees from
Anatolia after 1923, and remember that the Revolt of Pactyas,
like the Lydian War of Miletus in Solon's time and the Fall of
Samos later (p. 164), dispossessed many Greek families, to be
'desirable aliens' elsewhere. These, like the numerous industrials,
were a substantial element in the *demos* with which Solon and
Cleisthenes had to deal. Under Peisistratid rule they were personal
protégés of the ruler—what the Romans called *clientes*.

Writing, partly at least, for Athenians, Herodotus had no need
to dilate on the history of Athens: when he discusses it, he is
seeking for causes in the main current of events. But from these
allusions the political situation at the fall of the Peisistratid
tyranny can be reconstructed. There were the old 'Eupatrid'
families, led by Isagoras (v. 66) but of diverse origin, displaced
from elsewhere during the migrations, without the race-bond
which made the Dorian conquest oligarchies so strong. Such
were the Gephyraeans, the families of Miltiades, Isagoras, and
Hippocleides (v. 66; vi. 126–7), Pesistratus, and probably the
Alcmaeonidae. Solon's policy of re-uniting land-ownership with
commercial wealth had added to these a 'new nobility' like that
of Tudor England. The Alcmaeonidae, noble but quite self-
centred, had gold, won in Sardis under Croesus and invested at
Delphi and otherwhere; Peisistratus, the revenue of mines in
Attica and on the Strymon, and the support of mineworkers and
peasant proprietors; both competed for the support of the un-
privileged *demos*, day-labourers, tenant-farmers, industrials, sea-
farers, and merchants. Already under obligations to Lydia, the
Alcmaeonidae sought Persian help for a moment (v. 73), but
Artaphernes' jest—'where do they live?'—revealed them as

persons lately without earth or water to offer, unlike Hippias in
Sigeum. But Cleisthenes stepped into Hippias' place as 'protector'
(*prostates*) of the *demos*, and ally of democratic Eretria against
Sparta and Sparta's middle-Greek friends (v. 79–81). Consequently, Athenian reaction against tyranny was not followed by
relapse into oligarchy, as at Corinth and Sicyon, but by a new
forward step towards political equality. For in Attica there had
been neither race-feud nor conquest; immigrants had been incorporated as 'desirable aliens', bringing skill and wealth. Cylon's
attempt at an Isthmus-tyranny was a fiasco. Peisistratus had risen
as 'protector', not oppressor or partisan any more; and Cleisthenes transferred to his own 'company' the leaderless clients of
the Peisistratidae.

In dealing with Cleisthenes, Herodotus had the peculiar advantage that he lived early enough to converse with *Cleistheneioi*, and
to be unaffected by later uses of the terms *prostates* and *hetaireia*;[1]
he was not an Athenian, but all the more interested in the method
of admitting 'desirable aliens' to citizenship: no one, indeed,
could have made a better Athenian than he. But, as elsewhere,
he uses synonyms for political terms; his ten *phylarchoi* are no
doubt the *strategoi*—as he calls Ion *stratarches* for *polemarchos* (viii.
44; cf. *Ath. Pol.* 3), and the members of the pre-Solonian Council
prytaneis tôn naukrarôn (v. 71), not *bouleutai*: compare *hetaireia* and
moira below.

The problem of Cleisthenes was to deal with the mass of
'desirable aliens' whom the flight of the Peisistratidae had left
without *prostates*: they were, in Greek, *pelatai*. Just so the exiled
Tarquins had left in Rome a mob of *clientes* without political
patronus. Herodotus clearly distinguishes two stages of political experiment. First, Cleisthenes appropriated these patronless clients
to his own *hetaireia*, a word which Herodotus uses (as it is used
in the Gortyna Code 10. 38)[2] but quite without colour, for any
kind of association (v. 71; iii. 70), and applies here to the mass of

---

[1] Myres *Melanges Glotz*, ii. 657–66.
[2] At Cyrene (early fourth century) it is a subdivision (*Suppl. Epigr. Gr.* ix, no.
3, ll. 18–28, ἐς φυλὰν καὶ πάτραν ἐς Θε ἐννῆα ἑταιρήας . . . ἑταίρους δὲ τοὺς Θηραίους).

pelatai of the Alcmaeonidae. In v. 69 he used another colourless word *moira*, 'section'. This device failed: it would merely have perpetuated Peisistratid tyranny under an Alcmaeonid label; as it would have perpetuated tyranny in Rome if the Claudii had become *patroni* of the *clientes* of the Tarquins.

It was the second-thought of Cleisthenes that was epoch-making. In Rome the *plebs* was provided with local ward-*patroni*, the *tribuni plebis*, with all the privileges of a patrician *patronus*, including a seat within the Senate-House—if they brought their own stools—and unlimited right of *auxilium*, day and night. In Athens the ten tribal heroes were immortal and blameless *pro-statai*, for all members of the demes respectively entrusted to their care. The Blessed Ten were selected by Delphi: the leading case was Ajax of Salamis, an alien of Aeacid descent and Aeginetan origin, but 'a neighbour to the city, and a stout ally'. Domicile and loyalty were to be the test of fitness as Athenian, for 'strangers, and serfs, resident aliens', and all 'men of mixed breed'. The distribution of existing communes, the *demes*, among the new tribes was 'ten by ten' as equity required.[1] No total number is mentioned, but it was far greater than 100—Strabo (396) says 174. The old racial grouping of class and kinships retained social and religious meaning only; but Herodotus' slip of the pen about the *phylarchoi* is excused by the survival of this name for the commanders of the new tribal cavalry—the 'Knights' of Aristophanes.

The comparison of the work of Cleisthenes of Athens with that of his mother's father, Cleisthenes, tyrant of Sicyon, has caused offence to those who have not seen that such a travesty is deliberately ironical like the traditional 'oppression' of the Athenians by Peisistratus, their political liberator (i. 59). Doubtless the comparison had been made; but on each of the six points the superficial parallel covers flat contradiction. At Sicyon, race-feud (absent at Athens) and religious prejudices were exacerbated; Delphi gave a curse, not a blessing; the Epic was banned, not

---

[1] If the text MSS. δέκα should be altered, let us read not δέκαχα (Lolling) but δέκα δέκα δὲ καὶ—a phrase to defeat any copyist. For equitable distribution, the ten largest *demes* had to be distributed first, then the ten next largest, and so on; at the end a few little *demes* could be used to level up the ten groups.

canonized—Herodotus seems to contrast a 'Peisistratid recension';[1] new tribe-names were opprobrious, not saintly; and the whole plan *failed*, whereas at Athens it was tribal reform that initiated the great achievements of Herodotus' own time. Here is more than Sophoclean irony; the 'teller of myths' simply states the facts and leaves us to *think*.

On the other hand, on one point Herodotus has committed himself. In what sense was Cleisthenes 'overlooking the Ionians' and setting Athens apart? In his new tribes there was room for all, as there had been welcome for all in Attica before the Ionian cities were founded. Is this another irony, in view of their mixed origin (i. 146)? Account must be taken of Herodotus' own low opinion of the Ionians. But the new Athens was to be something wider and greater; and so it grew to be, until the reaction towards restricted citizenship in Herodotus' own time (p. 184).

ix. The failure of Cleomenes to check the new democratic movement (v. 72–76) is followed by the Athenian counter-attack on his satellites, Chalcis and Thebes (v. 77–78), the outbreak of the long feud with Aegina (v. 79–90), and the further intervention of Cleomenes himself in support of Hippias (v. 90–95). For details see p. 185. The medism of Hippias, and the demand of Artaphernes for his restoration as a Persian vassal, brought Athens into direct and open conflict with Darius (v. 96) on the eve of the visit of Aristagoras.

In all this Athenian story there is little that does not directly bear on the main issue—the causes of Athenian advancement and embroilment with Persia. In the later narrative also the references to Athenian affairs are strictly relevant, and so restricted that it is sometimes difficult to find their places in Athenian history.

x. For example, Herodotus' dependence on Athenian sources for Eretria after its devastation in 490 B.C. is sufficient explanation of his almost complete omission of Eretria from the narrative. This is most notable in the story of the 'double battle' with Chalcis

---

[1] In vii. 8 a collected edition of the oracles of Musaeus is ascribed to their agent Onomacritus, and Cleomenes captured their arsenal of such texts (v. 90).

and Thebes, in which the Athenians, after defeating the Boeotians, crossed into Chalcis and took it (v. 77). How did they cross the Strait? What Herodotus relates is surely the Athenian 'task' in a larger battle between Chalcis and Eretria, in which Eretria held the Strait for her mainland ally. The date, approximately given by the first appointment of *strategoi* at Athens[1]—in 504–503 B.C.—to command the new Cleisthenic levies, is immediately after the transfer of sea-power from Naxos to Eretria; the defeat of her old rival Chalcis was Eretria's first use of this advantage.

Another example is the Raid on Sardis, when Athens provided the commando and landing-craft; Eretria, as sea-power, the naval escort (p. 198). It was part of the exceptional fortune of Athens to be the residuary heir of two great precursors, Eretria and Miletus, both devastated by the Persians, and to be also the source of almost all our information; the historians of Eretria and Miletus are lost.

xi. The quarrel between Athens and Aegina similarly has provoked rearrangements of Herodotus' own story. It is, however, essentially clear and consecutive. Thebes, defeated by Athens (v. 79) after the withdrawal of Cleomenes, begged help from Aegina. At first Aegina prevaricated, sending only the token-help of 'the Aeacidae'. Even the second appeal only led to 'un-announced war' of raids and counter-raids (v. 81), the only meaning of the phrase before the fourth century.[2] The 'old quarrel' in which Epidaurus and Argos were involved, was raked up to inflame Aeginetan opinion; Athenian reprisals were blocked by Cleomenes' intervention, and Corinth in turn frustrated Cleomenes.

xii. *Herodotus and Athens.* Herodotus probably came to Athens about 450. He was already widely informed about the Persian Wars; he had been born a Persian subject and was a citizen of a league-city, but unhappy there. Alternative prospects were indefinite travel or naturalization elsewhere. Solon had recognized as qualification for acceptance at Athens that a man must have

---

[1] *Ath. Pol.* 22. 2.
[2] Myres, *C.R.* lvii (1943), 66–67.

been disfranchised for life in his own city; Cleisthenes prescribed only that he must be 'a neighbour and a stout ally' like Ajax of Salamis. At Athens Herodotus became known to Sophocles; he had much family information about Alcmaeonids and Philaids; he emphasizes the democratic services of Athens, and the dependence of these on the democratic inclusive movement since Peisistratus. The reaction after 451–450 B.C. presumes that there had been laxity before; everyone knew that Cleisthenes himself, Themistocles, Miltiades' son Cimon, and Pericles on his mother's side had been of 'mixed breed'. Pericles himself acted as if he expected the liberal régime to continue. What prevented Herodotus from remaining at Athens? He did not apparently resume his travels: he may have already written down much that he had seen; he had no special reason for going to the West. But was he free to stay in Athens? Had he been a candidate, and rejected? and was Thurii the next-best-thing that his Athenian friends could offer him? In a word, had Herodotus hoped to become a *Kleistheneios*, and was he just too late?

BIBLIOGRAPHY

JACOBY, F. *Atthis*, p. 152 (Herodotus' account of Peisistratus). 1949.

MacGregor, M. F. 'The Pro-Persian Party at Athens 510–480 B.C.', *Harvard Studies, Suppl.* i.

Robinson, C. A. 'The Struggle for Power at Athens in the Early Fifth Century', *Am. J. Philology*, lx (1939), 232.

——— 'Athenian Politics 510–486 B.C.', ibid. lxvi (1945), 243.

Wade-Gery, H. T. 'The Laws of Kleisthenes', *Class. Quart.* xxvii (1933), 17.

——— 'Miltiades', *J.H.S.* lxxi (1951), 212.

Munro, J. A. R. M. *Class. Quart.* xxxiii (1939), 84.

SPARTA

References to early Sparta are rare and allusive. It is the leading state of the migratory Dorian breed (i. 56), Macedonian in origin, but propagated eventually from Dryopis and the Doris of Parnassus (viii. 43, 73). From early troubles, within and without, Sparta had been delivered by Lycurgus, with Delphic sanction (i. 65). After successful wars elsewhere—the only mention of the

Messenian struggles is in the Samian story (iii. 47)—the war with Tegea, on the threshold from Laconia into the rest of Greece, enforced a complete change of policy, symbolized by the discovery of the 'bones of Orestes' (i. 67–68). It is for us, as well as for Lichas, to read the riddle, in the light of Cimon's discovery of the 'bones of Theseus' in Scyros (Plut. *Cimon* 8). The composition of this episode, the counterpart to the story of Peisistratus (i. 59–64), is pedimental, a triptych between prologue and epilogue (pp. 84–85). It is in no sense a compendium of Spartan history, but the announcement of what was, for Herodotus, the 'cause' of Sparta's subsequent domination.

Sparta's position at the head of the 'lot of Temenos'—the regions conquered by the Dorians—rested, that is, for Herodotus, on the institutions and mode of life (*eunomia*) initiated by Lycurgus, and in particular on the double control of elders and elected ephors over the kings. The phrase does not mean '*the* ephors and *the* councillors' objectively, but 'the ephor-and-council' constitution peculiar to Sparta.[1] The council was older than Lycurgus: the ephors' authority grew up later.

But the greater Sparta of the Peloponnesian League needed more than this; mastery of the iron industry—still a novelty to the Spartan intelligence officer (i. 68)—and acceptance of the Spartans as heirs to Orestes, of the pre-Dorian House of Atreus. So, too, in old Kenya the Masai warrior-class was at the mercy of their iron-working Wanderobbo helots: they could not make nor mend their own spears.

Later references to Spartan history are likewise inquiries into causes: the war with Samos, which began the downfall of Polycrates (iii. 40, 48, 54–57); the anomalies of Cleomenes' birth and accession (v. 39–48), where the accessory figures are Anaxandrides and Dorieus, and the brief portrait of Cleomenes himself is central (v. 42); the anomaly of the double kingship, its cause (v. 51–54) and other Spartan curiosities (vi. 55–60) leading to the quarrel between Cleomenes and Demaratus, and eventual 'revenge' of the latter (v. 61–84). The king-lists introduce

---

[1] τοὺς ἐφόρους καὶ γέροντας i. 65.

respectively Leonidas before Thermopylae (vii. 204) and Leotychides before Mycale (viii. 131). Gorgo supplies two anecdotes,
as daughter of Cleomenes (v. 51) and wife of Leonidas (vii. 239),
and Leotychides another (vi. 72) of later date and double import,
explaining his successor Archidamus, king at the outbreak of the
Peloponnesian War, but presented as a 'retribution' for wrong
done to Demaratus. So rarely does Herodotus 'digress' on one of
the landmarks of Greek history.

Foreign Policy. The Ionian appeal to Sparta was intelligible on
military grounds, for Sparta was the strongest Greek state. But
Sparta had failed Croesus and merely warned Cyrus; it had
interfered with Polycrates and repelled Maeandrius; and though
it had been deposing tyrants in mainland Greece, those democratic leaders were of quite different significance from the Persian
agents deposed by democratic Ionians. But now one of the kings,
Cleomenes, was a vigorous and quite incalculable personality, on
whom events turned in his troubled life and myths hovered after
his death: and Herodotus, looking for a tragic hero in his narrative, devotes much care to trace to its causes his meteoric career
(p. 77).

Even the chronology is obscure. That Cleomenes 'reigned no
long time' is not true (v. 48). The visit of Maeandrius (iii. 148)
was not later than 517 B.C., and the second visit to Aegina not
earlier than 492 B.C. Probably Herodotus reflects speculation
among the friends of Dorieus, that so eccentric a person as Cleomenes 'could not last long', and for Dorieus there were western
informants (v. 47) not easily checked. Did Dorieus pose in the
West as King of Sparta?

Still more uncertain are two more events in his reign.

The *Plataean Alliance* with Athens (vi. 108) is placed by Thucydides (iii. 68) in 519 B.C. But the historical background is not
519 B.C. but 509 B.C. For under the Peisistratidae Athenian relations with Sparta were 'as friendly as could be' (v. 63) till Delphi
intervened: there is no other evidence that Cleomenes was active
in central Greece so early; and the alliance is the act of the
'Athenian people' without any mention of the Peisistratidae.

The Argive War is more difficult. Pausanias' phrase 'forthwith' after Cleomenes' accession probably mis-renders 'recently' (vii. 148); i.e. not long before 490 B.C. Even if Demaratus was concerned (Paus. ii. 20), it need not have been long before his quarrel with Cleomenes. Grote connected it with the 'double oracle' and so with the Ionian Revolt. If Argos had been tempted to help Miletus, the short way for Sparta to keep trouble out of Peloponnese was to disable Argos; and the same applies if Argos was suspected of medism in 492 B.C. But if Argos was already disabled in 500 B.C., there was nothing at home to prevent Cleomenes from 'marching to Susa' as Aristagoras proposed. On the other hand, before his Argive victory Cleomenes had only a record of defeats. And the stages of Argive recovery support the latest possible date for the disaster. Argos pleads impotence in 480 (vii. 148-9); only volunteers went to help Aegina about 488 (vi. 92); and Argos was not openly opposing Sparta again till 472 B.C. (ix. 35).[1]

Why did not Sparta medize? The question is inevitable, in view of what had passed. Sparta had been founded as a conquest-state, dominant in Laconia and in Messenia. Later it had been challenged beyond those borders by Tegea and by Argos; by Elis and Mantineia. The alternative policy of vassalage by prudential consent was successful until it was challenged by Athens. The new principle of resistance to Spartan domination was the creed and practice of *isonomia*, of which Athens claimed later to have been the protagonist, and probably was, though the federal plan for Ionia, ascribed to Thales (i. 170), anticipates the reform of Cleisthenes. Further, the cities and interests which supported Spartan dominion, and looked for support from Sparta in their own, were the *anciens régimes* in Greece and the island world as far afield as Samos. There were therefore occasions for rivalry between Sparta and Persia for the acquisition of such supporters; Cleomenes' attempt to re-establish Hippias at Athens, with the risk that the Alcmaeonidae might medize, as indeed they momentarily did; and the Persian attempt to re-establish him, when

[1] For the earlier date, however, see Wells, *J.H.S.* xxv. 192–203; *Studies*, 74–99.

Sparta was thwarted by her own allies: both alike were aimed at the new democracy. But, in the event that the democratic movement became uncontrollable by Sparta alone, Sparta's only resource was to bring in (or *let* in) Persia, and look forward to a satrap's portion in peninsular Greece. Demaratus had encouraged medism in Aegina (vi. 61) and when exposed and expelled he went to Persia (vi. 67, 70). He had been a great personage in Sparta, and an Olympic victor; and he remained an important adviser of Xerxes (vii. 3, 101–4, 209, 234–9; viii. 65).

Hitherto Sparta had missed all earlier opportunities of defending Greek independence: with Croesus (i. 81, 83), with Phocaea and Pactyas (i. 142), with Polycrates (iii. 54–56), with Maeandrius (iii. 145), with Aristagoras (v. 51), with the Scythians (vi. 84). Then in 492 B.C. the heralds of Darius (vi. 48; vii. 133) were killed both at Sparta and at Athens, an insult and a sacrilege which closed all possibility of understanding. At about the same time Sparta on the appeal of Athens, which had been in open enmity with Persia since the raid on Sardis (v. 99), took hostages from Aegina which had medized: and this was the occasion of open breach between Demaratus and Cleomenes, and of the deposition and exile of Demaratus (vi. 51, 60–61, 67–70). It is reasonable to suppose that it was the 'irresponsible' Cleomenes who was responsible for this sudden and irremediable breach with Persia.

The Thessalian and Arcadian visits of Cleomenes (vi. 74). Herodotus gives these as voluntary movements. But he hints that the Spartans 'were in panic' after the withdrawal of Demaratus: probably when they realized how they were compromised with Persia. The order of events puts them in relation to the Macedonian campaign of Mardonius: and this was good reason for Cleomenes to make both a military reconnaissance of the north, in case Darius should advance farther; and a political reconnaissance in Peloponnese to discover whether the time had come for a democratic as well as nationalist movement, with himself as champion, to force Sparta also to conform to his policy; and also whether a 'new model' army of highlanders could be raised there, personally devoted to himself. Both incidents support a late date for Cleomenes' death, and consequently for the resumption of hostilities between Athens and Aegina.[1]

The Death of Cleomenes. As reputed 'causes' of the madness and death of Cleomenes, Herodotus has collected other incidents besides the Argive War; sacrilege at Eleusis (vi. 75), and at Athens (v. 72), corruption of the priestess at Delphi (vi. 75), and the local Spartan excuse of strong drink (vi. 84). The Argive episode (vi. 76–82) illustrates his unscrupulousness in war and his sardonic humour. It seems likely that his career, if not his life, had ended before Marathon; a festival would not have detained him had he wished to reach Marathon in time. His outstanding service to his own country, and to Greece, was that he turned Sparta from the easy road to Medism at the small cost of reversing his policy towards Athens.

The Double Kingship. Inlaid in the retrospect of Cleomenes' antecedents are constitutional details, the more valuable for their rarity, and for Herodotus' personal knowledge (iii. 55). *The Votes of the Spartan Kings* (vi. 57) incurred the censure of Thucydides (i. 20), but without reason. What Herodotus had to explain was the provision for the kings' votes if they were absent from the Council, of which they were ex-officio members. If the kings were to go on field-service the proxy-votes were indispensable. There were three possibilities. If both kings were present, each voted once in his own right. If one king was absent, the 'most proper elder' voted as his proxy as well as in his own right. If both kings were absent, the 'two most proper' elders voted as their respective proxies, and also each in his own right. Herodotus correctly describes this extreme case as 'giving two votes and a third, their own': i.e. the personal vote of each, and the two royal proxy-votes. Thucydides misread this as giving each king two votes, like the heads of some Oxford colleges.

In his account of hereditary criers, pipers, and cooks (vi. 60) Herodotus' humour flashes out. Criers are appointed 'not for

---

[1] Recently Miss Daphne Hereward suggests *Sellasia* for *Thessalia*: *C.R.*, lxv (1951), 146.

clear voice'; of the others, no need to speak: Herodotus had
tasted the 'black broth', and the music was no better. Like their
double rations and field allowances, the other privileges of the
kings are all related to their military functions; adoptions and
disposal of heiresses concerned prospective recruits; public roads
carried the troops; sacrifices, representatives abroad, direct access
to Delphi, and custody of responses, meant early, exact, and
confidential 'intelligence'.

Demaratus, the other king, has the further interest for Herodotus, that he was destined to be a leading adviser of Xerxes, and
that in this capacity he always represents the cause of moderation
and common sense, in dramatic contrast to the brilliant but
unscrupulous Cleomenes.[1]

AEGINA

It has been said that among Greek states Aegina is the 'dark
horse' because it is the 'black sheep'. With one exception, our
authorities draw on Athenian memories of a long and bitter feud;
a bad conscience survived the ruthless end of it. The public of
Herodotus was familiar with the profane aspects, and with the
clause in the Thirty Years Truce 'to let the Greek states go free'
on which the Spartans declared war (Thuc. i. 139). To this or
some such clause Aeginetan exiles had appealed in 432 B.C.
(Thuc. i. 67).[2] Herodotus sets his tragedian's skill, as well as his
learning, to enhance the facts by relevant myths, oracles, 'curiosities' like the long dress-pins (v. 88), as ulterior causes. In the far
past, he just alludes to the Aeacidae, the culture-heroes of Aegina
—whose 'ark of the covenant' fared ill in battle in Boeotia (v. 81)
but better at Salamis (viii. 64, 89)—and to Athenian propitiation
of Aeacus (v. 89).

For commentary on the Aeacidae we turn to our sole non-
Athenian witness. Pindar celebrates no less than eleven Aeginetan
victors. Their city is 'famous for ships' (*N.* v. 31; *Ep.* i. 1), the

---

[1] v. 75 at Eleusis; vi. 51 at Aegina; origin and quarrel with Cleomenes
vi. 65-72, 84; in Persia vii. 3, 103-4, 209, 234-37, 239; viii. 65.

[2] λέγοντες οὐκ εἶναι αὐτόνομοι κατὰ τὰς σπονδάς (Thuc. i. 67); τοὺς Ἑλληνας
αὐτονόμους ἀφεῖναι (Thuc. i. 139).

'long-oared fatherland' (*N.* vii. 86), but also a 'dear field for strangers' (*N.* v. 11) and full of them (*N.* iii. 3: cf. *N.* v. 31). Its walls are fortified with high excellence' (*I.* v. 44). Long ago it was *Oenopia* and *Oenone* (Hdt. viii. 46), the 'vine-land' where 'goodness grows, with fresh shoots like a vine, among wise and just men, to the buxom air' (*N.* viii. 41). This repute it owes to the 'divine born' Aeacus, son of Aegina and sister of Thebe (*I.* viii. 18: cf. Hdt. v. 80), and his seed, Telamon and Peleus, Ajax and Achilles, famous from Nile-springs to Hyperboreans (*I.* vi. 20–24). Their sanctuary, very ancient (*N.* vii. 50) and 'right-regarding', stands by the altar of Zeus Hellanicus (*N.* v. 31; cf. Hdt. ii. 178 at Naucratis), who is also *Xenios*, protector of strangers, and has Saviour Themis as consort (*Ol.* viii. 21). 'Doing justice to strangers' (*Paean* vi. 130–1) and 'prince of ships', 'prudent and sagacious' (*I.* viii. 24). Aeacus 'made ordinances for gods and men'; 'a hard struggle is it, when the full scale turns many ways, to decide with upright mind, not against the fact; but some ordinances of the immortals this sea-girt land provides, a divine pillar to strangers from all-where— and may recurring time not weary so doing'. Aegina is thus 'city of justice' (*P.* viii. 22) and guarantee of 'kindly Quiet, great city, daughter of Justice, holding the supreme keys of counsel and war' (*P.* viii. 1–4). All this points to a code, inherited from the old sea-league of Calauria, but reconstituted by 'divine-born' Aeacus, in the generation of 1260 B.C., adopted by Dorian conquerors, widely accepted like the later 'Sea-law of the Rhodians', and sanctioned by some international court of justice in Aegina itself, 'overstepping neither rule nor right of strangers' (*Ep. Isthm.* i. 4–6). An inner circle of neighbours includes Epidaurus, Nemea, Megara, Salamis (as home of Telamon); but Corinth and Athens are quite outside. There may be allusion (*P.* viii. 8–12) to a naval victory, which 'threw insolence into the bilge'; it has been referred to the battle of Cecryphaleia (458 B.C.), for the future was uncertain (viii. 95–98) and Aegina fell within a year.

This is very different from Athenian outlook on Aegina, the 'eye-sore of Peiraeus', so long resented, and cruelly extirpated at last.[1] In Herodotus (v. 83) even for justice Aeginatans had resorted in early times to their mother-city Epidaurus, a side-step to the fame of Aeacus.

Another aspect of Aegina's greatness is concealed in Herodotus' allusion to Pheidon of Argos (vi. 127), who 'made measures for the Peloponnesians and was most insolent of all Greeks'; for the system of coinage used in Aegina was on Pheidon's standard.[2] It dominated the Cyclades and Crete, Peloponnese (except Corinth), central and northern Greece, except Euboea—with which Corinth compromised with its famous 'colts'-money with Pegasus as badge. From this commercial system Athens was transferred by Solon to its Euboic rival, and Aeacid Salamis (and for a while Nisaea) was annexed by Peisistratus (cf. i. 59), so that Thebes and Aegina were no longer 'nearest' economically. Athens, biding its time politically, accepted Delphic advice during the 'unproclaimed war' to propitiate Aeacus by a shrine (v. 89).

The commercial importance of Aegina is further illustrated (ii. 178) by its separate sanctuary of Zeus at Naucratis, like those of Samian Hera and Milesian Apollo; it was, moreover, the only European state represented there at all. On the other hand, Aegina had few colonies—a couple of factories, Hatria and Spina, near the mouth of the Po, and Cydonia in Crete, seized from exiled Samians (iii. 44–59), which had a colonial issue of 'Pheidonian' coins, on Aeginetan standard, with Aeginetan 'tortoise' symbol.

Like other Dorian states, Aegina seems to have been ruled by an aristocracy; but unlike its mainland neighbours, it had no tyranny; democracy was fostered by Athenian intrigue. This helps to account for the submission of Aegina to Darius in 492 B.C. (vi. 49) like other rules-of-privilege; though better conserved than most, the government of Aegina felt its position insecure. And this in turn explains the vacillation of Sparta, accentuated by quarrel between the Royal Houses.

---

[1] Wilamowitz, *Pindaros*, 61–66.

[2] Strabo 376, probably using Ephorus, says that Pheidon struck *his own* coins in Aegina; but known Aeginetan coins are after Pheidon's latest date.

The sequence of events down to this point has been confused by mistranslation of the phrase 'unproclaimed war' (v. 89). Though in the fourth century the words mean 'truceless', i.e. inexorable, the phrases of Thucydides for the period of tension in 432 B.C. (i. 146; ii. 1) describe a state of hostility without formal declaration of war. Macan[1] antedates the seizure of the sacred ship (vi. 87) and gives this as the reason why the Athenians withdrew from the Ionian Revolt and why the Corinthians lent ships to them (vi. 89). Walker[2] brings down the events of v. 81–83 to about 491 B.C., referring the 'former misdeeds' either to the medism of 492 B.C. or to some earlier offence. Both dislocations are needless. Athens and Aegina had been 'at daggers drawn' from before 500 B.C. to 492 B.C., but only open medism gave Athens opportunity to call in the Spartans.

Arguments, as to date, from the Delphic message to Athens (v. 89) to tolerate aggression for thirty years, have no value; for the Athenians did not accept the warning, though they propitiated Aeacus forthwith. This unpleasant but not dangerous phase had begun before the visit of Aristagoras and helps to account for the inaction of Athens after the raid on Sardis. But only in 492 B.C. did Aegina become a Persian vassal and incur the chastisement of Cleomenes (vi. 50), and only after the death of Cleomenes (vi. 85–94) was there open war with Athens.

Once more the *List of Sea Powers* supplies a missing link. After the destruction of Eretria in 490 B.C., Aegina 'ruled the waves' till the 'crossing of Xerxes'. The period of transition (vi. 87–93) is marked by the democratic revolt and re-establishment of oligarchy in Aegina (vi. 91); and tension, if not open warfare, between Athens and Aegina was the occasion of the naval programme of Themistocles in 483 B.C.

The silence of Herodotus after the Athenian failure to change the government of Aegina (vi. 88–93) continues till 480 B.C. (viii. 144–5) when the two cities are again—or perhaps still—at war, and Themistocles has financed a new fleet for Athens. These 200 ships are a measure of the 'sea-power' which Aegina estab-

---

[1] *Hdt.* V–VI, Appx. VIII, p. 109.   [2] *C.A.H.* iv. 157.

lished after the fall of Eretria. The same reticence—or a lack of information—obscures the movements of Aeginetan ships in the battle of Salamis: all we know is that by general consent Aegina made the largest tactical contribution to victory (viii. 91–93, p. 272).

BIBLIOGRAPHY

ANDREWES, A. 'Athens and Aegina', *B.S.A.* xxxvii (1937), 1.
DUNBABIN, T. J. *'Εχθρὴ παλαίη*, ibid. 83.
WELTER, G. *Aegina*. Berlin, 1938.

THE IONIAN REVOLT (v. 28–vi. 48)

From the Fall of Samos (iii. 128) to the Revolution in Naxos (v. 28) Herodotus is silent on the main course of Greek history. After the Scythian adventure there was a 'remission of troubles' and nothing to say. When he resumes the story another state, Naxos, is in the foreground, and Miletus, Persia's chief protégé hitherto, is the 'show-piece' of Ionia. Both had recently passed through political changes; an old friendship had been broken; and the exiled oligarchs of Naxos were seeking Persian help through Persia's friend on the coast.

The date for the fall of Samos in Eusebius' list (517 B.C.) is in accord with Herodotus, and the short Spartan episode (517–514 B.C.) is transitional. Sparta had been already at war with Polycrates; Maeandrius, his underling and would-be successor, was repelled by Cleomenes (iii. 148); but though open breach with Persia was avoided, as at the revolt of Pactyas (i. 182), the collapse of the Samian protectorate left anarchy in the Aegean. The enterprises of Dorieus in Libya and Sicily were probably attempts to deal with the multitude of dispossessed persons; but order was restored by the recognition of Naxos as protector, with an oligarchic government which lasted till it was expelled in 505 B.C. Before this we only know that Naxos had been under an adventurer Lygdamis—the name is Carian and he had helped Polycrates in Samos—supported by Peisistratus: but his tyranny, the counterpart of that of Polycrates, had given place to restored oligarchy, probably in 515 B.C.

As Naxos was succeeded in sea-power by Eretria, which, like Athens, must have been a democracy by 505 B.C.,[1] it looks as if the expulsion of the Naxian oligarchy was part of the same change of fortunes; and also as if Aristagoras' description (v. 31) of Paros and the other Cyclades as dependencies, and of Naxos as stepping-stone to Euboea, referred to the sea-power which he was asking Artaphernes to restore.

It must be remembered that Eretria, like Chalcis, was more than a normal city-state. Like Athens in Attica, it was the metropolis of all south Euboea except Carystus and Styra, and its countryside was divided like Attica into *demes*. Chalcis similarly held all north Euboea except Histiaea. Hence the abnormal strength and wealth of the two rival cities.

Herodotus' retrospect of the history of Miletus fills out the picture. The Naxian exiles were guest-friends of Histiaeus and counted on restoration by his help and Persian support. Miletus then was oligarchic as well as medist. But this was a recent compromise, due to an arbitration by Paros, one of the satellites of Naxos, which had ended two generations of party-feud (v. 28). These take Miletus back to the days of Cyrus and before, when it had made its own agreement with Persia.

Of the earlier history of Miletus only a few incidents are preserved. In the *List of Sea Powers* Miletus follows Egypt (60 years, probably 664–604 B.C.) and is followed by Lesbos and Phocaea; but these numerals are damaged.[2] If Phocaea had 44 years' sea-power, ending with its destruction about the time of Cyrus' capture of Babylon (538 B.C.: i. 164–7), its dominance began about 582 B.C., close after the Battle of the Eclipse (585 B.C.: i. 74) between Alyattes and Cyaxares of Media. In 545 B.C. Miletus renewed with Persia its former treaty with Lydia (i. 141). It was early in the rule of Polycrates that he prevented Lesbos from intervening in the affairs of Miletus (iii. 39): a glimpse of

---

[1] Evidence is (1) war on Chalcis which was oligarchic; (2) friendship with Athens; (3) friendship with democratic Miletus; (4) a medizing opposition in 490 B.C.; (5) expulsion of oligarchs from Naxos after transfer of sea-power. Myres, *J.H.S.* xxvi (1906), 88–96.

[2] l.c, 88, 102, 104, 110.

the period of *stasis* (v. 28) which lasted two generations, and was not over when Histiaeus spoke at the Bridge (iv. 137).

It must be noted that one of the main resources of Peisistratus was the gold-field of the Strymon valley (i. 64); and that the fall of the Peisistratidae is closely linked in time with the concession of the Strymon country to Histiaeus (v. 11) after the Scythian Expedition. The blocking of that concession and the internment of Histiaeus (v. 23-24) probably shook the city's confidence in Darius, and Histiaeus played on this. Off-shore from Myrcinus lay Thasos, of which the mother-city was Paros. The Parian arbitration was early enough to give Miletus a government-of-affairs and great prosperity before 500 B.C. As Paros was only second city in the Cyclades after Naxos, it may be connected with the change of sea-power from Naxos to Eretria; Miletus, that is, returned to an ancient friendship (v. 99) without forfeiting Persian protectorate. This was the more desirable because the fall of Sybaris—another ancient friend—in 510 B.C. was a grievous blow to Miletus (vi. 21), for Croton its rival and conqueror was a western partner of Samos. The Naxian oligarchs, however, thought they could still count on Milesian help in 501 B.C.

Thus, for Herodotus, the immediate cause of the Ionian Revolt was the appeal of the Naxian exiles; but the occasion was the personal grievances of Aristagoras and Histiaeus; and the underlying motive the democratic deposition of the Persian agents; and it was this that gave Aristagoras his convincing argument to the Athenians, who had already experienced some years of democratic freedom.

Aristagoras underestimated the strength of Naxos. The Persian expedition failed, and on its return to Ionia found disaffection everywhere. Histiaeus had warned his fellow tyrants at the Bridge that they held their places by favour of Darius against the general will. Since then, the revolution in the Cyclades, the rise of Eretria, and the establishment of Cleisthenes' democracy in Athens had altered the whole balance of parties. Aristagoras had quarrelled with Megabates; Histiaeus was plotting to return to the coast; but discontent with the tyrant-system was general, and neither of them was master of the situation. Hecataeus, with wider geographical knowledge, deprecated evacuation, except on the plan—which was not adopted—of creating an island-citadel in Leros, fertile, well-watered, with two fine harbours, as outer guard to Miletus and Branchidae. Herodotus, too, thought the revolt ill advised and ill managed; but he lets fall a few phrases which reveal a federal organization (v. 36, 106, 108, 109).

A widespread series of homogeneous electrum coins of this period, on the Milesian standard, but probably minted in Chios, was probably a federal war-issue.[1] There were abstentions and secessions—Lebedus, Ephesus (v. 100; vi. 17), Cyzicus (vi. 33)—and Samos eventually deserted (vi. 13, 14) followed by Lesbos.

The order of battle at Lade (vi. 8) displays the full naval strength in geographical order; Miletus (80 ships) on the right, nearest the home-port, is supported by Priene (12) and Myus (3); Chios (100) in the centre by Teos (17) and Erythrae (8); Samos (60) and Lesbos (70) by Phocaea (3) on the left and nearest to their own harbours northward. This is the first occasion on which Herodotus deploys a Greek force: we shall see that on battle-order he is uniformly precise and illuminating.

Like Croesus (i. 46–56) the Ionians looked oversea for help from mainland Greece. Besides the mission of Aristagoras himself to Sparta, when he failed like Maeandrius (v. 49–54), and to Athens, where he succeeded (v. 55, 97), Herodotus notes his recall of the interned Paeonians, to reinforce his Strymon dependency (v. 98), and gives also, in separate contexts, a Delphic joint response, cursing Miletus (vi. 29) and warning Argos of disaster (vi. 77): it looks as though Aristagoras had visited Argos as well as Sparta. Naturally there is no mention of appeal to Eretria. The visits of Aristagoras are emphasized by pendant retrospects of recent events in Sparta (v. 39–48) and in Athens (v. 56–96), like those in the Lydian story (i. 59–70).

---

[1] P. Gardner, *Proc. Brit. Acad.* iii. 108; *J.H.S.* xxxi (1911), 151, pl. vii; xxxiii (1913), 105; R. Jameson, *Rév. Num.* (1907–8; 1911), 60; *B.M. Cat. Coins, Ionia*, pp. xxiv–xxv.

Of the sequence of events in the six years' struggle, Herodotus says little, but enough, describing only the initial raid on Sardis; the extension of the Revolt to the Hellespontine cities (498 B.C.); the Ionian expedition to Cyprus (497–6 B.C.) which marked the climax of the movement, but failed through local jealousies; the threefold Persian counter-measures; the withdrawal of Aristagoras to the Strymon; the return and recapture of Histiaeus, whom the Ionians repudiated (495 B.C.); and the belated arrival of the Phoenician fleet, to blockade and recapture Miletus 'in the sixth year' (494 B.C.).[1]

The Burning of Sardis. The narrative of this commando-raid is full and precise (v. 99–100). Only the twenty transports were Athenian; as Eretria 'ruled the waves', her escort of five war-ships was sufficient, and their admiral, by his death, fully implicated the 'sea-power', as Darius' reprisals show. Another glimpse of Eretrian hostility, a sea raid into the Levant, is given by Plutarch. The landing, probably at Scala Nova on the seafront of Ephesus— which had not revolted but supplied the guides—concealed the operation; the raiders at once gained the high ground of Mt. Coressus, circumvented Ephesus itself, crossed the Cayster river higher up, and reached Sardis through Tmolus undetected. The reed-shanties of the gold-washers in the lower town were fired at the circumference so that the blaze spread inwards and concealed the assailants.[2] But from the steep acropolis the garrison broke out, and the raiders withdrew, shedding homewards their Ionian auxiliaries, but losing heavily before they reached their ships. The measure of success was the prolongation of the Revolt for six years. But the secret was out; further surprise impossible. Both Eretria and Athens had done their utmost; they now realized the magnitude of the Revolt, and perhaps its futility. Moreover, Persia had friends in mainland Greece, and Eretria

---

[1] Plutarch (*de Mal. Herod.* 24) puts the siege of Miletus in the first year; but if it had begun then, it was postponed by the raid on Sardis, the object of which was to destroy the Persian siege-train and war-stores. In any event, Milesians knew, from their war with Alyattes, that land blockade need not hurt them so long as they held the sea.

[2] Compare the use of a fire-signal at the Eurymedon (Diodorus, xi. 61) and more recently at Suvla Bay.

had to face its successor in sea-power, Aegina, in a losing quarrel; for Aegina surrendered to Persia (vi. 46).

The Campaign in Cyprus (v. 104, 108–16) was an obvious extension of the Revolt. This large and rich island lay within sight of the Phoenician coast and had been in close intercourse with it since the fifteenth century. But it had been colonized from the Aegean almost as early. A Minoan city close to Salamis on the east coast became very wealthy in the fourteenth century, but was devastated and replaced in the twelfth by an Achaean colony from the Attic Salamis. A similar city was the forerunner of Phoenician Citium (*Kittim*). Other Greek settlements were at Soloi on the north coast and Paphos and Curium in the west. Idalium and Tamassus in the interior behind Citium seem to have been Phoenician, but at Amathus on the south coast, a third language was in use. Cut off from the Aegean, after the migrations, by Phoenician sea-power, the Greek cities retained kingships, chariot-fighting, a dialect akin to Arcadian, a syllabic script derived from the Minoan, and a tradition of Epic minstrelsy, from which in the eighth century the 'Cyprian verses' were retransmitted to Ionia. In the *List of Sea Powers* Cyprus holds the sea for a generation, probably 745–709 B.C., giving place to Phoenicia under Assyrian overlordship. To this sea-power probably belongs the active commerce with the Syrian coast at Minet-el-Beida, with Cilicia, and also with Rhodes and Crete. Under Amasis, Cyprus became an Egyptian protectorate, but was conquered by Cambyses, with advantage to the Phoenician cities; so Greek discontent gave the revolted Ionians their opportunity to establish an outer guard against attack by sea. But the ancient grudge between Phoenician and Greek cities, and prompt Persian counter-measures, wrecked the Ionian enterprise, and nothing is heard of Cyprus till its ships follow Xerxes to Salamis (viii. 58, 100).

The Forward Policy of Darius and Mardonius (vi. 42–49). From the Ionian Revolt Darius had learned three lessons.

i. The 'tyrant'-system had failed—as Histiaeus foreknew—and was replaced by 'home rule all round' (vi. 42–3), so long as the

Greek cities kept the King's Peace: what Artaphernes insists is that they shall submit to justice and 'not harry each other'. Not even Athens could grant them more, and it was under this wise protectorate that they fought for Xerxes.

ii. The tribute was reassessed as a land-tax and therefore did not hamper industry or commerce. This was a return to the old tribute under Croesus; and, being reckoned not by local measures but by Persian *parasangs*, it was on the same scale for all. Such a tribute was compatible with the political independence now guaranteed. The same applied to the Delian 'tribute of Aristides' (Thuc. v. 18. 5) with a similar provision for settling quarrels. Persian tribute was not, however, easy to collect, when Athens by treaty precluded the King's officers from entering the coast districts (Diod. xii. 4. 5), and consequently it fell into arrears. But it was reaffirmed in the Athenian treaty with Darius II in 424 B.C. (Isocrates, *Panegyric* iv. 120). Herodotus, therefore, is correct in insisting that the 'tribute of Artaphernes' remained in force till his own time (vi. 42). It is, moreover, not unlikely that Aristides used the Persian assessment as an accepted basis for his own.[1]

iii. Thirdly, Persia realized that the heart of Greek nationality was not in Ionia at all, but oversea—the sea-power of Eretria and the new democracy of Athens; and meanwhile Hippias had come to add his testimony to that of Histiaeus (vi. 94).

Thus the 'very pacific' measures in Ionia covered a 'forward policy' as well as reprisals against Eretria and Athens (vi. 44).

The Hellespont cities were punished like the Ionian (vi. 33). Only Miltiades, an Athenian adventurer, hereditary chief of the Thracian Dolonci in Chersonese, but already compromised by his advice at the Danube Bridge (iv. 137–8) and recently disturbed by a Scythian raid, escaped through Imbros to Athens (vi. 33, 40–41). In this quiet way is the hero of Marathon introduced, with his exceptional experience of warfare and Persians. Mardonius, too, appears now (vi. 43) as the new-model governor of pacified Ionia, and exponent of democracy within empire.

[1] M. Cary, *C.Q.* xxxix (1945), 87; A. W. Gomme, *Thuc. Commentary*, 334–5.

We compare the first appearance of Themistocles later (vii. 143).

Mardonius traversed Thrace with a large force; his fleet took Thasos; and a later phrase (vii. 85) shows that Persian suzerainty was extended to the frontiers of Thessaly. But the fleet was wrecked off Athos, and Herodotus thought the expedition a disaster and a warning; though Thasos, with its mines, was disarmed (vi. 46–47) and a general summons followed, to all Greek cities, to accept Persian overlordship (vi. 48).

Among the islands that medized was Aegina, in the heart of the mainland area, a vassal latterly of Sparta, and recently involved in hostilities with Athens. To Athenian protest Sparta replied through King Cleomenes by seizing hostages from Aegina (v. 49), and Herodotus intervenes once more to explain the new situation and the political difficulties of Cleomenes (vi. 49, 51–93). These have been considered already (p. 186).

Wider Implications. Persia's failure to recover Naxos for oligarchy had destroyed the prospect offered by Aristagoras of a dominion in the Cyclades and Euboea (v. 31); but the Raid on Sardis justified reprisals against Eretria and its accomplice, Athens. The defection and destruction of Miletus had deprived Darius of his principal instrument within the Greek world. Consequently he had to foster other hot-beds of medism; reactionary elements in Eretria (v. 100) and the Cyclades (vi. 96), the governing cliques in Thebes (ix. 86; Thuc. iii. 62) and in Aegina (vi. 49, 73). Argos, which had refrained from helping Miletus (vi. 19), had been friendly with the Peisistratidae (i. 61), now Persian vassals, but had been put out of action by Cleomenes (vi. 76–83) and was biding its time (vii. 148–9; ix. 12). Persia's hope, everywhere, was in the old rules-of-privilege based on class-differences.

In retrospect, Sparta ranked as organizer of national defence and contributor of the essential land force. But the champion, in Greece, of old-time parties and reactionary interests, which looked to Persia in Ionia and the island-world; the state whose own protectorates were being threatened by the democratic movement; and the obvious 'quisling' to be envassalled and confirmed as Persian agent for the maintenance of peace in a medized Greece, had neglected, hitherto, every opportunity of challenging Persian aggression (p. 188). The medism of Aegina was a crisis of the same kind. Demaratus and Leotychides were for dealing with it in the same way. Demaratus, in fact, did medize, and became a Persian counsellor, like Hippias and Alexander son of Amyntas; a tragic figure, because he knew what his countrymen were fighting to defend. Only the personality of Cleomenes stood fast. But it was a close thing for Sparta, and it was yet another piece of characteristic audacity to murder the Persian envoys. After that, not Demaratus himself could have interceded.

BIBLIOGRAPHY

GARDNER, P. 'The Coinage of the Ionian Revolt', *J.H.S.* xxxi (1911), 151; xxxiii (1913), 105.
DE SANCTIS, G. *Aristagora di Mileto, un problema di storia antica*, 63. Bari, 1932.
LARSEN, J. A. O. 'Sparta and the Ionian Revolt', *Classical Philology*, xxvii (1932), 136.

MARATHON (vi. 94–140)

The Date. After the fall of Miletus, the reforms of Artaphernes and Mardonius (vi. 42–43) fill the years 494–493 B.C. The European campaign of Mardonius and the first attack on Thasos follow in 492 B.C.; the second siege (vi. 46–47) was in 491 B.C. with the mission of the heralds (vi. 48) which took some time, but was connected with the preparations for the seaborne attack on Eretria and Athens. The Athenian appeal to Sparta against Aegina followed 'at once' (vi. 49), and the deposition and medism of Demaratus soon after (vi. 37, 61, 66–69). It is difficult, besides all this, to find room for Marathon in the autumn of 491 B.C., as proposed by Munro, not, as usually reckoned, in 490 B.C.[1] Further, the Egyptian Revolt (vii. 1) was in the fourth year after Marathon (487 or 486 B.C.); it was still in progress when Darius died (486 B.C. : vii. 4)[2] and ended the second year thereafter

---

[1] J. A. R. Munro, *C.A.H.* iv. 232–3. C. J. Cadoux, *J.H.S.* lxviii (1948), 118, supports 490 B.C. against Munro.
[2] Fotheringham, *Monthly Notes R. Astron. S.* lxix (1909), 446 ff., 542.

(485 B.C.: vii. 7). Xerxes' expedition was in the fifth year after that (481 B.C.: vii. 20, 37, 51). This confirms 490 B.C. for Marathon. Yet Thucydides sets Marathon in the twentieth year after the expulsion of Hippias, which was in the fourth after the death of Hipparchus (Thuc. vi. 59), one hundred years from the Four Hundred in 411 B.C. (viii. 20, 68: 510 B.C.); and he sets Xerxes' invasion in the tenth year after Marathon (i. 18) and 'about fifty' before 432 (i. 118).

Strategy. Mardonius, though he had not failed utterly in Europe, had gravely miscalculated the land-route into mainland Greece (vi. 43–45). But the heralds brought back surrenders enough to justify his 'forward policy': and there was another route to Eretria and Athens (vi. 95) directly through the island-world as displayed already by Aristagoras (v. 31). The reference to horse-transports, a new type of sea-craft, indicates the special scope of the expedition, and explains the delay in launching it (vi. 95). On this route Naxos was a necessary stage (vi. 96); Delos a sanctuary to be propitiated (vi. 97, 118). Carystus, an Eretrian outpost, and the farthest point beyond which Datis could not conceal whether he meant to attack Eretria first, or Athens, offered brief resistance (vi. 99). Eretria was surrendered by partisans of Persia (vi. 100–1); the 4,000 Athenian *cleruchs* in Chalcis took warning and withdrew. When and where they joined the Athenian home-army is not recorded.

At this point difficulties begin; for the literary traditions preserved in the *Vita Miltiadis* of Cornelius Nepos (marked 'N' below) are not easy to combine with the narrative of Herodotus. The battle fresco in the Painted Portico at Athens (Pausanias i. 15. 4) had canonized much eyewitness, but its influence on either story cannot now be determined. It was tripartite, like a narrative in Herodotus, the central struggle at the marsh being flanked by the charging Plataeans on the left and by the capture of the ships on the right: the point of view was thus approximately the burial mound (*soros*), looking eastward. Above the combatants, among whom Callimachus and Miltiades alone were named, Athena, Heracles, and the hero Echetlus looked down on

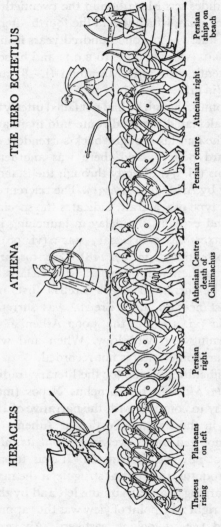

THE HERO ECHETLUS

ATHENA

HERACLES

Theseus rising | Plataeans on left | Persian right | Athenian Centre death of Callimachus | Persian centre | Athenian right | Persian ships on beach

FIG. 12. MARATHON PANEL IN THE PAINTED PORCH (STOA POIKILE) AT ATHENS: RECONSTRUCTED FROM PAUSANIAS

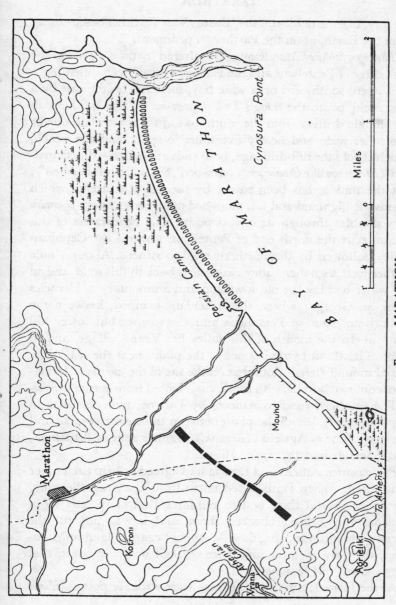

FIG. 13. MARATHON

━━━ Athenians and Plataeans (east).   ▭▭▭ Persians: ◠◠◠ ships along beach.

Based on Greek Staff map.

the fray, like the deities on the 'Darius Vase',[1] with Theseus rising from the Earth, as on the Parthenon pediment.

The topography of Marathon is little altered by time. Between the high ridge of Pentelicus and the Euboean Strait, a confused highland opens southward on a wide bay, sheltered on the east by a long rocky point, the 'Dog's Tail' (*Cynos-oura*). This has held up the shingle drifting from the south, to form a coast plain one or two miles wide and nearly five miles long. Behind the beach, which checks the hill-drainage, both ends are marsh—the 'fennel-bed' (*Marathon* like *Crommyon* 'onion-bed', *Sicyon* 'cucumber-bed') ; but the middle has been raised by the silt of a stream which drains the highland and has ploughed out a torrent-bed (*charadra* now double) through its own deposits. The headwaters of this stream skirt the north end of Pentelicus, towards the Cephissus valley, followed by the northern road to Athens. About a mile farther west a smaller valley cuts nearly back to this road, and on the watershed lay the old township and a sanctuary of Heracles (now St. George) where the Athenians camped, between the Aphorismos spur of Pentelicus and the steeper but lower hill Kotroni. In the mouth of this valley lies Vrana village, and in front of it, about two miles out in the plain, near the sea, is the burial mound (*soros*), doubtless on the site of the carnage. It contains confused burials, with small vases looted from earlier graves.

The southern road to Athens, by Pallene, more familiar to Hippias (i. 62), leaves the plain between the western marsh and the steep slope of Agrieliki (*Argaliki*), another spur of Pentelicus, and descends into the upper Ilissus.

Preliminaries. Athens and Eretria had agreed to help each other if attacked. When Datis sailed north from Carystus, therefore, the Athenians did their best to reinforce Eretria (p. 203). But treachery in Eretria checked them, and it was not till the Persian squadron moving down-channel began to land at Marathon, the only open landing-place on their own east coast, that they moved out to meet it there.

At the Heracleium the Athenians were strongly posted (*idoneo*

---

[1] Furtwängler–Reichhold, ii, pl. 88.

loco N 5. 2) blocking the northern road and commanding the southern in flank. Scattered trees were cleared and collected into an entanglement (*arborum tractu* N 5. 3), to reinforce the natural entrenchment of the torrent-bed against cavalry. There were other trees still standing towards the eastern marsh.[1]

For utmost shelter the Persian ships lined the beach from the rocky base of Cynosura to the torrent mouth—about three miles —and perhaps also west of it. At 30 feet each abeam, 600 ships (vi. 95) in single rank would require just over 3½ miles, but they may have been at anchor, two deep (cf. vii. 188, πρόκροσσαι). Cavalry transports would be next to the marsh, where there was grazing. The transports of the corps which guarded the whole camp may have been west of the torrent, which protected all that lay east of it.

Arrival of the Plataeans. The whole force of Plataea was about equivalent to one Athenian tribe. Its arrival is sufficiently explained by Herodotus (vi. 106–8); and the date of the Athenian alliance has been discussed already (p. 186). The Plataeans knew what awaited them, if the Athenians were defeated, from their powerful and long-hostile neighbours in Thebes, ringleaders of the *ancien régime* throughout Boeotia. In the order of battle their proper place was on the left, with clear line of communications and retreat by the northern road, and so they were depicted in the Painted Portico.

Polemarch and Strategoi. Herodotus was not an Athenian, and is elsewhere not precise in his use of official terms (p. 180). In Solon's college of nine *archons*, the *polemarch*, elected like the others, was 'war-lord' in a general sense. To command the new tribal battalions, under the Cleisthenic constitution, ten 'corps-leaders', *strategoi*—whom Herodotus calls *phylarchoi* (v. 67)—were elected, like the Roman *tribuni militum*, and, with many changes of function, they remained elective throughout; but at first their duties were tribal, and 'of the whole force the commander was the polemarch' as before (*Ath. Pol.* 22. 2). From 487–486 B.C. onwards the nine archons were chosen by lot out of an elected panel.

[1] Suidas χωρὶς ἱππεῖς.

Yet, Herodotus says, in 490 B.C. Callimachus was 'elected by lot to be polemarch'. His concern is not with constitutional history, but with the divine chance that the man with the right name—'fine fighter'—and the right judgement was in command at Marathon. But has Herodotus blundered? Even after the nine archons for any year had been elected as a 'college' or cabinet, it had still to be decided who was to 'go to the war office'. What the current practice was we do not know: perhaps the nine posts were always assigned by lot; perhaps, with invasion in prospect, no one much 'wanted the war office'. Anyhow, the nine 'tossed up', and the right man got it. But this man was not Miltiades.

That Miltiades was 'tenth' of the tribal commanders in 490 B.C. made him chief-of-staff, consequently in position to supply information and influence decisions. Moreover, on his own 'day' of command, in tribal rotation, he was orderly-officer, responsible for intelligence, routine, and transmission of the polemarch's orders. In the council of war all tribal commanders' votes were equivalent to that of the polemarch. Herodotus does not say that he was bound by a majority vote; nor that there was a parity vote, or a formal vote at all; only that there was a division of opinion, and that the 'worse' opinion, opposed to Miltiades' plan, was gaining ground (ἐνίκα). We, like Miltiades, have to remember that *strategoi*, like *tribuni militum*, were political as well as military officers; and that it was a similar 'rot' that had just destroyed Eretria (vi. 100). Inaction now meant delay, and the growth of treason in Athens. It was for the polemarch to decide, and the sooner the better. He quite properly supported his chief of staff and a majority of the commanders supported him, each offering to transfer to Miltiades his own turn (πρυτανηίη) as orderly-officer. On this crucial occasion Herodotus has taken peculiar pains to ascertain the real 'cause', and states it in Miltiades' words to Callimachus (vi. 109). The same phrase is used by Themistocles to Eurybiades (viii. 69).[1]

The Shield Signal. When the Persians 'were already in their ships' (vi. 115, 121–4) a signal from a polished shield was ob-

---

[1] Compare H. Berve, 'Miltiades', *Hermes Einzelschriften*, ii (Berlin, 1937), 78 ff.

served, from the battlefield, and regarded as a message from Persian partisans in Athens. Herodotus rejects vigorously the rumour that it was sent by the Alcmaeonidae, but has no explanation. If it was relayed from the city, it must have been sent from the ridge of Pentelicus—from no other point are both Athens and Marathon in view—and if so, such signals could not be observed by the Greeks till they left the Vrana valley for the plain. The precise moment is therefore irrelevant: signals could have passed unobserved—and probably had—ever since the Persians landed. Such signals can have had but one purpose, to inform them of affairs in the city; and the Persian reaction was to withdraw, wholly or in part, from Marathon, and attempt a landing in Phalerum Bay (vi. 115) before the Athenian army could return. That army, moreover, would be held in position at Marathon if a striking force was left there to threaten Athens through the passes. This force had its own naval escort and transport in case of reverse. Since it acted also as rear-guard to cover the re-embarkation of the main body, it was necessarily posted, with its ships, on the left or western flank of the Persian array, where it was also farthest along the southern route to the city; that is, towards the western marsh, and probably west of the torrent-bed. This southern route was only covered in flank by the Greeks at Vrana.

Though signals from the ridge were invisible from the Greek position, re-embarkation was in full view. Moreover, in a tradition preserved by Suidas,[1] Ionians in the Persian force had been signalling from trees in the plain (i.e. east of the *charadra*) that the cavalry had been withdrawn; and this fact diminished the risk of deploying into the open ground. This was the moment for which Miltiades had waited; and he could not wait longer, whether it was 'his day' or not, lest Persian cavalry should land at Phalerum.

The Battle. The Athenians deployed as in normal routine, with the right wing under Callimachus leading, and the Plataeans from in rear on the left. As Callimachus was supported by his own tribe *Aiantis* (Plut. *Mor.* 628 d) and the other tribes followed

[1] s.v. χωρὶς ἱππεῖς.

'by number', Miltiades was in the left wing, for his tribe *Oeneis* was eighth from *Aiantis* on the roll.[1]

On entering the plain the right wing held close to the steep slopes of Aphorismos and Agrieliki. The left, with the Plataeans, deployed towards the torrent-bed with Kotroni in rear. The line of battle thus faced south-east. Eleven thousand men, four deep— the usual formation—would cover 2,750 yards, about the distance from the foot of Agrieliki to the torrent; so there were no men to spare, and any extension or reinforcement of the wings, whether deliberate or not, had to be at the expense of the centre (vi. 111).

Normal Persian deployment would place the heavy infantry in the centre, the archers and other light troops on either wing: beyond these, the cavalry, in open ground. As the only part of the Athenian line which had serious losses was the centre, the *soros* certainly marks where these occurred.

With the point of encounter thus fixed, it is clear why the torrent-bed, though a conspicuous feature, is not mentioned. It was not *on* the battle-field at all, but bounded it, and this natural feature had also been reinforced *arborum tractu* (N 5. 3). It also put out of action any cavalry who may have been still ashore. In many respects Marathon was 'good riding country' (vi. 102); but Hippias had forgotten the *charadra*.

The tactics of Miltiades were indeed original (*nova ars* N); for he alone of the Athenian leaders had experience of Persian warfare, itself a rare combination of inherited skill. Of this, Aristagoras had given a caricature to Cleomenes (v. 49). First, the horsemanship of folk originally (and still in part) nomad (i. 125); second, the same nomads' powerful bow, but handled now by light infantry kneeling in scrub-country, protected and camouflaged by wicker screens—Birnam Wood coming to Dunsinane; thirdly, the compact mass of spearmen, characteristic of their sedentary neighbours, Sumerian and Elamite. From these elements Persian genius had created a mode of attack invincible hitherto: the enemy was first herded together by cavalry on

[1] Paus. i. 32–33.

either flank, and demoralized at long range by a barrage of
arrows 'that covered the sun' (vii. 226); then the phalanx of
'immortals' gave the *coup de grâce*. For heavy infantry to charge,
without such preparation by cavalry and archers, seemed to
Persians to be 'madness and downright suicide' (vi. 112). But
Miltiades had discovered the counter-move. Against cavalry he
strewed felled trees along his exposed flank (*arborum tractu* N 5. 3), at
the same time clearing such obstructions from his front. The other
flank was protected by a steep hill-side (*montium altitudine* N 5. 3).
Against archery, the Athenian in bronze helmet, breastplate, and
greaves was fairly immune, even erect, and invulnerable if he
crouched behind his bronze shield. When he came within bow-
shot, he dropped on the knee till the archers had found the range;
then, at the word, sprang forward, sprinting (*dromô*) till he was
within the barrage; then he crouched again, by signal, till he had
his second wind, and the arrows found him; then 'at the double'
once more. In this last rush even 'immortals' went down—turban,
trousers, and all—before a wave of one-man-power *tanks*.

The Sequel to Marathon. As soon as the fighting was over, the
Athenian force returned full-speed to Athens, and camped by
another shrine of Heracles at *Cynos-arges*, on the hill-ground
beyond the Ilissus. The fame of this march was enhanced by
ancient notions of the shape of Attica, which doubled the ratio
between the two sea-sides of the triangle (about 70 miles) and
the land-side connecting them (under 20 miles, 22–25 by road).[1]
That the Persian vanguard was already in the offing is evidence
that it had begun to leave Marathon Bay at least the dawn before
the battle. At 5 knots for 70 miles its vanguard would take
14 hours. Plutarch's belief (*Arist.* 5) that the fleet was driven
inshore by the weather may be well grounded, for an east wind
would normally be followed by a north-westerly gale, and this
may explain the immediate retreat from Phalerum. But there is
no reason to doubt that the Persians intended to land in rear of
the Athenian army, and that this was why they withdrew from
Marathon.

[1] Myres, *Greece and Rome*, xii (1943), 33–42.

Herodotus, an exile or a traveller since early manhood, was no trained soldier, but as a military historian he has been unduly disparaged. He gathered information where he could get it, in the taverns, on the quay-side—at best, in the club. But he knows how an army was marshalled and led; how the rank-and-file watched and discussed the commanders, and drew their own conclusions from orders they did not understand. By the time of his visit to Athens, most of the 'Marathon-men' were dead and strangers were shown the painted war-memorial. That his battle-pieces are as intelligible as they are is testimony to his industry and common sense.

Epilogue to Marathon (vi. 118–40)

At first sight Book VI ends in an untidy string of anecdotes; but comparison with the last chapters of Book IX reveals a symmetrical arrangement which cannot be accidental. There were two matters which had to be traced to causes: the shield signal, and the fate of Miltiades. These are treated in pendant sections (vi. 121–4, 125–31, 132–6), each threefold, with a picturesque central episode; both enframed between the exoneration of the Alcmaeonidae (vi. 121–4) and the annexation of Lemnos, Miltiades' principal countervailing exploit. This *Epilogue* punctuates the main narrative between the aggression of Darius and that of Xerxes, and leaves the field clear for other leaders; for neither Miltiades nor the Alcmaeonidae reappear. The Lemnian story (vi. 137–40) resumes earlier references to Lemnos (v. 26; vi. 34–41).

Agarista's Wedding. To his defence of the Alcmaeonidae against the scandal of the shield signal, Herodotus appends a retrospect of the family, whose renown is for him the counterpart of the antecedents of their opponent (vi. 34–41, 103–4). It is composed in three parts: the central episode of 'Agarista's Wedding'—an anecdote based on the widespread fable of the 'Dancing Pea-cock'[1]—enframed between an earlier anecdote, the enrichment

---

[1] Rhys Davids, *Buddhist Birth Stories*, i. 291; cf. E. Peters, *Der Griechische Physio-logus* (Berlin, 1898), rev. *Edinb. Rev.* (Vol. 231, No. 472, April 1920), 340; Macan, *Hdt.* V–VI, Appx. XIV.

of Alcmaeon by Croesus, and an almost contemporary dream of the younger Agarista before the birth of Pericles (probably 493 B.C.).

The Parian Expedition (vi. 132–5)

This episode, also, is constructed in three sections. Between the attack on Paros and the trial and death of Miltiades stands the anecdote of the priestess Timo, the *cause* of Miltiades' failure; interpolated, on Parian authority, but with Delphic sanction, between narratives 'generally accepted' in Greece.

It is characteristic of Herodotus that his account of a personage so significant as Miltiades is scattered in four distinct contexts: his conduct at the Ister Bridge (iv. 137–8); his family history, domain in Chersonese, and expulsion from it after the Ionian Revolt (vi. 32–41); his leadership at Marathon (vi. 103–4); and his failure at Paros (vi. 132–40), with his annexation of Lemnos, which belongs to his career in the north. In each he is the responsible agent and *cause* of events; but those events are distinct and disconnected, like his own career. The adventurer-state ruled by Miltiades in Chersonese was founded by permission of Peisistratus, but was neither a colony nor a cleruchy—nor a public domain like that of Histiaeus on the Strymon; the Peisistratid hold on Sigeum was similar (v. 94). A modern parallel is Sarawak under Rajah Brooke. The founder was protected by Croesus against Lampsacus; the victor of Marathon had saved Darius, though unwillingly, at the Bridge. Athens had thus already peculiar relations with the Persian overlord of Hellespont. His 'tyranny' over the Thracian Dolonci and the Greek cities in Chersonese was inherited and personal, so that Athenian citizens who suffered under him there could prosecute him at Athens, where he retained his citizenship like a *cleruch*. Before the Revolt he had been a Persian vassal, though a disloyal one; betrayed by a Parian (vi. 133) after it, he fled to Athens, where his family had property and wealth. His quarrel with the Alcmaeonidae, who led the popular party, made him prominent among the 'notables' (*Ath. Pol.* 28), and he had the support of Aristides, who was to be archon in 479 B.C., and whom he left to clear the field of Marathon (*Marm. Par.* [*F.Gr.H.* 239 A 49]; Plut. *Arist.* 5).

For Miltiades, with his wider experience, the defeat of the Persians at Marathon was but the turning-point of the struggle. Their conciliation of Delos made it necessary to purge the islands of medism if Attica was to be secure. Athens was, moreover, the residuary heir of Eretria. Naxos had evaded formal surrender to Datis (vi. 96), but Paros, the next in importance, had contributed a ship (vi. 133). Moreover, Aegina was in the same relation to Persia as Naxos had been from the fall of Polycrates to the rise of Eretria to sea-power (p. 194); and Aegina had not only medized, but was trying to escape the consequences. Further, whether Cleomenes was dead or only incapacitated, Leotychides was prepared to support Aegina against Athens, and to allow Greek freedom to go by default, as before. It is in accordance with his practice elsewhere, and especially in regard to Aegina, that Herodotus only gives that aspect of the campaign which reveals the *causes* of Miltiades' fall, not of Athenian change of policy. But by 489 'sea-power' had passed from Eretria to Aegina. Where Miltiades failed to recover the heritage of Eretria, Athens had to wait for Themistocles. In this perspective, Herodotus' careful inquiries into the tragedy of Miltiades are explained. He was writing an obituary, not the sequel to Marathon. Current stories were contradictory; even the nature of Miltiades' wound, and the charges against him, were uncertain; only the oracle was indisputable; and there Herodotus leaves it. What a contrast to the Alcmaeonidae!

It has been commonly supposed that the island-campaign belongs to 489 B.C. But with Aegina alert and hostile, prompt naval action was necessary, and utter secrecy. It must be assumed that the Athenian fleet—of seventy ships as in the war with Aegina (vi. 89)—was ready, in view of the Persian attack. Miltiades alone, after his eminent services at Marathon, and with his interests in Lemnos and Chersonese, was in a position to put all enemies on a false scent. Marathon fight was early in

September.[1] If the blockade of Paros was begun forthwith, it should be over by mid-October; but its abandonment, after a set back, was inevitable, like the Persian siege of Naxos in 501 B.C.

At Paros, as at Marathon, Nepos (8), certainly drawing here on Ephorus,[2] is more copious and coherent. The Parian expedition was part of a larger scheme. It was not only in Eretria and Athens that there had been 'something rotten' (vi. 100, 109). Some of the islands were recovered, others compelled to submit. Only at Paros was a regular siege required, as at Andros in 480 B.C.; and the city was on the point of surrender, when fire-flashes— perhaps from a forest-fire in Myconos—were read by both sides as portending the return of the Persians. The Parians withdrew their surrender; Miltiades, already wounded, retired. The fine was to refund the cost of the expedition: other accusations were not upheld, but it was not only at Delphi that a bad end was expected for Miltiades. After this fiasco, 'sea-power' passed without controversy from Eretria to Aegina.

BIBLIOGRAPHY

MACAN, R. W. *Herodotus IV–VI*, ii. 198 ff. (1895).
CASSON, S. *Klio*, xiv (1914).
HOW, W. W. *J.H.S.* xxxix (1919), 48 ff.
LUGEBIL, K. *Jhrb. f. klass. Philol. Suppl* v (1871), 539.
LEHMANN-HAUPT, C. F. *Klio*, xviii (1922), 65 ff., 319 ff.
KROMAYER-VEITH. *Antike Schlachtfelder*, iv (1914), 581.
MAURICE, SIR F. *J.H.S.* xlix (1929), 100.
BERVE, H., 'Militades'. *Hermes Einzelschriften*, ii. (Berlin, 1937).
WADE GERY, H. T. 'Miltiades', *J.H.S.* lxxi (1951), 212.

BOOKS VII, VIII, IX
THE EXPEDITION OF XERXES

After the string of footnotes to Marathon (vi. 118–49) the curtain falls at the end of Book VI, and rises forthwith on the third act of the Herodotean trilogy, the story of the expedition of Xerxes (Books VII–IX). Here the narrative is more continuous,

---

[1] Dinsmoor, *A.J.A.* xxxviii (1934), 444–5.
[2] *F.G.H.* 70, F. 63; cf. Steph. s.v. 'Πάρος'.

and the general structure simpler, than in Books V and VI, but it makes use both of parallel narratives and of pedimental balance of episodes.

The transition from Book VI to Book VII, like that from the first to the second main drama at v. 28, is deliberately close-knit; for the last of the footnotes to Marathon brings the story back to the occupation of Lemnos by Miltiades, an outpost against ulterior aggression founded by the victor of Marathon himself. The first episode of Book VII is also transitional, with Darius' wrath and preparations, the Egyptian revolt and its suppression, and the palace intrigue which prepared the way for the accession of Xerxes (1–4). The real break, and opening of the *Prologue*, is at the death of Darius (vii. 4).

Like the earlier 'dramas', Books VII–IX are a story with a hero: not Xerxes, who has no heroic quality, but his disastrous counsellor Mardonius; more fully responsible, and therefore more guilty, because he sinned against the light. For it was he, the flower of the new imperial college and son-in-law of Darius, who had made so fair an entry, in vi. 43, to supplement the remedial finance of Artaphernes by 'establishing democracies' in Ionia. For all the emphasis of Herodotus on the disaster of Mount Athos, he had completed the work of Megabazus, and left behind him a friendly vassal in Macedonia (vi. 44–45; cf. vii. 173, 175; viii. 136–44).

Xerxes' initial reluctance to resume the offensive in the West was overcome by a combination of circumstances, which Herodotus presents, after his manner, as personal 'causes'—Atossa, Mardonius, Demaratus who had supported his cause before Darius, the Aleuadae, and the Peisistratidae with their sinister agent Onomacritus. Atossa had been a 'power behind the throne' before the attack on Samos (iii. 133–4; cf. 139), and Aeschylus in the *Persae* has portrayed her forcible personality. Mardonius supported the reasonable demand for reprisals, by appeal to Persian prestige and Xerxes' self-esteem, by misrepresentation— as Demaratus knew (vii. 102)—of the fertility and wealth of Greece, and by his own ambitions and enthusiasm. The Aleuadae were typical of those displaced representatives of the old order from the least politically conscious region of northern Greece: the Peisistratidae had their own failure at Marathon to avenge, and their knowledge of Athenian affairs to exploit in personal reprisals. Onomacritus, with his bad record, has to be judged by Herodotus' own opinion about forged oracles (p. 52)—the greater the respect due to the 'voice of God', the graver the guilt of the 'false prophet'. But of all these distinct types of the 'Lie', as Darius had known and hated it, and feared lest Xerxes should be beguiled by it, Mardonius is, for Herodotus, the most significant. He, if no other, knew the risks; but his obstinacy and self-esteem learned nothing from experience. As the story unfolds and the end must come (ix. 41–42, 66), even his colleague Artabazus stands aloof.

The Prologue (vii. 1–19), in which Xerxes' mind is made up for him, is more fully dramatized even than the *Debate of the Conspirators* (iii. 80–82). It is also carefully constructed as a composition of antithetical elements, a–f : g : f'–a', set between the years before Xerxes was established on the throne (i. 1–4, 6) and those of eventual preparation (20).

(*a*) The suppression of revolt in Egypt (7) removed the only external obstacle; (*a'*) the Magian interpretation of the Fourth Dream, all internal check on loyal enthusiasm (19).

(*b*) At the First Council, Xerxes intends to fight (8); in the Third Council (*b'*) he reaffirms this finally (18).

(*c*) Mardonius encourages him (9), and (*d*) Artabanus opposes (10); after the Second Dream (*d'*) Artabanus opposes again (16), but after the Third (*c'*) he replaces Mardonius (*c*) in support (17).

(*e*) After the First Council, Xerxes still intends to fight (11); and so too (*e'*) after the Second Dream (14).

(*f*) Within this balanced composition stand (*f*) the First Dream (12) and (*f'*) the Second (14), both commanding Xerxes to fight; (*g*) between these, Xerxes tells the Second Council that he has changed his mind (13). Paradoxically, this central incident shows the King weakly struggling against the Fate of the Empire:

it was 'in him', as Miltiades told Callimachus, at all events to postpone disaster, and he did not. Artabanus is in the same condemnation, for he qualifies his conversion by obstinate, though loyal, belief that Persia is invincible; somehow, Fate will see to it that the Greeks do not win. Here is 'insolence' at its extreme.

This *Prologue* is a test of Herodotus' insight into the crisis and the leading personages, and must be compared with his ultimate verdict on Xerxes, his officers, and his people in the much disputed *Epilogue* (ix. 107–22). It is also a notable example of pre-Socratic experimental philosophy; to detect a false dream, or a false oracle, is as important for Herodotus as to interpret the true. Whatever the source of his story, Persian or Ionian, it has been transmuted into the form and substance of Attic tragedy.

The character of Artabanus, like that of Mardonius, is drawn with insight and probably with knowledge. He had tried to dissuade Darius from the 'Scythian Expedition' (iv. 83) and had supporters now; for the Councillors had 'joyfully saluted' when the King changed his mind (vii. 13), though they displayed 'all zeal' at his final decision (19). The later intervention of Artabanus (46–52) shows him still oppressed with misgivings, which were reasonable, as to physical obstacles (49) and risk of revolt (51); and therefore he is left as Xerxes' civil viceroy—'to thee, above all men, I entrust my royal power' (52)—and as a tragic foil to Mardonius.

PERSIAN PREPARATIONS (vii. 20–138)

This section is planned on an impressive scale and carefully executed. The structure is pedimental, and its articulation clearly marked, though the latter half, from the climax onwards, is (as so often) less formally presented than the earlier. It begins with a geographical comparison of Xerxes' expedition with other great enterprises—the Scythian Expedition, the Raid of Mysians and Teucrians into Europe—and it ends (138) with a shorter estimate of the dual scope of the expedition itself and the apprehensions which it provoked in Greece: this connects with the contrasted behaviour of the Athenians (139) and the pendant story of Greek preparations (140–75).

Persian preparations had begun three years before, with the canal at Mount Athos (22–24), the bridge over the Strymon(24), and the double bridge at the Hellespont (34–36). There was another great physical obstacle, the frontier range of Olympus, Pelion, and Ossa; but this needed no attention from engineers, for Poseidon—if it was he—had torn open the Pass of Tempe (128–30). Only some clearing of forest was necessary in Perrhaebia (131). These western obstacles are accordingly described in their place at the end, when the army is ready to deal with them.

Within this frame, reinforced by the mission (32) and return (131) of the heralds—who had been sent from Sardis at the end of the first phase of the advance, and rejoined Xerxes at Therma at the end of the fifth—the progress of the expedition itself is recounted in five sections: (i) Critalla to Sardis (26–31); (ii) Sardis to Abydus (32–43); (iii) Abydus to Doriscus (44–104); (iv) Doriscus to Acanthus (105–23); (v) Acanthus to Therma (124–7). Among these, the third—Abydus to Doriscus—is central: it marks the point where the adventure has really begun, by the twofold review of the whole force (44–58, 59–105), including the formal 'Catalogue' (61–99).

The significance of this centre-piece is emphasized by two rhetorical episodes: Artabanus reviews the risks and problems of the expedition and is transferred from the staff to the 'home-front' (46–52); Demaratus looks ahead with an estimate of Spartan courage and Greek steadfastness under the 'rule of law' (101–4). Compare the structural use of speeches throughout the Scythian Expedition. And within this central section Xerxes on his throne, overlooking the Hellespont and his army as it passes over, is presented, in a popular phrase, as the agent of Zeus himself for the devastation of Greece (56). The momentous occasion is signalled, as in Scythia, by portents (57).

Whether the *Catalogue* was expressly written for this place or was an older draft is uncertain. The point of insertion is marked, like the description of Egypt (ii. 1; iii. 1), by the repetition of a phrase (60, 100). It seems to be derived from a Persian army-list, and to give the provincial assessments for service, not actual contingents. It does not always agree with the list of provinces in Book III. There have been many attempts to go behind the immense figures; the best is that of Sir Frederick Maurice[1] based on the daily traffic capacity of the road from Sestus to Cardia: his total for fighting effectives is 150,000.

The Hellespont Bridges (vii. 34–36)

Between the Sea of Marmora and the Aegean the channel makes a dog's-leg turn, first from west to south, round Nagara Point; then, three miles lower, from south to south-west, round the precipitous Kilid-Bahr headland. Xenophon describes the strait as eight stades wide (4,824 ft.: *Hell.* viii. 4. 8. 5), probably referring to the distance from Sestus to Abydus. As the banks are firm rock, they cannot have been eroded appreciably, nor can small streams have advanced their alluvial deposits much into deep water with a strong current. The European shore is precipitous and inaccessible here, and the current rapid and irregular up to 2 knots. But a little west of north from Nagara Point—a low spit of hard rock, too narrow for more than one roadway— a small valley breaks the steep European bank, with good access to the interior, and so to the isthmus of Gallipoli. The narrowest point is where this stream flows out over a gravelly delta, but there is firm beach westward at 11 cables (6,600 ft.) from Nagara Point, for nearly 3 cables (1,800 ft.), and eastward for 2 cables (1,200 ft.) till it is closed by a spur from the high ground.

Starting from Herodotus' numbers for the ships under each bridge, and assuming that the shorter (down-stream) bridge was at the shortest crossing—namely from Nagara Point to firm beach west of the stream—the 314 ships give an average ship-interval of 21·01 ft. Of such units 360 give the upstream bridge a length of 12·6 cables; and this is the distance from the eastern end of the European beach to a point about half-way along the shelving shore between Nagara Point and Abydus Point. Beyond the latter the coast turns south-east, the channel widens, and any further landing-place is incommoded by Abydus Point. In these positions the two bridges were nearly parallel, almost 1½ cables (900 ft.) apart at the European end and about 2 cables (1,200 ft.) at the Asiatic.

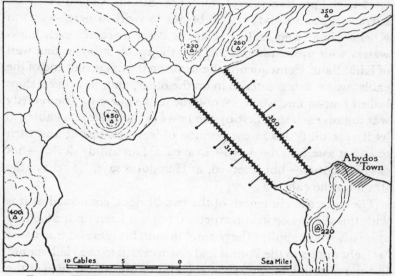

FIG. 14. THE BRIDGES OF XERXES IN THE HELLESPONT

Based on British Admiralty Chart No. 2429, with the permission of the Controller of H.M. Stationery Office and of the Hydrographer of the Navy.

The dimensions, estimated above, allow a very small interval between ships, for a trireme was about 15 ft. abeam. But many—probably most—of the ships were not triremes but penteconters, much lighter craft, and certainly narrower. Moreover, no allowance has been made here (1) for the catenary sag of the bridges, due to the current, increasing their overall length; nor (2) for closer packing of ships at either end, and (3) to support the wider spans provided for through-traffic. The necessary headroom for these spans was the main reason for the immobilization of ships-of-the-line (triremes), which had a higher freeboard than pentecomters, as well as larger displacement.

The catenary curves of the bridges, horizontally, due to the current, are of interest in another connexion. Under the upstream bridge 'towards Pontus' the ships were lashed four-square to the cables, because the current flowed evenly between banks, accelerated only slightly as the channel narrowed. The strain was therefore evenly divided between the two ends, and ships so secured were in the position of least resistance. But off Nagara Point the current is more rapid; it also begins to swirl to north-west: at Khelia Liman and south of Nagara Point there are even backwaters with upstream current, like the much stronger one west of Kilid Bahr. Consequently the strain on the upcurrent end of the cables was much greater than on the other, and, moreover, ships lashed four-square would be oblique to the current. The remedy was to lash each ship first by the bows to the upstream cable; to let it veer till it was in the position of least resistance; and then to lash it astern to the downstream cable; an untidy device—not easily forgotten—but it served, as Herodotus says, 'to relieve the strain on the cables'.

The difference in length of the two bridges, connected as it is with this difference in construction, has not been understood by some who have applied the phrase[1] to both bridges and translated 'at right angles to the Pontus and downstream to the Hellespont'. But the meaning of ἐπικαρσίας is certain from iv. 101, where the northern and western sides of the 'Scythian square' are drawn inland from the ends of the coastal side (described as ὄρθια, 'erect') and 'at right angles to them'. How a bridge could be constructed 'at right angles to' an *area* a hundred miles away has not been explained; and no bridge crossing the Hellespont could be 'down stream'. The alternative is to take the two phrases separately, and apply them each to a different bridge: the genitives being adverbial and replacing the cumbrous phrase τὰς μὲν ὑπὸ τήν πρὸς τοῦ Πόντου γέφυραν, κτλ. in the sense of 'Pontusward', i.e. upstream, and 'Hellespont-ward', i.e. downstream; each describing the distinct construction of one bridge. The phrase which follows 'to relieve the strain on the cables', though applicable to both bridges, had—as we have seen—peculiar

[1] τοῦ μὲν Πόντου ἐπικαρσίας, τοῦ δὲ Ἑλλησπόντου κατὰ ῥόον.

application to the downstream, i.e. Hellespont-ward bridge. This rendering is confirmed by the subsequent phrase πρὸς τοῦ Πόντου τῆς ἑτέρης, a partial expansion with similar genitive. The reason for this economy of moorings was that each bridge, being to leeward of the other, needed no moorings on its inward side. So far as possible penteconters replaced triremes[1] by reason of their lower freeboard and wind-resistance. A south-westerly gale would fully compensate the current and make downstream anchors necessary.

Other illustrations of Persian organization

Though Herodotus loves to dwell on defects in the Persian administration, occasional incidents illustrate a higher degree of preparation for emergencies than he has understood. In addition to the bridges and the canal, he makes casual mention of the bridges over the Strymon, which had been ordered in advance (vii. 24) and were 'found' already in place (vii. 114), and with these should be connected the human sacrifices so often associated with bridge-building in the Nearer East, which he describes with the explanation that such rites, known also in Persia, were to appease 'the god under the earth'.

In the same district the 'King's Way' was shown long after, a paved causeway across the outlet of Lake Bolbeis, between the Strymon and Acanthus (vii. 115), which the natives had failed to break-up and restore to cultivation in Herodotus' time— another glimpse of eyewitness. It was still visible in 185 B.C. (Livy xxxix. 27).

The supply-depots, proclaimed and organized in advance, down to the poultry-coops (vii. 119), and the strict control of provisions (vii. 120), supplement the general description (vii. 21) of the 'home-front'. More specific and unexpected are glimpses of the surveying and medical services. At Artemisium the Greeks saw with surprise the reconnaissance of the reef *Myrmex*—one of a

---

[1] All MSS. have τρίχον, and this may well be original, and account for the omission of τριηρέων. But MSS. Εὗρον for Ζεφύρον in the previous sentence may result from the same blemish, leaving only -ύρον and τρ . . . legible.

class of nicknames from floating animals familiar to Greek sailors of all ages—and the erection of a stone column on it, after which marking of the obstruction the whole fleet passed by. A recent Greek traveller has detected traces of its base. In a collision before Artemisium also (vii. 181) Pytheus, son of Ischomachus, was propelled from the prow of his ship into that of the enemy and 'all cut to butcher's meat as he fought'. But the Persians restored him, 'healing his wounds with myrrh and winding him in shield-straps of cotton fabric', an early record of a surgical bandage.[1] The 'myrrh' was no doubt the fragrant antiseptic *ladanum*, collected still on many a hill-side in Anatolia from a species of *cistus* which smears the grazing goats with its exudation till they have to be cleaned from this encumbrance. The honourable treatment accorded to Pytheus on his recovery is also to the Persians' credit.

Another detail of organization is that the bread-corn was provided ready-ground, economizing a vast expenditure of time in corn-grinding, which was moreover women's work (vii. 23).

Doriscus to Strymon: the Threefold Route (vii. 108–14)

Attempts to identify three parallel routes in this section (vii. 121) like those on the march from the Strymon to Therma (vii. 113–14) have not been successful. It has been suggested that one column was transported by sea, so that Xerxes, who passed inland of the coast towns, might be on the middle route. There is no reason to suppose that any force moved by the Hebrus valley and north of Mount Rhodope, which is very much longer, and was only used by Megabazus (v. 15) in order to outflank Paeonian opposition. But with rugged and partly unpacified highland on the right hand, a flanking column must have moved through the foot-hills. The main through-route, traversed by Xerxes himself, passed inland of the coast cities—compare the phrase used in vii. 42 of Antandrus, which was certainly 'by-passed'—and the description of the chain of lagoons along the sea-front suggests that these were encountered by a coastal column moving direct

---

[1] But Achilles bandages Patroclus about 500 B.C. on the Sosias vase no. 1; Pfühl, *Malerei und Zeichnung*, p. 137, no. 410.

from town to town, and conscripting contingents for the fleet (vii. 110), whom Herodotus distinguishes from levies in the high-land interior. Farther west, where the coast plain was obstructed by Mount Pangaeum, the King's route 'passed the very walls' (vii. 112), so by contrast he left the eastern towns at some distance. In vii. 113 the topography is obscured by Herodotus' notion of the lower course of the Strymon (to be considered later (p. 226); the Angites river bounds Mount Pangaeum on the north rather than the west, and the Strymon lies west rather than south. It is possible that here the inland column did not return to the coast, but used an easy pass north-east of Mount Pangaeum into the Angites valley, before moving up the Strymon (as in vii. 124), without going near Acanthus.

The very detailed topography of this and the following section, as far as Therma, suggests that Herodotus may have traversed this country himself. It is supplemented by his description of Thrace and Paeonia (v. 1–10); by his information about the royal family of Macedon (v. 17–22; vii. 137–9); and by his account of the operations of Artabazus in Chalcidice (viii. 126–9).

Strymon to Therma (vii. 113–14)

Though there is much topographical detail in this section, it is not very easy to follow because the orientation of the whole map is awry, for a reason which is apparent on the ground. Mount Pangaeum, a very prominent feature from the east and south-east, projects beyond the general trend of the Thracian coast opposite Thasos and forces coast-land traffic to converge on the 'Nine Ways' (*Ennea Hodoi*) near the mouth of the Strymon river. As Mount Pangaeum projects thus seaward, a traveller following the coast road (or coasting) westward looks up the Strymon valley—a deep wide trough with its axis north-west to south-east —before he reaches the crossing at its mouth. Consequently the Strymon appears to flow more nearly from west to east than it actually does, and this illusion is enhanced by the long high Athos promontory beyond it—actually to south-west. Moreover, in summer, seen from the 'Nine Ways' the sun sets up-valley.

Further, Pangaeum is bounded on its far side, actually trending north-east to south-west, by the Angites tributary of the Strymon; and as this appears to be the western boundary of the high ground, and emerges from an upper valley in the main Thracian escarpment, it is easily taken as joining the Strymon at right angles and as descending from the north.

On the other hand, Herodotus correctly describes the coast west of Strymon as lying east-and-west: 'towards the sunset', as it does during the winter and spring (vii. 115). From the mouth of the Strymon the course of this coast to south-west, being lowland, is not visible. Argilus is actually on the foot-hills of the Dysorus ridge (v. 17) which bounds the Strymon valley southwestwards farther inland.

Xerxes, tied to the coast by his sea-borne food-supply, did not take—or not with all his forces—the direct route westward along Lake Bolbeis to Therma, but crossed the alluvial ground (*Syleospedion*) between Bolbeis and the Strymon gulf, where the 'King's Way' had already been built. He thus passed by Stagira, on the coast near the north horn of the bay of Acanthus which opens east, and so reached Acanthus on the isthmus of Mount Athos. The pass through the east–west range which defends the Chalcidic promontory from sea to sea, behind the fosse of Lake Bolbeis, is almost eight miles east of Stagira. So far all is clear, taking into account the misplacement of the Strymon valley to a position nearly parallel with the axis of Lake Bolbeis, which made this seem a more direct route to Therma than it actually is.

But how, on this route, had Xerxes the 'gulf towards Poseideium' *on his left*? The gulf round which Xerxes was advancing was the bend of the coast from the Strymon-mouth to the seaward eastern end of the main ridge of Chalcidice. But Poseideium is the name of the western promontory of Pallene, the third, south-westerly peninsula of Chalcidice, about forty-five miles distant and quite out of the picture here. Noting that the giant Syleus, the namesake of the coast plain, was a son of Poseidon, must we supply a forgotten coast-town or Poseidon-sanctuary on this coast?

Or does this phrase refer to the farther line of advance from Acanthus to Therma? For in vii. 124 Xerxes leaves the fleet to pass through the canal and round the two other promontories, and himself moved direct to Therma, by an inland road,[1] a difficult cross-country route, through the headwaters of the streams which fall into the Gulfs of Singis and Torone. On this route he could look down between the promontories, and west of them in due course, and so see *on his left* the wide bay closed southwards by Cape Poseideium prominent between Potidaea and the Thermaic gulf. This is sufficient indication of his route, *if he went this way*.

But in vii. 124 Xerxes and his land-force are immediately described as traversing Paeonia and Crestonia to the river Cheidorus (or Echeidorus) which rises from Crestonia, flows through Mygdonia, and issues by the marsh on the Axius river, about ten miles west of Therma, draining, that is, the western slope of Mount Dysorus, the escarpment overlooking the Strymon valley (v. 17). Note that this is again something quite different from the great direct route—afterwards the *Via Egnatia*—which leaves the coast at the 'King's Way', follows the south shore of Lake Bolbeis, and descends on Therma from the north by a short pass through the Cissus watershed.

It would seem, then, that we have here fragments of description of three roughly parallel routes:

(i) A coast route from the Strymon to Acanthus and thence inland across Chalcidice to a point where it overlooked Cape Poseideium and its bay and so north to Therma, keeping utmost initial and final contact with the fleet and also allowing Xerxes the opportunity of seeing the Canal.

(ii) A direct route diverging from (i) south of the 'King's Way' and 'cutting inland' along the future Egnatian Road to Therma direct. If Xerxes used this, the central and principal route, his visit to Acanthus was a digression, with the very natural object of viewing the Canal.

[1] τήν μεσόγαιαν τάμνων τῆς ὁδοῦ.

(iii) A circuitous flanking route guarded against raids from the interior; not by Acanthus at all, nor by the 'King's Way', but direct from the Strymon mouth, up valley to the pass through Dysorus; then by the western slope of Dysorus north of Lake Bolbeis, descending by the Cheidorus valley on Therma from the north. A vivid phrase of eye-witness betrays Herodotus' own acquaintance with this route where he describes how on 'crossing Dysorus there you are in Macedonia'[1] (v. 17).

Writing concisely, Herodotus has compiled characteristic glimpses of all three routes in one composite account of 'Xerxes and his army', all converged at the Strymon Bridge but diverging, some at once, some later, after crossing it, and reuniting at Therma. Two further points may be noted here:

The anecdote of the lions and camels (vii. 125-6) is much too detailed to be legendary. The familiar coin-type, a lion pulling down a wild bull, had probably appeared on the silver of Acanthus before Xerxes' time; but the great ox-horns, exported to Greece, are evidence of eyewitness, and confirm the persistence of wild cattle in this region. The vivid representations of lions in Minoan art, the stories of heroic lion-killing, and the frequent reference to the lion in Homeric similes and in Greek personal names, combine to confirm the survival of lions in south-eastern Europe to a rather late date. Where did Alexander get his lion-skins?

The description of the four Macedonian rivers (vii. 127) is important for fifth-century topography, because the convergent deltas have greatly changed the shore-line of the gulf and shortened the journey into Greece. But the principal settlements remained unchanged, along the edge of the western foot-hills, and Thessalonica, which later superseded Therma, lay far enough within the eastern spurs to escape obstruction.

The Frontiers of Thessaly (vii. 128-30)

The reconnaissance of Tempe by Xerxes and the description of the frontiers of Thessaly need to be correlated both with the

[1] ὄρος ὑπερβάντα εἶναι ἐν Μακεδονίῃ.

actual topography and with the larger outlines of peninsular Greece as they appeared to ancient geographers and strategists.[1]

Strabo's account (334) of the 'Line of Eudoxus', the base-line of all ancient maps of Greece, illustrates the extent to which positions fixed by co-ordinates served as the corner-stones of a rectangular construction within which topographical features were displayed. This base-line was drawn straight from the Acroceraunian mountains north of Corcyra through the Isthmus to Sunium, and was oriented east to west. At right angles to it was drawn a line from Sunium to Therma (Thessalonica), which lies actually only a little west of north and is not exactly followed by the coast-line except in its Attic and Thessalian sections. Westward from this meridional line and parallel with the 'Line of Eudoxus' were drawn the north frontier of Attica, from Oropus, which struck the shore of the Corinthian Gulf at Creusa (*Livadostro Bay*); the north frontier of Locris from Thermopylae through Mount Oeta; the south frontier of Thessaly through (or parallel with) Mount Othrys, and the north frontier of Thessaly from Olympus through the Cambunian mountains to the watershed range of Pindus, where the west frontier of Thessaly was laid down similarly at right angles, running south till it met the south frontier west of Othrys. Other subdivisions were interpolated in this 'grid' as required; the traditional division of Thessaly itself with its four 'tetrarchies' is a good example. The method is the same as is used to construct the 'Scythian Square' (iv. 99) and the relevant comparisons with Attica and South Italy, and it is presupposed in the mistaken orientation of Thermopylae (vii. 201) plotted from north to south because it traverses a frontier running from east to west.

Thessaly was thus deemed, in general conformity to fact, to be a rectangular area, with its sides east, north, west, and south; from Olympus along the Cambunian mountains, with the Volustana Pass from Servia at the bend of the Haliacmon to the headwaters of the Titaresius about the middle of the north side, as Tempe is of the eastern; and along the south face of Othrys from

[1] Myres, *Greece and Rome*, xii (1943) 33-41.

the Pagasaean gulf to the head of the Spercheius. For this south front a double bearing is given 'towards midday sun and south wind' (*notus*), as for the south face of the 'Scythian Square' (iv. 99). Eastward this boundary crossed the entrance of the gulf, and joined the eastern sea-front at Cape Sepias. The gulf, like Lake Bolbeis farther north, counted as a submerged area within this square.

Between this south frontier of Thessaly and the open north frontier of Boeotia lie two narrow strips of country roughly parallel, from east to west: (i) *Malis*, consisting of the Spercheius trough-valley between Othrys and Oeta; the latter being regarded as its southern boundary and as lying from east to west; (ii) *Doris*, the upper valley of the Boeotian Cephissus, similarly regarded as lying from east to west between Oeta and Parnassus, and continued westward into northern Phocis and eastward into Opuntian Locris, with a sea-front on the Euboean channel. Actually the Cephissus swerves to south-east, round the foot-hills of Parnassus, till it reaches the flooded Copais. It is divided from the Malian Gulf and the north Euboean channel by Mount Callidromus, the eastward prolongation of Oeta; and the seaward outlet of Copais is south of Larymna. Probably the whole course of the Cephissus was plotted as lying east–west, with the Copais flood-land on its southern bank, between the broad eastern face of Parnassus and the sea; and Callidromus was represented as lying east–west from Oeta. This picture of Doris is supplemented in detail in its relations with Phocis and Delphi (viii. 31–32 and 43).

The results of Xerxes' reconnaissance (vii. 130) were as follows: (1) Xerxes himself was impressed only by the fact that having but one outlet Thessaly might (by a great engineer) be flooded. The fear of this he imputed to the Aleuadae, who had medized: they may have feared what Xerxes would do, or they may have suggested this remedy for Thessalian resistance. (2) The Thessalians begged the Greek leaders to help them to hold the 'Olympic entrance' (vii. 172), and the Greek advance-guard was sent by sea to Halos in Achaea Phthiotis, where Alexander of Macedon warned them that if they stayed they would be outnumbered, and where they learned that there were other entrances. These are (*a*) from the Haliacmon valley by the Volustana Pass to the Europus, the northern tributary of the Peneius; (*b*) from the coast road at Dium, westwards over the ridge north of Mount Olympus, into the Titaresius tributary of the Europus: this joins the other road at Oloosson and so leads 'past Gonnus' (vii. 128, 173) because it is here that this route joins that by Tempe, and crosses the Peneius just inside the pass. This is the 'upper road' of Herodotus (vii. 128): he does not mention the northern route in either passage (173): but as Xerxes himself used the 'upper road' it is probable that one of the flanking columns used the coast road by Tempe and the other moved by Berrhoea and the Haliacmon. The strategical aspect of this Thessalian topography is postponed by Herodotus till he has dealt with the Greek preparations (vii. 173–4), where he refers to the warning of Alexander and the decision not to defend Tempe.

GREEK PREPARATIONS (vii. 145–71)

This section is as carefully constructed as the *Persian Preparations*, but has likewise been overloaded. Enframed between the account of Athenian initiative, courage, and loyalty (vii. 138–44) and of the involuntary medism of the Thessalians (vii. 172–4) is the fivefold 'Narrative of Missions', wherein Syracuse is central, preceded by Sardis and Argos, followed by Corcyra and Crete, and enhanced by speeches, between a retrospect of the rise of Gelo, and a forecast justifying his decision to retain a free hand. The mission to Argos is elaborated by a comparison of versions, and by the later episode at Susa, with Herodotus' own reflections. The opening section on Athens, too, is expanded by the story of the two oracles, which introduces Themistocles, and enhances the contrast with Thessaly, where the Aleuadae used Persia for their own ends, and where the topography made defence impracticable.

These five 'Missions' are a graduated analysis of typical attitudes. (*a*) What the Greek spies discovered at Sardis was that the

Persians were not only terribly well prepared but were discriminating already in favour of their friends in Greece; for Herodotus, their reception illustrates once more the boundless confidence of Xerxes. (*b*) Argos was not only playing for safety, as the oracles advised, but had a grievance against Sparta, and a long-term policy of friendship with Persia. (*c*) Gelo was defending Greek freedom in his own way, but had his hands full on his western front. (*d*) Corcyra was the strategical base and reserve for Greek sea-power, ready to strike east or west as need might arise. So, too, in 1915–18 the Allied naval headquarters were at Corfu, not at Malta or Suda. (*e*) Crete was living in the distant past and had no interest in the present conflict. Finally, Thessaly would have resisted if adequate help had been sent; it also had its own feud with Phocis.

The panegyric of Athens (vii. 138–44) is significant, for it is from this point onwards that, alongside Spartan conduct of the land defence, looms up Athenian insistence on a collateral sea-front, and predominant participation in it. The defeatist opposition of Delphi requires separate examination below, in connexion with the whole political situation in northern and central Greece. What is central here is the new personality of Themistocles, with his twofold policy of evacuation in Attica and of naval offensive, for which he had made provision by the recent Navy Act. This also has its place—if we can find it—in the general history of Greece in the years between the two wars, and must be considered separately.

Herodotus rightly insists that Persian naval superiority over the rest of Greece was such that, but for the Athenian fleet, no fortification of the Isthmus could have prevented naval landings in Peloponnese; Sparta's allies would have been invaded and defeated in detail; and Sparta itself must have either surrendered or been destroyed. And this prospect, in the event of the Athenian fleet being detached or defeated, has to be taken into account in estimating the reluctance of many Greek states—of Argos, in particular—to take part in a national defence. In northern Greece the position was even worse, as the naval operations

themselves showed; for though it was eventually possible to concentrate a considerable fleet at Salamis, quite insufficient naval
forces were sent as flank-guard for Thermopylae.

The pessimism—or worse—of Delphi illustrates the same predica-
ment, but to be fully appreciated it must be presented against
the wider background of political trends in northern Greece.
Here much is obscure. The situation in Thessaly is instructive;
the democratic movement had already gone so far that the
Aleuadae were in exile and had medized. In Thebes—so the
Thebans plead in 432 B.C.—a narrow clique[1] was in control,
while the majority (by implication) were on the side of freedom.
Of the other districts and their cities there are no details; but we
may infer the same tension and *stasis*, and temptation to the
privileged minorities to ensure their own position with Persian
help.

The position of Delphi was more complicated. This was not one
of the immemorial sanctuaries, though Apollo claimed to have
cast out an earlier power, and Aeschylus[2] knows of some chthonic
cult, with a voice which had the force of law. Of Demeter, however, there is no further trace at Delphi. Apollo's coming is
ascribed in legend to Cretan adventure; and there are traces
—but not more—of Minoan contact, all the more remarkable
because the whole Corinthian Gulf remained otherwise so secluded
during the Bronze Age. It was indeed only in the periods of
migration and colonization that Delphi rose to wider repute,
through its successes as adviser to Sparta throughout, and of
Chalcis and Corinth in their western adventures.

The older cult-centre of northern Greece was quite different,
the sanctuary of Demeter at Anthela, at the inner gate of Thermopylae. Here warm springs revealed the Earth-Mother close at
hand, and 'hither the tribes went up' to annual festival, with
revision of usage and correction of lapses, like the *Althing* of
Scandinavian Iceland. Here the *hieromnemones* 'holy remem-
brancers' like Icelandic 'speakers', spoke for twelve groups of

[1] Thuc. iii. 62—a narrow clique—δυναστεία ὀλίγων ἀνδρῶν.
[2] *Eum.* 2 πρωτόμαντιν Γαῖαν, ἐκ δὲ τῆς Θέμιν.

tribes from as far north as the Perrhaebi, as far west as Aenianes and Dolopes, and as far south as the barrier of Cithaeron and Parnes. There were Ionians too among these Amphictyonic corporators, probably the ancestors of those mainland Ionians who are barely noted in the *Iliad* (xiii. 685) among other middle-Greek peoples, and were probably pushed into Euboea by the 'migration from Arne' a generation or more after the Fall of Troy. Athens in later times was included in the Ionian name, but as a 'colony'; Sparta, and other Dorians of Peloponnese, as 'colonies' of the aboriginal Doris north of Parnassus. The ancient league of Calauria, farther south, was enlarged in the same way, Argos personating Nauplia and Sparta Prasiae. Such outliers, and any of the historic city-states within the Amphictyonic area, could be represented at the festival by *pylagoroi*, 'speakers at the Gates'—a clear indication of the home and primary function of this Amphictyony. But one of the first duties of this league-council was to maintain ancient privileges, and among them those of other cults within the league-area. As Delphi rose to fame, for the reasons and in the period already noted, Delphic business at the festival grew until it was found convenient to hold a by-meeting there; and this in turn gave occasion for Amphictyonic influence to be exerted in Delphic policy. Yet there were never *delphagoroi*.

But here there was a further complication. The 'Dorian Invasion' of Peloponnese was not a self-contained adventure. It was only the southern and providential extension of a general exodus from the Pindus highlands, which followed on the 'Migration from Arne', and, about a generation later, drove a broad wedge of Doric-speaking tribes into the heart of the Thessalo–Boeotian area, reaching the Maliac Gulf. Phocis, Locris, and Malis spoke Doric of a sort, like Doris, and held all together in an anti-Thessalian and anti-Boeotian block. And Delphi was the leading sanctuary of Phocis, though not its place of political meeting.

Yet again, within Phocis itself, there was controversy between the Delphians and the other Phocians over the management of the sanctuary, as there was between Pisa and the rest of Elis about Olympia.

Thus, on any occasion when the oracle of Delphi was consulted on a matter of public concern, there were these three regional trends of opinion and interest, represented on the spot or easily consulted: the policy of the Amphictyonic Council or a majority within it; the policy of the Phocians, usually dominated by their quarrels with Thessaly and Boeotia; and the local politics of Delphi, usually seeking for external aid against Phocian encroachment. The best-known occasion is in the middle of the fifth century, when Athens and Sparta are drawn into the quarrels of Delphi and Phocis and general war results (Thuc. i. 107).

With the rise of Persia yet another complication appears. The foreign repute of Delphi was already such that Gyges had acknowledged its favour and probably sought it; Croesus had trusted its advice; Miletus had incurred its censure in the Ionic Revolt (vi. 19). It was Persian policy to respect and favour the cults of subjects and neighbours; and this policy had its reward in the surrender of Pactyas by Cyme at the bidding of Branchidae (i. 157-9) and in the censure of Miletus above noted. It is Apollo who 'told truth to the Persians' in the letter of Darius to Gadatas.[1] It was therefore nothing new if Delphi used its influence to restrain Greek resistance to Xerxes, especially if that resistance seemed to be futile.[2] This was not peculiar to the Athenian inquiry: the Cretans also (vii. 169) and Argos (v. 77) were advised to stand clear. And it has been argued that the Persian visit to Delphi to 'make an inventory' of the Temple treasures was in fact not in order to remove them, but to protect them against looting (viii. 35-39; cf. p. 262).

It is characteristic of the Greek view of the gods that though Delphi had discouraged the principal Greek loyalists at this crisis, Apollo received his thank-offering nevertheless after the war was won. Apollo was not to suffer for the mistakes of his priests: 'the unworthiness of the minister affecteth not the efficacy of the sacrament'.

---

[1] Tod, *G.H.I.* 10.
[2] Casson, *Class. Rev.* xxviii (1914), 145-51.

Themistocles (vii. 143)

The introduction of Themistocles is slight, almost casual, as 'a certain Athenian' who put forward an alternative view of the two oracles, and carried his point, because he had already provided Athens with a new-model fleet for use against Aegina, by allocating to it the profit from the silver-mines at Laurium. Of the man himself Herodotus has only to say that he 'was called' a son of Neocles, and that he had only recently (νεωστί) risen to the first political rank. He is not even made personally responsible for the further decision to build yet more ships to meet the Persian fleet, and to fight it at sea (144). Both these positive statements need elaboration. Neocles was of an old Athenian family (the Lycomedae), but Themistocles' mother was a Carian or a Thracian, and Themistocles himself therefore a *Kleistheneios*, born either in 523 B.C. (Plut. *Them.* 31, *Cim.* 18) or in 513, and admitted to citizenship under the new constitution. He commanded his own tribe at Marathon (Plut. *Arist.* 5), however;[1] so in 482–481 he was not quite new to public life. The earlier date would just allow him to be elected an archon in 493 (Dion. Hal. vi. 34), but it was as one of the archons of 483–482 that he promoted his Navy Bill, and this is in accord with the later date for his birth, and with Herodotus' use of νεωστί (cf. vii. 148).

The fortification of Piraeus (Thuc. i. 93; Paus. i. 1–2) was a corollary of the new naval policy; for Herodotus had described Phalerum as 'ship-yard then' in 490 (vi. 116).

Further information from the *Life of Themistocles* by Cornelius Nepos is as different from all this, in its perspective, as is Nepos' account of Miltiades. Here Themistocles' mother is of Halicarnassus—in Caria but not of it; his father disinherited him; he frequented the lawcourts and political meetings (without indication of date); but his first public office was in a war with Corcyra; after that, he drove 'the pirates' off the seas with the fleet he had persuaded Athens to build. If his *primus gradus capessendae rei-*

---

[1] But he is not in Plutarch's list of *strategoi* (*Moralia* 305 c). A Schol. to Thucydides quoted by Hude (ed. Teubner 1927, p. 73) says he was archon: Πρὸ τῶν Μηδικῶν ἦεξε Θ. ἐνιαυτόν.

publicae was his exploit abroad with the new fleet, it must have occurred between 482 and the general truce of 480 (Thuc. i. 136). That he had western interests or connexions is inferred from the names of his daughters *Italia* and *Sybaris*, and from his threat to withdraw the Athenians to Siris (viii. 62). If the state of war between Athens and Aegina was still 'undeclared', the phrase *maritimos praedones* would cover Aeginetans attacking Attic vessels at sea; it was in any event good training for the new squadrons to patrol the corn-route, which had been unprotected since Miltiades withdrew from Lemnos. But there is no other evidence for either of these exploits. The ostracism of Aristides in this year reflects an internal crisis, allayed, like the quarrel with Aegina, by the recall of all ostracized leaders in 481–480, and the new rule that in future such persons were not to stray too far; i.e. not to take refuge behind 'the iron curtain' (*Ath. Pol.* 22. 8).

With the later history of Themistocles we are not concerned here except to note that the discrepancy of dates among the sources continues, and is part of the general problem of that generation.

The episode of the spies sent to Asia (vii. 146–7) differs from the rest in its generality. It illustrates three points: (1) the immense preparations of Xerxes; (2) his unbounded confidence and reliance on these preparations as propaganda to shake Greek resistance; and (3), as a special illustration of this, his treatment of the corn-ships bound for Aegina and Peloponnese. The two names slip out almost unawares. Only two chapters earlier (145) Herodotus has stated that Aegina and Athens had suspended the greatest of quarrels among Greek states; but his audience knew, as well as he did, that Aegina had been among the chief Greek states which surrendered to Darius before Marathon; and in the very next chapter he proceeds, with similar reserve of phrase, to present the policy of Argos—second city of Peloponnese—in very compromising guise. To a Persian, corn-ships bound for 'Aegina and Peloponnese' might indeed be 'bringing corn to *us*'. The Great King knew how to look after his friends; the bridges had been expressly constructed so as to pass friendly traffic in either direction (vii. 36); and Persian commissariat need not respect political frontiers. Corn was stored where it would be wanted.

The Mission to Argos (vii. 148–52) presents several difficulties. The statements of Herodotus, not all vouched for by him, may well be historical; but the chronological perspective is uncertain, by reason of Herodotus' use of 'lately' (*neôsti*) in the principal episode. The main statements, separately, are as follows.

(*a*) Argos, on some occasion 'lately' after the victory of Cleomenes (vi. 76–83; p. 187), consulted Delphi on general policy (vii. 148) and was advised to keep quiet. At that time Argos was 'hated by its neighbours, but dear to the immortals', enjoyed, that is, the favour of Delphi, and might in due time 'save the body' of Greece as its 'head'. If this occasion was 'soon after' the victory of Cleomenes, it might well be the visit of the heralds of Darius in 492–491 B.C., when Argos, still paralysed by defeat, may have been tempted already by the prospect of Persian vassalage and protection, as in 480 it admittedly was. This would be consistent with Herodotus' statement that Argos had early information about Persian designs (vii. 148). The heralds of Darius may well have offered the initial recognition of Argos as an ancestral friend of Persia. Similar speculations as to early Sparta are noted by Herodotus himself (vi. 54).

(*b*) Argos was also visited, like other Greek states, by the heralds of Xerxes in 480—unless it was one of the states left uninvited because already secured to Persia (vii. 32)—and it might be expected that any earlier declaration of friendship would be rehearsed then and confirmed as preamble to further proposals. Before replying, Argos may well have consulted Delphi again; but if it was now that it received the oracle quoted in vii. 148, the occasion was not 'soon after' the victory of Cleomenes, but at least thirteen years later, and ten years or more after Cleomenes' death.

(*c*) Argos was further invited in 480 to join a Greek league already formed; for the members of it are called *synomotai*, 'sworn allies' (vii. 148) and their oath is recorded (vii. 132): approximately they represented the 'right-minded' Greeks (vii. 145). That Argos was not among them suggests that its policy was already suspect, and this may have given the Argives time to consult Delphi now, as Herodotus describes. Though Delphi (now or earlier) advised neutrality, Argos bargained with the League for a thirty years' guarantee of security, not unlikely in view of relations with Sparta, but less likely than 'soon after' the victory of Cleomenes; also for a share in the High Command, a debating 'point of honour' on which negotiation might well break down, and actually did. All this is quite compatible with an offer to the heralds of Xerxes—or to a special mission, which was rumoured—of neutrality or vassalage; for in 480 Argos had only partly recovered its fighting strength, and another disaster would have been final: on the other hand, if Xerxes won, and Argos became leading state in a Greek satrapy, 'the head might save the body'. Security Argos must have, either from Sparta or from Persia, and Herodotus' judgement, that the Argives were in grave peril, that they behaved very badly, but might have behaved worse if they had medized or had invited the Persians into Greece, was as far as he ventured to go. For he was writing at a later time (460–452 B.C.) when Argos had become the ally of Athens against Sparta, for the same recurrent reason—its own security—and was reinsuring itself once again with Persia. It might be nineteenth-century Austria.

The date of this affirmation of Persian friendship, though important both in Argive and in general history, can only be determined more precisely as an episode in the famous Embassy of Callias. In itself it was not more than a formal salutation of the new King of Persia, and renewal of earlier assurances of friendship, about which it proves little. Walker[1] selects the earliest possible date, soon after Artaxerxes' accession, because he prefers a high date for any understanding with Persia, and uses this episode to support it; but his argument proves too much, except on the fourth-century theory that the 'famous peace' resulted from Cimon's victory at the Eurymedon. The alternative, that the peace closed the period of Athenian aggression against Persia, and consequently belongs to 449 or later, has this in its favour,

[1] *C.A.H.* v. 469–71.

that a treaty of non-aggression between Persia and Athens left uninsured a state not included in the Delian League, in the event of Persian hostility to other Greeks; for the treaty between Argos and Sparta in 451 B.C. was a mere truce, not an alliance against a third party, as far as we know.

The Mission of Callias. What Argos, never having been included in the League of Freedom, needed to know was whether external —that is, Persian—help would be forthcoming in the event of attack by other Greek states. More than ever was this needful, if Athens was negotiating the peace-treaty with Persia which is supposed to have been the occasion of the Mission of Callias.[1]

The Mission to Gelo of Syracuse. This episode, central in Herodotus' narrative of the Missions, raises the larger question how far the Carthaginian attack on Sicily was planned to synchronize with the expedition of Xerxes and to co-operate with it. That Darius was believed to have had western projects is clear from the use which Herodotus says he made of Democedes (iii. 129–38), and from Histiaeus' project for an Ionian colonization of Sardinia under Persian sanction (vi. 2). That Greeks from the Aegean had been looking again westward for fresh settlements, in view of Persian aggression, is no less clear from the Phocaean refugee-settlement in Corsica about 540 B.C. (i. 165–6), from the Samian settlement at Dicaearchia in Campania (p. 164), from the adventures of Dorieus in North Africa (c. 517) and at Heraclea Minoa (c. 513: v. 42–48), and from the project of Histiaeus for a colony in Sardinia (vi. 2) and that for a new settlement at Cale-Acte after the Ionian Revolt (c. 493: vi. 22–24). That Carthage too was taking precautions against rivals at sea is shown by its vigorous intervention against Dorieus, and its first treaty with Rome in 509–508 (Polyb. iii. 22).

To appreciate the allusive story in Herodotus, account must also be taken of the complex historical background of Greek settlement in the West. For there were as many different kinds

---

[1] The relevant texts are collected by G. F. Hill, *Sources for Greek History 478–432 B.C.*, 2nd ed. 344, and have been re-examined by H. T. Wade-Gery, *Harvard Studies, Suppl.* i (1940) 121–56. See also Gomme, *Thuc. Comm.* 331–5; Cary, *C.Q.* xxxix (1945) 87.

of Greeks east of the Adriatic as there are of Europeans in the New World called America.

i. From the heel of Italy to the Strait of Messana lay the ancient 'Achaean' refugee-settlements, perhaps coeval with the trans-Aegean, and later reinforced by Ionian immigrants and by the long-term friendships of Sybaris with Miletus (vi. 21), Croton with Samos, and Siris with Athens (viii. 62) and Colophon. That these 'Achaean' cities were established before the great colonization of the eighth century follows from heroic foundation legends, from difference of dialect, and from the absence of any other kind of Greek colony between Tarentum (with its offshoot Heraclea) and Rhegium. But they received large accessions at that time.

ii. From Euboea came Cyme and its daughter-cities in Campania, and later, after the quarrel between Eretria and Chalcis, the cities of north-eastern Sicily, from Naxos, the oldest, to Catana and Leontini southward, to Zancle northward, and thence along the north coast to Himera, defended by its strong-flowing river against Phoenician Panormus, and connected up-valley with the south coast.

iii. Neck-and-neck with the Chalcidians came Corinthians to Syracuse, probably reinforced by refugees from the First Messenian War; as its offshoots, Acrae and Casmenae, seem to have been from the Second. Later again, beyond the south-eastern promontory, Syracuse founded Camarina, but was debarred from further expansion here by Gela, and northward by the Chalcidian group. Probably there had been agreement—perhaps Delphic like the Papal division of the New World between Spain and Portugal—to respect the Simaethus river as frontier, broken only later by Chalcidian Leontini.

iv. Within the Corinthian area thus defined, Megara, an uneasy neighbour at home, had intruded at Thapsus on the coast, and later had fallen back inland into a partnership with Sicel natives at Hybla. Eventually these 'hyphenated' Megareans flitted to Selinus far to the west.

v. Meanwhile, along the south coast, Rhodians and other

Triopian Dorians, had settled at Gela (690) and thence at Acragas (580).

vi. To complete the picture, Tarentum was founded from Sparta in 707, Corcyra from Corinth about the same time, Alalia in Corsica from Phocaea (560–540), and Velia in South Italy after 540.

Though, in general, cities of similar origin were linked by common speech, manners, and cults, there were a few anomalies. Chalcidian Leontini lay south of the Simaethus valley. Camarina, with its access to the interior strangled between Gela and its own mother-city Syracuse,—like British South Africa between Portuguese and German dependencies—quarrelled with both. Selinus had bitter feud with its inland neighbour Egesta, a half-Hellenized Sikel town. Between Chalcidian and Corinthian cities there was no love lost anywhere.

The foundation of Selinus and Acragas, and then of Heracleia Minoa by Dorieus (513), marked a new hostility towards the Phoenician settlements in the west end—Mazaca, Motya, and Panormus—and provoked reprisals which culminated in the attack on Himera in 480. In face of this danger, Acragas and Gela held close together, and put an uneasy constraint on Himera.

Of the internal affairs of the western cities little is known till the rise of the tyrants, first at Acragas 570–564, then at Gela c. 499. These western monarchs differ both from the commissioners of Cyrus and Darius in Ionian cities, from the leaders of anti-Dorian popular parties in Corinth and other Isthmus-states, and from the Peisistratid rule in Attica. In Sicily, with a large native population, already partly civilized, there had been a good deal of intermarriage, and a new breach between thoroughbred and half-breed classes. In neighbouring towns the thoroughbreds rallied to each other, and in face of quarrels between cities of different antecedents, and the standing dangers from Phoenicians in the west and from native chiefs in the interior, power passed into the hands of military adventurers, who had their own lieutenants, intermarried among themselves, and seem to have been tolerated, if not supported, by the aristocrats, who had wealth though not numbers.

At Gela, Cleander became 'tyrant' about 499 B.C. and was succeeded by his brother Hippocrates in 491.[1] Cleander had controlled Himera through Gelo, son of Deinomenes, as 'independent general': Hippocrates added Naxos, and ruled Leontini through Aenesidemus and Zancle through Scythes, whose name perhaps betrays him; he had been Darius' commissioner in Cos, and returned to Persia later. With these strong points in hand, Hippocrates planted Thero, son of Aenesidemus, at Acragas to guard the western front, and attacked Syracuse. Though he occupied the Olympieium across the Great Harbour, Corinth and Corcyra sent help in time to save the city; but Camarina was surrendered, 'enslaved', and depopulated. On the death of Hippocrates (491–410), Gelo became guardian of his young sons and soon after 'tyrant' of Gela. His marriage with Demarete daughter of Thero of Acragas, and that of Thero with the daughter of his own brother Polyzelus, confirmed their union of interests.

After Hippocrates' death a democratic revolution at Syracuse was suppressed and Gelo became 'tyrant' there also: the Syracusan *demos* was expurgated as a 'most ungracious neighbour', and its place was filled by transferring to Syracuse the aristocracies of Leontini, Megara, and Camarina, and trustworthy families from Gela itself. With Thero guarding the west since 485 and watching Himera, Gelo attacked the other Chalcidian cities; he also 'liberated the Emporia' (v. 42–43) on the Libyan coast (Polyb. iii. 23. 2) and established Heraclea Minoa in western Sicily: in these unfinished enterprises of Dorieus, however, Sparta had refused to co-operate, as Gelo afterwards complained (vii. 158).

The Chalcidian cities, threatened by this Dorian aggression, were without a leader and short of men. Both, however, were provided unexpectedly in 492–491. In Rhegium a Messenian exile, Anaxilaus, made himself tyrant, married a daughter of a

---

[1] The dates adopted here are on the later of the two ancient reckonings.

local magnate Terillus, and gave his own daughter to Hiero, brother of Gelo, who dissuaded him from attacking Locri, but did not prevent him from intervening disastrously in Sicily. About the same time, Zancle, facing Rhegium across the strait, promoted a colony at Cale-Acte on the north coast, and issued a general invitation. The only known applicants were the Samian democrats exiled after the battle of Lade in 494 (vi. 23), who put themselves at the disposal of Anaxilaus. Scythes being absent—probably on errands of the new colony—Anaxilaus persuaded the Samians to occupy Zancle, meaning to reinforce it against Hippocrates. Hippocrates, however, arrested and interned Scythes, confirmed the Samians in Zancle—thus splitting the Ionian forces—and enslaved the original Zanclaeans. Cadmus, son of Scythes, who succeeded his father as commandant for Hippocrates, was later Gelo's intelligence officer at Delphi. But Anaxilaus expelled the Samians, and refounded Zancle as 'Messana' with exiles from Messenia like himself (Thuc. vi. 4. 5; Paus. 4. 33. 6 ff.).

Himera had long been an uneasy neighbour of Acragas and Gela. Thither Scythes escaped from Hippocrates on his way to Persia; and from Himera about 481 Thero expelled Terillus. It was this fresh hostility that determined Anaxilaus and Terillus to call in the Phoenicians from Panormus with the whole force of Carthage. As Scythes had paid another visit to Himera, and returned to Persia, it looks as if a Carthaginian attack and Himera's collaboration were concerted; but there is no other evidence, except Gelo's refusal to co-operate with the Aegean Greeks without a similar common plan. When this was refused, all he could do was to post his own envoy at Delphi, with instructions for either event.

What is notable about the western situation is that whereas in the Aegean the trouble with Persia had arisen from the Ionian Revolt, and Ionian states, Eretria and Athens, had taken a leading part in the fight for freedom, in the West it is the Ionian element that calls in the Phoenicians, and Dorian states who resist them. But the paradox is explained by the earlier history of both, and by the eventual weakness of the Chalcidians. Through the action of Anaxilaus and Terillus, what might have been a normal feud, between Greek states with different ancestry and traditions, became poisoned by appeal to the national enemy, and led to the ruthless reprisals of Hiero, and long after to the situation which tempted the Athenians to intervene.

The Mission to Corcyra (vii. 168) resembled that to Syracuse in this, that Corcyra lay far enough west to be directly threatened by a Carthaginian victory. Its fleet was large enough to act as a strategical reserve for either front, and was rightly so used; for there is no reason to regard the sixty ships, sent as far as Peloponnese, as the whole force available. Their excuse, that they were prevented by head-winds from passing Malea, may have been well founded, but Corcyra's normal ill-feeling towards Corinth, and recent action in Sicily to save Syracuse from Hippocrates, must be taken into account; and also that war with Athens in which Nepos says that Themistocles had used the new fleet (p. 237).

The Mission to Crete (vii. 169–71) added nothing either to Greek forces or to our knowledge of events in the south. Not only Crete took no part in Aegean affairs, but there is a great silence about the Sporades, though Artaphernes had tried to attack Rhodes;[1] the warning of Delphi to Cnidus (i. 174) had been effectual; and Cos had a Persian commissioner, Scythes (p. 243).[2] The connexion is looser than usual, and Herodotus recognizes this, and apologizes for it as an 'insertion'.[3]

---

[1] Lindian Chronicle, C. 32, l. 65 (Artaphernes); D. 56–57 (Datis: Mardonius).

[2] The phrases from petition and response in this passage are iambic, and unusually full:

> vii. 169 . . . ἄμεινον εἰ σφι τιμωροῦσι γίνεται*
> ὦ νήπιοι μέμφεσθε . . .
> ὑμῖν ὅσ᾽ ἐκ τῶν Μενελάου τιμωρ[ιῶν]
> Μίνως ἔπεμψε μηνίων δακρύματα
> οὐ γὰρ συνεπρήξαντο . . . αὐτῷ . . .
> τὸν ἐν Καμίκῳ θάνατον . . .
> ὑμεῖς δ᾽ ἐκείνοις τὴν ὑπ᾽ ἀνδρὸς βαρβάρου
> γυναῖκ᾽ [ἀν]αρπαχθεῖσαν ἐκ Σπαρτῆς [· τότε].

> * Or   . . . γίνεται
> τιμωρέουσιν εἰ σφ᾽ ἄμεινον Ἑλλάδι . . .

[3] For the Tarentine disaster (170) see Diod. xi. 52: for the 'many statues' at Olympia Paus. v. 26. 3–4.

The Cretan Mission illustrates the indifference of outlying parts of the Greek world to the Persian issue. Crete was very little developed, either culturally or politically, still under Dorian régimes of privilege for the most part, and unaffected by the democratic movement; and between the greater Dorian cities deep-seated feuds persisted till long after the Persian Wars. Dorian settlements, moreover, lay mostly in the western and central districts. In the eastern peninsula, of which Praesus was the principal city, not only old traditions survived, but an old language represented by three inscriptions in archaic Greek letters.

The story of Minos and the 'expedition to Camicus', well dated to the second generation before the Trojan War, has nothing to do with the Fall of Cnossos about 1400, but belongs to the period of the Sea Raids (c. 1250–1190) and of the withdrawal of the survivors of Hesiod's 'Age of Heroes' to the 'Blessed Isles' (W.D. 170–2), where Sicily, Sardinia, and Tyrrhenia perhaps bear the names of the Shakalsha, Shardana, and Tursha in Egyptian records. The archaeological record of the Lasithi highland, where Minoan folk held out long, is instructive commentary on Herodotus' account of the Praesians.[1] Stories of these western adventures were obvious material for propaganda in connexion with the Sicilian project of Dorieus; and this recent fiasco may have confirmed Cretan reluctance to venture oversea.

Thus the 'Five Missions' are more than a survey of the limits of Greek resistance. They are typical tensions throughout the background of the struggle which is to follow.

THERMOPYLAE AND ARTEMISIUM
(vii. 175–239; viii. 1–21)

The advance of Xerxes through Thessaly to the Spercheius valley followed the threefold order of march; less easily recognized, however, south of Larissa, except by the topography.

---

[1] Pendlebury, *B.S.A.* xxxviii. esp. 140–1.

i. An inland column followed the Apidanus, west of the moorland ridge of Cynoscephalae, i.e. by Thaumaci.

ii. Xerxes himself went by Halos and the coast road to Lamia: he was now in enemy country, and kept close to his fleet.

iii. The main south road is between these flanking routes, through Pharsalus and Meliboea, and over the western spur of Othrys by a one-day pass to Lamia, probably the line of the railway, which skirts a serviceable lake within the highland.

The Spercheius is easily crossed by ford at Anticyra above its confluence with the Melas, which defends Trachis town on the west. Here there is wide alluvial ground, defended on three sides by the Melas, the Spercheius, and the Asopus, and hither all three columns converged.

Topography (vii. 172, 198–200)

The general ignorance among Greeks of the topography of northern Greece is shown not only by the first plan of campaign (vii. 172-4) but by the neglect of the bypass at Thermopylae, and by Herodotus' own notion that the famous 'Gates' lay north and south (vii. 176-200). But correctly oriented, Herodotus' description only needs to be supplemented by the subsequent accumulation of silt from the Spercheius and Asopus in a broad plain at the foot of the old coast bluffs. For instead of forming a symmetrical delta in front of the trough-valley, this silt was—and is—diverted southward by the swell and current (vii. 198) entering the Euboean Gulf from Artemisium, and settles in more sheltered water along the Locrian coast. This alluviation had already begun, because Herodotus describes 'marshes' as well as sea at this point, but the Asopus still followed the coast, and only reached the sea at Anthela, instead of joining the Spercheius as now. Thus the Phoenix river, then a tributary of the Asopus (vii. 176, 200), now enters the sea separately. The ophthalmia which disabled two of the Spartans is a local disease affecting reed-cutters in these marshes.[1]

[1] vii. 229: Grundy, G.P.W. 312-13.

Essential features, all securely fixed by Grundy, are:

1. The coast road, and its 'cart-track only' between truncated bluffs and marshy coast, with a wider section between inner and outer 'gates'.

2. Herodotus distinguishes between the 'mountains of the Oetaeans' and 'those of the Trachinians', and says that Ephialtes' track passed between them (217) and *crossed* the Asopus 'which flows through the gorge', beyond which 'began the path called Anopaea'. The name 'Callidromus' he does not use, and its significance is only revealed in Burn's description[1] of the peculiar long trough lying parallel with the watershed ridge which steeply overlooks the upper Cephissus valley: this is the 'fair course' between the Asopus and a point nearly south of Anthela. From it descend the headwater of the Phoenix and the other ravines which lead down to the coast road.

3. But how did Ephialtes reach the Anopaea (Callidromus) section of his route? Herodotus is quite explicit. He *crossed* the 'Asopus which flows through the gorge' (216–17), that is, the upper course of that same stream which pours into the gorge and out of it into the plain. The notion that Ephialtes led the Persians up the gorge ignores (*a*) the extreme difficulty of passing a large force *by night* through a 'slit' only 12 feet wide at narrowest; (*b*) the probability that Thermopylae was fought some time after the full moon on which the Carneian feast began; (*c*) the certainty that the three-days storm off the coast, and the rain deluge which followed it, had not left the Oetaean mountains dry, and the consequent probability that the gorge was in spate and quite impassable.[2]

The alternative is to accept Herodotus' statement that Ephialtes' path had the Oetaean mountains on the right and the Trachinian on the left; for while this ceases to be true as soon as the Asopus is crossed and Anopaea begins, it exactly describes any track which entered the hills by the Melas valley west of the citadel of

---

[1] *B.S.A.* xliv. 315–16.
[2] For a different view, A. R. Burn, *B.S.A.* xliv (1949), 313–16; *Studies presented to D. A. Robinson*, p. 480.

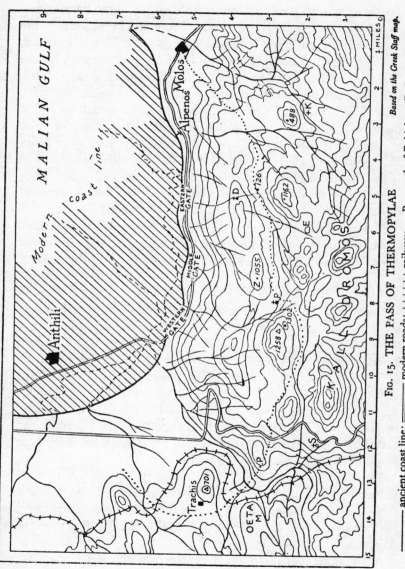

MALIAN GULF

Modern coast line

Anthili

Alpenos Molos

EASTERN GATE

MIDDLE GATE

WESTERN GATE

Z 1055

1258

1302

1258

1126

1162

488

+K

+D

+D

+E

A L D R O M O S

+S

K A L

+P

+P

Trachis

701

OETA

M

E. Elatovonni

1 MILES

FIG. 15. THE PASS OF THERMOPYLAE   *Based on the Greek Staff map.*

—— ancient coast line; +++++ modern roads; ━━━━ railway; ⋯P⋯ path of Ephialtes. D. Drakospilia.
Z. Zastani ridge. E. Elatovonni.

Trachis, circumvented that section of the Trachinian barrier, and crossed the Asopus above the gorge. From the Persian camp the distance is not much greater than by the gorge or the modern road.

4. The path of Ephialtes descended from the Anopaea by the 'Lairs of the Tail-eyed' and the 'Stone of the Black-Rump', landmarks on one of the ravines which reach the sea across the coast road. The 'Tail-eyed' Cercopes, when Heracles makes an end of them on a temple metope at Selinus, are human, dwarfish, and very properly slung upside down. But originally they were probably double-headed monsters, like the *amphisbaena* described within living memory in a cave of the Karpass in Cyprus. They have left their name in the village of Drakospilia ('serpents' caves') on one of the tracks from Callidromus to the coast.

Melampygus was an epithet of Heracles, and also described one of the many eagles which give their names to peaks in Greece (*Aetos, Aetomyti*). This rock has still to be sought along the descent.

The Greek Strategy and the Decisions of Leonidas

Herodotus' story is coherent and intelligible with one omission : though he mentions the Locrians, he does not say where they were posted, or what they did. Their obvious duty was to defend Locris; the way to defend Locris was to hold the strong position of Trachis town, commanding the passes at either end of the 'Trachinian cliffs'; and Herodotus expressly notes that Trachis was not in Persian hands (vii. 201 μεχρὶ Τρηχῖνος) but was garrisoned by the Locrians (203). In this position the Locrians and Leonidas' force mutually covered each other, on either side of the gorge of the Asopus.

The Locrians, however, could do nothing positive to help Leonidas, without deserting their own stronghold and opening their passes to the enemy. Even in this, moreover, they failed because they could no more command the Melas valley than the Anopaea.

As the same roads were the highways into Phocis, the Phocians also were properly placed in reserve (vii. 212), and if Xerxes intended to use the Asopus valley, it must be held against him on both banks. The 'track' of Ephialtes, after it left the Asopus, was therefore within the Phocian sector; but it was not their only concern, and when Hydarnes' force appeared the Phocians who guarded it very reasonably withdrew towards the main road into Phocis. They may or may not have appreciated the significance of the 'track' for Leonidas on the coast road, but they had to avoid being outflanked themselves. It is the old, old story of a blow delivered at the junction between divisional commands.

The Thebans, and the Dismissal of the Allies by Leonidas

Controversy comes therefore to a head in Plutarch's *ex parte* defence of the Thebans against the *malignitas* of Herodotus. Plutarch certainly had other sources—for example in the Ionian Revolt (p. 198 n.) : but here he has not demonstrably anything but Theban tradition. Thebes had ancient feuds both with Athens and with Phocis; as Herodotus says of Phocis and Thessaly, they were certain to be on opposite sides. Whatever earlier Theban policy may have been, Thebes did actually medize, and became Persian headquarters at the battle of Plataea. The Theban defence later (Thuc. iii. 62), a 'clique of a few men' ($\delta\upsilon\nu\alpha\sigma\tau\epsilon\acute{\iota}\alpha$ $\acute{o}\lambda\acute{\iota}\gamma\omega\nu$ $\acute{\alpha}\nu\delta\rho\hat{\omega}\nu$), admits the essential fact that Thebes was oligarchic because reactionary; and this remains characteristic till the fourth century, except during the brief Athenian supremacy. This medism of Thebes helps to explain the exceptional loyalty of Thespiae and Plataea, the latter probably now brigaded with Athens, for the defence, if necessary, of the Cithaeron passes. It explains also the reliance of Leonidas on Locrians and Phocians.

Where were the other Boeotian contingents? The answer is that they were dominated by Thebes, and the only chance of preventing them from medizing, or annoying Leonidas, was to prevent Thebes from giving them the lead or the necessity to medize. If the disloyalty of Thebes had been foreseen, it must have influenced the whole plan of campaign, like the indefensibility of Thessaly; but Leonidas appears to have had no previous anxiety about his immediate rear, and therefore had to take emergency action after his arrival at the front.

The Decision of Leonidas. As in Thessaly, the Greek High Command overestimated the facilities for defence. It was again a question of topography. With the forces at his command, it was Leonidas' decision to hold Thermopylae at all that led to disaster; his retention of Locrians, Phocians, and Thebans explains itself on the ground, as has been seen; and his decision to let the other allies retire was the only way to minimize this disaster.

The Greek High Command also underestimated Persian efficiency. The forces of Leonidas were not the whole Greek levy, nor even the whole Spartan army; but they were all that could be spared from the festivals of Carneia and Olympia, and they were thought to be sufficient to hold Thermopylae till the main bodies arrived. What spoiled all was the rapid advance of Xerxes' striking force (vii. 206); the whole campaign was over in eighteen days from Therma, about 140 miles in fourteen days' march. The four days' pause before the attack was not only to allow the Greeks to disperse, if they were so minded, but to concentrate four days' route-column at the battle-front. Troops and equipment were doubtless still arriving (as at Plataea) while the attack went on. Moreover, when the narratives of the movements by land and by sea are combined, it becomes clear that within these four days fall the three days of the Storm, which certainly meant bad weather at Thermopylae also. And it is only on the fourth day that there is mention of 'whips'; the first three attacks (two on the first day) were delivered by shock-troops, as the corps-names show.

A third misfit was unavoidable, the coincidence of the attack with the great festivals. In the Greek view of life, these things mattered. Even in our time, the sinking of the Greek cruiser *Helle* on the Virgin's Day at Tenos, and the Italian invasion of Albania on Good Friday, caused bewilderment, because, as men said, these things 'are not done'. The Spartans had already risked all by delay before Marathon: conversely the Argives in 419 B.C. tampered with the calendar 'keeping the same day' during their raid on Epidaurus (Thuc. v. 54).

The narrative of Thermopylae, realistic and vivid as it is, is nevertheless composed on the pedimental scheme already familiar

(p. 81). The 'Prologue', indeed, does not quite balance the 'Epilogue', for there is no preliminary reference to Demaratus; but his warning to Sparta (239) may be regarded as an 'aside' to the final reference to Leonidas. There is no doubt about the deliberate double contrast between the two kings.

Thermopylae and Artemisium

Herodotus emphasizes the connexion between sea defence and land defence: 'the whole struggle of the fleet was for the Euripus, as it was for Leonidas' force to hold the Pass' (viii. 15). For the land defence was hopeless if the Persian fleet forced the channel, and sea defence was useless if the Persians secured the pass.

There are difficulties in Herodotus' account; he names or implies a few individual sources—Pytheas, Scyllias, and the Athenian squadron—and probably he had more. Wherever these observers were, we may expect detailed information; where they were not, there may be blanks in the story. Moreover, the detailed narratives have been pieced together by him on his own general notion of the larger operations, for which he had not necessarily any comprehensive authority at all. In naval warfare, especially, distances are large, and it is hard to see what is going on afar, even within view.

With superior numbers, it was Persian strategy to outflank and envelop; and this was not necessarily an afterthought, though at Thermopylae local information, at the last moment, suggested a method. Similarly, pauses in the Persian advance result partly from unforeseen accidents and from losses; but also from the intention to keep land- and sea-forces working in conjunction. As the fleet could move much more rapidly than the army, eleven days passed before naval movements began. Similarly the fleet at Aphetae waited for news of the squadron sailing round Euboea; but eventually attacked, without waiting longer, on the third day of battle at Thermopylae, because it was the only chance to cut off the Greek fleet, now likely to retire as soon as the pass was forced. It is curious that it is nowhere argued that if the Greek fleet could hold the narrows it could detain the Persian land-force indefinitely, since the Persian commissariat was mainly sea-borne. But just this is the significance of the 'deep-sea squadron', outflanking the Greek fleet at Artemisium.

Epilogue to Thermopylae (vii. 234–9)

Between the fighting at Thermopylae (vii. 233) and the naval operations at Artemisium (viii. 1) Herodotus interposes a short but composite section, mainly concerned with Demaratus, who had already warned Xerxes (vii. 209) of the desperate resistance he must expect. The first story (vii. 234–7) is an obvious counterpart to that warning, of which he is reminded by Xerxes, and asked what further forces the Spartans have, and how the King should proceed. His advice, to occupy Cythera by sea, and then attack Sparta in rear, is rejected by the Persian admiral Achaemenes (236), whose attempt, however, to destroy the King's trust in Demaratus fails (237).

Then follows the mutilation of the body of Leonidas, at the express order of Xerxes, to gratify his exceptional resentment. Disconnected as it is from the burial of the other Spartans (228), it has peculiar meaning where it stands, as foil to Xerxes' exceptional trust in Demaratus. Similar postponements of part of an episode are (1) the failure of Sparta to assist Croesus (i. 70), because the Spartan field-force had been destroyed by the Argives (i. 82); (2) the postponement of the actual building of the bridges till Xerxes is ready to cross the Hellespont (vii. 36), though the preparations were described together with the digging of the canal at Mount Athos (vii. 22–24).

But it is the final chapter (vii. 239) that has most troubled commentators.[1] It has been supposed that Herodotus meant to insert vii. 239 after 220. But if so, why does it stand after 238?

---

[1] Powell translates (p. 596) as if the verb ἐξέλιπε, here alone in Herodotus, meant that the λόγος 'stopped' intransitively. But if the subject may be understood, so also may be the object. It is suggested that the subject is τὸ πρότερον, and that ἐξέλιπε means 'lost touch with' what follows now—compare vii. 83, where, if one of the 'Immortals' ἐξέλειπε τὸν ἀριθμόν, his place was filled; the metaphor is from continuous linkage. So, too, in an 'eclipse' (vii. 37) the sun became invisible ἐκλιπὼν τὴν ἐκ τοῦ οὐρανοῦ ἕδρην. Compare the Samians' desertion at Lade: ἔκλειψιν τῶν νεῶν (vi. 15).

The answer is that the reference to ch. 220 is a back-reference merely, and that the incident is deliberately in place here. For the story is a pendant anecdote about Demaratus, the honest man who retained Xerxes' confidence by telling the truth, however unwelcome, and—for whatever reason—told unwelcome truth to the Spartans also. They too, like Xerxes, failed to accept the warning at first, and their eventual acceptance was not the work of Leonidas—whose heart and muscles were better than his head —but of his wife Gorgo, daughter of Cleomenes. She had already saved one Spartan king from a blunder (v. 51). A tragic occasion! The girl 'Bright-Eyes' is grown up, and unequally mated; Leonidas is King of Sparta—*and it might have been Cleomenes, with Demaratus as his colleague.* Truly the evil that men do lives after them. Herodotus, searching for causes, reveals here the full tragedy of Thermopylae.[1]

Thermopylae and Artemisium: Chronology

Herodotus has solved the problem of describing simultaneous operations, by narrating:

   (i) the movements of the fleets until the Persians who had survived the storm were established at Aphetae, facing the Greek fleet at Artemisium;
  (ii) the advance of the Persian land-forces (which had begun eleven days earlier, I–XI) from Therma to Malis (vii. 210) with four days' pause there (XII–XV);
 (iii) the arrival of the Greek forces at Thermopylae, and Leonidas' disposition of them there;
  (iv) the four days' battle, and immediate sequel (days XVI–XIX). Then he recurs to
   (v) day XVI at Aphetae and Artemisium (viii. 1–5) and narrates the sea-fighting of days XVI–XVIII, followed by the retreat of the Greek fleet (viii. 6–21). Then

---

[1] The chapter has been 'condemned' by Macan because the word (ἐξέκνησε) recurs only in Theocritus and in Aeneas Tacticus 31. 14. But is there any other occasion in Greek literature when anyone has to scrape the wax off a tablet? The word is of troglodyte antiquity; the English equivalent of *kna-* is *gnaw*.

(vi) the two narratives are correlated on day XIX by the excursion of Persian naval crews to Thermopylae.

(vii) Finally, on day XX, Xerxes advances into Doris, and his fleet moves from Histiaea. The land-fight is thus enframed between the naval preparations (interrupted by storm), and the eventual sea-fight, supplementary to it and controlled by the course of events on land.

Artemisium. Though the general strategy is clear, there are difficulties in the narrative, all due to the fragmentariness of Herodotus' information, involving gaps, and perhaps also reduplication, as well as attributing to the Greek fleet as a whole the movements of a detached squadron. The main narrative is punctuated by 'days', which may be correlated (as above) with those of the land-movements, and numbered accordingly.

For eleven days (I–XI) after the land army began to leave Therma the Persian fleet remained at rest. On day XII it put to sea simultaneously, having plenty of sea-room, and in a long day's voyage (183) reached the beaches along the foreshore of Ossa and Pelion, from Casthanaia to Sepias. As the storm on days XIII–XIV–XV was on an east wind (185), it was preceded by a favourable north wind; the journey was easy, and the waves were setting nearly alongshore, till they veered with the wind towards on-shore. The disaster was due almost as much to this choppy swell as to the violence of the wind.

The same north to north-east wind made the beach at Artemisium untenable, and the Greek ships withdrew into the Euboean Gulf; not to avoid the Persians—for they had come expressly to oppose them—but for their own security. Herodotus says that they retired to Chalcis, and some no doubt did so (as will appear later), but it is unlikely that all withdrew so far; first because it was quite unnecessary for their safety, and secondly because it would have exposed the coast flank of Thermopylae, which it was their task to defend. If the Persians attempted to enter the Euboean channel, ships sheltering at Histiaea would take them in flank as effectively as at Artemisium. On the second day (XIV), the storm having abated, the Greek fleet returned to its post at Artemisium, and found surviving Persians already at Aphetae (192–4).

There was, however, good reason for sending *some* Greek ships to hold the Narrows at Chalcis, and also for recalling them later; and as Chalcis had been an Athenian *cleruchy*, and was the nearest port to Attica, this duty would normally fall to an Athenian squadron. If Herodotus had even some of his information from Athenian sources, this is the operation most fully within his knowledge; and the fifty-three Athenian ships which joined the main fleet at Artemisium on day XVIII (viii. 14) were probably not reinforcements from Attica but were *rejoining* 'according to plan', on information received across Euboea that the Persian 'deep-sea' squadron had been scattered by the storm (13).

Whatever ships went as far as Chalcis were sent 'to protect the Euripus' (183) against some new danger, not foreseen when the fleet had moved north, else they would have been left behind there. What this new danger was appears from the subsequent narrative, and also the precise moment at which it was realized by the Greek admirals.

On the day (XII) of their departure from Therma, if not earlier, ten Persian ships passed between Sciathos and the mainland, erected a sea-mark on the Myrmex reef, and cut off three Greek ships on patrol (vii. 179–83). From these ships therefore Greek headquarters had no report. But there were signals from Sciathos. What news did these convey?

It was on receiving these signals that the Greeks—or some of them—withdrew to Chalcis 'to guard the Euripus'. Against what new danger? At Artemisium they already protected the whole Euboean channel against attack from the north. But if what was signalled from Sciathos was a squadron of 200 ships detailed to pass outside Sciathos and Euboea, and force the Euripus from the *south*, the detachment of a squadron to 'guard the Euripus' is intelligible; and as the main fleet withdrew at the same time to shelter in the Gulf, all the ships kept company as far as Histiaea; and the absence of the Chalcis-bound squadron was not noticed by Herodotus' informants. Thus its fifty-three ships, on their return to Artemisium, were taken for reinforcements (viii. 14) and in fact they made up Herodotus' original complement (127— viii. 1) to the eventual total of 180 at Salamis, with losses replaced.

Further news of the 'deep-sea' squadron reached the Greeks on their return to Artemisium (day XIV), through Scyllias the diver. But if this had been the first intimation, it is notable that no counter-measures are recorded at this point, beyond a general disposition to withdraw again. This omission would be explained, however, if the Greek commanders already knew of the 'deep-sea' enterprise—by signals from Sciathos—before withdrawing from Artemisium themselves.

Confirmation of this view of the movements of the fifty-three Athenian ships is that at the moment of their arrival at Artemisium (14) came independent news of the destruction of the 'deep-sea' squadron. This gives an important limit of date, for it was more than a day's journey by land from the 'Hollows' to Artemisium; the disaster therefore occurred not later than day XVI and probably earlier. It was therefore not caused by the 'rain' storm—though certainly aggravated by it—but by the same wind-storm as fell on the main Persian fleet on days XIII–XV. The date of the disaster has been confused with that of the arrival of the news. As the same information, from watchmen on the eastern hills of Euboea, could reach Chalcis much earlier, the fifty-three ships, if they left Chalcis 'on information received', could arrive at Artemisium at the same time as the direct messenger. Now the earlier the date of the 'deep-sea' disaster, the more likely it is that the 'deep-sea' squadron was detached north of Sciathos (viii. 7), not sent back into the open from Aphetae; moreover, in the latter event, it could hardly have escaped the notice of the look-out men at Artemisium. Nor does Herodotus say expressly (as Diodorus does, xi. 12. 3) that these ships *started from Aphetae* (viii. 7); only that the news of their mission was reported from Aphetae by Scyllias on day XVI, by which time the disaster had occurred (viii. 8).

One further incident is probably to be connected with the

'deep-sea' episode (viii. 14). On the evening of day XVII, after the 'rain'-storm ('observing the same hour' (14) as the battle of day XVI), 'they'—either the main Greek fleet, or the newly arrived Athenians—fell upon 'Cilician ships' (not previously mentioned) and destroyed them. Who were these Cilician ships?

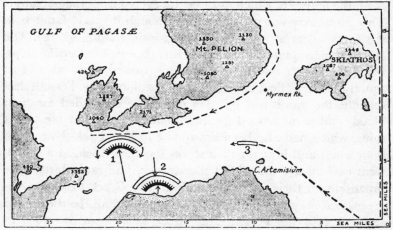

FIG. 16. THE BATTLE OF ARTEMISIUM

1. The earlier encounter. 2. The later encounter. ▬▬▬ Greek ships. ▭▭▭ Persian ships. 3. The Cilician squadron.

Based on British Admiralty Chart No. 1556, with the permission of the Controller of H.M. Stationery Office and of the Hydrographer of the Navy.

As the main Persian fleet took no part in this action, they must have been on some errand, and unexpected. Now if the fifty-three Athenian ships had time to return from Chalcis to Artemisium, there was also time for Cilician ships from the 'deep-sea' squadron to rally after the storm and retreat towards their own main body. Whether they were attacked by the main Greek fleet, or by the newly arrived Athenians before going to anchorage, is not clear from the grammar. But when the Greeks eventually retired, the Corinthians were leading, and the Athenians in rear. As they lay at Artemisium, therefore, the Athenians were nearest to the open sea and to arrivals from outside Euboea.

Meanwhile, after receiving from Scyllias confirmation of the departure of 200 Persian ships, and finding the swell more moderate, in the late afternoon of day xvi the Greek admirals decided to attack (viii. 9). The sunlight, from their port quarter, displayed the Persian ships against their beaches; it was also in the eyes of the Persians as they emerged by squadrons from their anchorages. Orders were to force an action, and execute a *diek-plous*, the nature of which must be discovered from the narrative. This manœuvre was not a new one, though it was unfamiliar to the Ionian fleet at Lade, who found it distressing (vi. 12). The two fleets presumably advanced in line abeam. The Persian ships, being the swifter and more numerous, turned outwards to surround the Greek fleet (viii. 10). Ionian sailors in the Persian fleet thought the game was up; Persian crews contended for 'first blood' and royal reward for an Athenian prize. But the Greek ships, which had also been advancing in line, backed water on both wings and brought their sterns together; then, at a signal, went each ahead radially at short range, and sank thirty ships broadside on their encircling course. The Greek losses are not given, and may be presumed to have been small. In the second sea-fight (16) the Persian and Greek tactics are described in similar terms but this time the Persians, turning inwards more smartly, let many Greek ships slip out between; then fell into disorder and rammed one another.

This manœuvre is perfectly clear: it throws some light on the movements at Salamis; and it was repeated by Cnemus in the Gulf of Patras (Thuc. ii. 83)—unsuccessfully, however, because Phormio's swifter ships closed the trap before the second signal. It is, however, quite different from the *diekplous* of later times, whereby the attacking fleet, in line ahead, 'crossed the T', in Nelson's phrase, passed through the enemy's line, and cut off one wing of it for total destruction.

In the second sea-fight, on day xix about midday (15), though the Greeks caused great losses, they suffered heavily themselves and were in no state to meet another attack (18). But they had to retreat unobserved, if possible, for their line of escape was across the enemy's front. The commissariat cattle collected from Euboea were slaughtered and put on board; fires were lighted, as if the crews were still ashore, and presumably stores were destroyed. Consequently, on the news that all was over at Thermopylae, retreat was immediate; the Corinthians leading, as they had farthest to go, and so lay farthest up channel; the Athenians covering the rear, and posting messages at the watering-places for the medizing Ionians. News of this withdrawal reached Aphetae from Histiaea, but was discredited. But when daylight showed the beach at Artemisium empty, the Persian fleet moved up the Gulf to Histiaea, and spent day xx in excursions to Thermopylae, instead of overtaking the Greeks at the Euripus.

Xerxes' Advance (viii. 27–32)

After this visit of the fleet, Xerxes and the main land-force crossed the coast range of Trachis into Doris, which is the long straight trough of the upper Cephissus, along the north face of Parnassus (viii. 32). Though the army is described as being 'divided' at Panopeus, this refers only to the force which skirted Parnassus to visit Delphi; of a coastal column there is no mention at all, but it is improbable that the coast-road, so hardly contested, was not used. Though the numerous small towns of Phocis were devastated, the mass of the Phocians withdrew into Tithorea, the upland plain of Parnassus, and into Ozolian Locris, by the pass which descends on to Amphissa, but they were not pursued beyond the watershed, a considerable climb (32). The Boeotian cities were protected by Macedonian commissioners sent by Alexander.

SALAMIS (viii. 26–144)

The story of Salamis is enframed, as usual, by a prologue and epilogue of subordinate episodes.

The Raid on Delphi (viii. 35–39)

Though it was Persian policy to conciliate the gods and priesthoods of other peoples, the burning of Sardis seems to have provoked reprisals on Greek sanctuaries (v. 102). The rich shrine of Apollo at Abae had already been devastated. Delphi, however, had discouraged Athenian resistance, and perhaps the mission to Delphi was a precaution (p. 235).[1]

The sanctuary of Athena Pronaea ('before the shrine') lies along the highway from Boeotia where it comes into view, round the base of the precipitous Phaedriadae, before it crosses the Castalia ravine. Many large fragments from the cliff lie round this enclosure and on the steep slope below. The chapels of the two heroes are not identified, as this whole approach to Delphi was replanned later, with a gymnasium and guest-houses.

The Greek Fleet in the Saronic Gulf (viii. 40–41)

While the advance squadron was at Artemisium, contingents from Peloponnese and the islands had reported at Troezen, where the land-locked Pogon harbour was protected seaward by Calauria Island. It is the best port of the Argive peninsula, and commands the Saronic Gulf, about thirty-three miles wide to Sunium.

The squadrons which retreated from Artemisium were, however, diverted by the Athenians, and put in to Salamis, to help with the evacuation of Attica; and here they were joined by the other contingents from Troezen.[2]

Some, but not all, of the ships lost at Artemisium had been replaced; but very few states except Aegina increased their contingents; and Aegina still kept ships in reserve for home defence. A few cities, which had no triremes, or inadequate crews, sent only penteconters.

Herodotus' list is in roughly geographical order: (1) Peloponnese; (2) Athens and Megara; (3) Ambracia and Leucas (colonies of Corinth); (4) Aegina; (5) Locris, Chalcis, Eretria, Styra, with Ceos and Naxos; (6) Cythnos, Seriphos, Siphnos, Melos; (7) Croton. The Naxian ships were deserters, and were attached like Ceos to the Euboean Ionians.

The Sack of Athens (viii. 50–56)

The evacuation of Attica was completed without interference: but a few poor or fanatical persons palisaded the Acropolis. The

---

[1] S. Casson, *Class. Rev.* xxxviii (1914), 145–51. But συλήσαντες must mean that the treasures were to be taken away.   [2] See note on p. 263.

Persians attacked with fire-arrows from the Areopagus spur, scaled the recess in the cliff north-west of the entrance, and massacred them in the temple. This was recognized as an atrocity: Athenian renegades were ordered to renew the temple services; and Herodotus notes that the sacred olive in the temple of Erechtheus shot up miraculously.

In the panic-stricken fleet at Salamis, Themistocles stated the strategical position. To retire, as proposed, to the Isthmus was to surrender Salamis and Megara, as well as Attica with the Athenian non-combatants, to uncover Aegina and the approach to the

[2] The total muster was as follows:

States	At Artemisium (viii. 1-2)	At Salamis (viii. 43-48)
Athens	127(+53)	180
Corinth	40	40
Megara	20	20
Chalcis	20	20
Aegina	18	30 (+home squadron)
Sicyon	12	15
Sparta	10	16
Epidaurus	8	10
Eretria	7	7
Troezen	5	5
Styra	2	2
Ceos	2 (+2 penteconters)	2 (+2 pent.)
Locris Opuntia . . .	7 pent.	
Ambracia	..	7
Leucas	..	3
Croton	..	1
Seriphos		1 pent.
Siphnos		1 pent.
Melos		2 pent.
Naxos	..	4
Hermione	..	3
Cythnos		1(+1 pent.)
All Hdt. items add only to .		365(+7 pent.)
Herodotus totals (viii. 2. 48)	271+pent	378
Add deserters		
Tenos (viii. 82) . . .		1
Lemnos (viii. 11) . . .		1

Isthmus, and to offer battle in open water with fewer, smaller, and inferior ships.

Within the strait at Salamis they would equally defend the Isthmus, Persian numbers would be unavailing, and if successful they would prevent the Persians from advancing farther at all. But it was the Athenian threat to withdraw altogether, if Salamis was not held, that decided Eurybiades to stay (63) and to invite the help of the Aeacid heroes of Salamis and Aegina (cf. v. 80–81).

Salamis: Political and Strategical

With the occupation of Attica, the initial and sufficient (though minor) objective of Xerxes' expedition was achieved, namely the punishment of Athens; and some Persians thought that this ended the matter. But Mardonius' ulterior aim was to annex all Greece: he was, or soon would be, in conversation with Argos; and Persian friends and vassals in northern Greece needed to be assured against reprisals; for the Athenians had extricated both their families and their fleet, and remained an urgent danger to the 'new order'. Though the season was late—the feast of Demeter at Eleusis would be on 23 September—there was still time to do something before winter, especially as the Greeks could not remain indefinitely at Salamis for lack of supplies for the fleet and the refugees.

Persian strategy still depended on co-operation between army and fleet. With the Greek ships withdrawn to Troezen, Aegina, and even Salamis, it was safe to bring forward any reserve vessels that had been guarding the Hellespont; and this movement may explain the three days' delay and the reference to vessels off Ceos and Cynosura, still working their way towards the battle-front. Another squadron from the islands had arrived on the day when the Acropolis was captured. There had also been several raids on the coast of Attica (Diod. xi. 145).

Greek squadrons had put into Troezen in the belief that the Peloponnesian land-force was awaiting the enemy on the strong defence-line of Cithaeron and Parnes (viii. 40). They found, however, that this land-force was fortifying the Isthmus, and intended to sacrifice all north of it; Athenian non-combatants were being evacuated to Salamis, Aegina, and Troezen, and the Athenian squadron had put in to Salamis (viii. 41). Naval reinforcements, concentrated at Troezen, were therefore transferred also to Salamis.

Persian Dispositions (viii. 65)

From Trachis the Persian fleet, after three days' rest at Histiaea, passed the Euripus in three days, a long period, because the current is seldom the same for more than a few hours. Once through the narrows, three more days brought a large part of it to Phalerum. But after experience of Aegean weather, every available shelter was used, and we hear later (viii. 76) of squadrons stationed about Ceos and Cynosura. There is no need to duplicate these places (p. 274).

Though losses at Artemisium had been heavy, the Persians had received reinforcements from south Euboea, Andros, Tenos, and other islands, sufficient (Herodotus thinks) to compensate them. But Herodotus reckons land-losses and sea-losses together, and gives only a general estimate of reinforcements from medizing districts of Greece.

The task now before the Persians was once more twofold: to break the Greek naval defence, and to force the line of the Isthmus. Artemisia alone of Xerxes' advisers doubted the superiority of the fleet—using the same phrase (viii. 68) as Aeschylus[1]—and advocated a blockade of the Greek force at Salamis. The other admirals were for immediate attack, and Xerxes misread the failure at Artemisium as due to his personal absence, which he now proposed to repair.

During the night the land-force began to move forward towards Peloponnese, though the Scironian cliff road had been demolished and the wall on the Isthmus was well advanced. Two anecdotes perhaps illustrate the Persian dispositions. The dust-cloud seen by Demaratus and Dicaeus in the Plain of Eleusis—estimated at

---

[1] *Persae* 728 ναυτικὸς στρατὸς κακωθεὶς πεζὸν ὤλεσε στρατόν ; Hdt. viii. 68 μὴ ὁ ναυτικὸς στρατὸς κακωθεὶς τὸν πεζὸν προσδηλήσηται.

30,000 men—indicates troops already on the move; and as the wind was north-west, it was off-shore, with calm in the Gulf, favourable to naval action (viii. 65). The mole and bridge of boats begun by Xerxes' engineers in the narrows between the mainland and Salamis portended an assault on the Athenian landforce and non-combatants in Salamis town, perhaps also a design to block the channel. It may have been begun before the battle, but was continued afterwards to mask Xerxes' decision to retire (p. 112 : viii. 97). As the mainland side of the narrows is shallow, with reefs and small islands, this project was much more easy to begin than it would have been to complete.

Herodotus enhances this account of the defences and defenders of the Isthmus with a masterly diagram of Peloponnesian ethnology (viii. 73) ; distinguishing (a) aborigines in Arcadia and Cynuria, the rough borderland between Argolis and Laconia, which was old-Ionic; (b) Achaean remnants of the pre-Dorian régime, now restricted (apparently) to the Achaean *riviera* along the Corinthian Gulf; four immigrant groups—(c) the dominant Dorians, (d) the Aetolians who had followed them into Elis, (e) Dryopes, already noted (viii. 43–46) as pre-Dorian aboriginals of the northern Doris, and (f) the Minyans from Lemnos, whose story had also been given (iv. 145–9).

The clear-cut division between Peloponnesians prepared to resist, and the rest who in effect were medizing (viii. 72), emphasizes (without mentioning names) the significance of the abstention of Argos (vii. 148–52).

There is no need to alter the description of the Cynurians (73) ; for οἱ περίοικοι means 'all the Argive *perioeci* there were', and this was probably the fact.

The topography of Salamis is simple. The gulf or bay between Salamis island and the mainland of Attica is roughly rectangular, about 5 miles east to west and 1½ miles north to south. It has steep shores north and south; at the east end, broken ground between the foot of Mount Aegaleôs and Piraeus harbour; at the west end, the town of Salamis on a low point between Ambelaki Bay to the south, and Georgio channel communicating north-westward with Eleusis Bay, which in turn opens into the Saronic Gulf by a reef-fringed strait about 22 miles from Salamis town. The eastward opening, about $1\frac{1}{4}$ miles wide, is divided into two channels by Psyttaleia Island: the more easterly, about half a mile across, is clear and direct; the other is oblique, and obstructed by Atalanti islet west of Psyttaleia, so that ships have to make a double turn to enter Salamis Bay. The shores of Ambelaki Bay greatly increase the length of coastline available for beaching or anchoring; and ships in this position stern-to-shore would deploy straight into line, with the right wing eastward, or into column to starboard.

The Greek position. As at Lade and at Artemisium, squadrons were presumably posted in an order relative to their respective bases. We may assume that the ships were beached or anchored prows seaward. Eurybiades and the Spartans on the right were therefore eastward nearest the open gulf and the sea route to Peloponnese; Aeginetans and Megareans next to them and other Peloponnesian contingents nearest their homes (Diod. xi. 18. 2); Athenians farther west, in front of Salamis town where their headquarters and non-combatants were; Corinthians, the only other large squadron, probably beyond them, towards Georgio channel and the back-way through the Bay of Eleusis into Corinthian home-waters—so that it was their obvious function to defend the back-way if the Persians tried to force an entry there. This all agrees, as will be seen, with the positions and achievements of each major squadron in the battle. What has to be remembered, however, is that when confronted with the enemy, i.e. facing south, the Spartans were on the extreme left, nearest the coast of Attica. The unidentified Heracleium which was the mainland end of the Greek line (Diod. xi. 18. 2) must have been between Peiraeus and 'Xerxes' seat', not on Georgio channel as some have supposed.

The Persian order of battle was determined by the threefold objective: to cut off the retreat of the Greeks by the western entrance, to confine them to the gulf by blocking the eastern straits, and then to enter and destroy them in the bay. Aeschylus

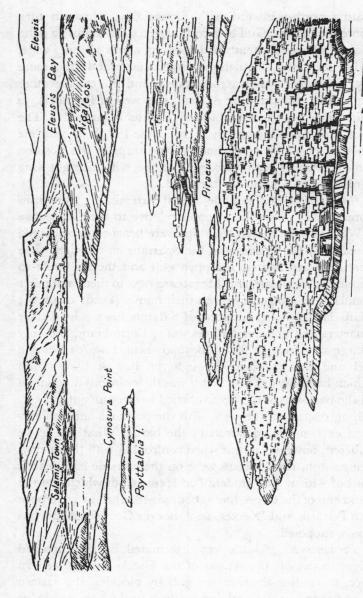

Fig. 17. THE BATTLEFIELD OF SALAMIS

From an air-view, over Phalerum bay, looking a little north of west.

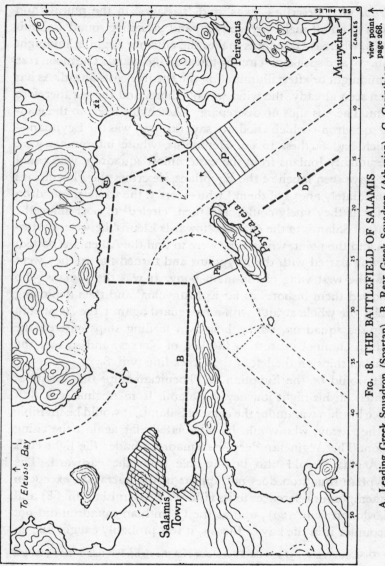

SEA MILES

Peiraeus

Murychia

view point
page 268.

A

P

D

Psyttaleia

Pᴇ

To Eleusis Bay

C

B

Salamis
Town

CABLES

FIG. 18. THE BATTLEFIELD OF SALAMIS

A. Leading Greek Squadron (Spartan). B. Rear Greek Squadron (Athenian). C. Corinthian
Squadron (returning from Eleusis Bay). D. Aeginetan Squadron. Ph. Phoenician Squadron.
P. Persian Centre. X 1. Xerxes Seat (traditional). X 2. Xerxes Seat (suggested).

Based on British Admiralty Chart No. 804, with the permission of the Controller of H.M. Stationery Office and of the Hydrographer of the Navy.

(*Persae* 367) describes 'exits' and 'passages' in the plural; and refers to an all-night voyage (382) and to 'sailing round' Salamis (368), whereas Herodotus makes the advance begin at midnight (viii. 76) and speaks of 'circling towards' the island. The moon rose at midnight or after, illuminating the enemy coasts ahead. As has been seen already, the wind was off-shore, and the sea therefore calm. There is thus no discrepancy. Aeschylus refers to the leading squadron—which Diodorus says (xi. 7. 2) was the Egyptian—which had farthest to go. Herodotus, whose informants were presumably Ionians from the easternmost squadron, who could not have seen much of the Egyptians, describes the Phoenicians immediately ahead of them,[1] who escorted the western squadron as far as they safely could, and then 'circled' to port along the coast of Salamis to the channel 'towards Eleusis' between Psyttaleia and the point, where they were to find the Athenians posted. Having parted with the Egyptians and turned north, they were now the west wing of the main body. It was the Ionians who followed them inshore 'as far as Munychia' and then deploying 'filled the whole strait'[2] with a rearguard against the Aeginetan deep-sea squadron, while their own leading ships entered the eastern channel nearest to the feet of Xerxes, and so met the Spartan ships on the left of the Greek line (viii. 85).

It would be the Egyptian or Phoenician ships that Aristides sighted on his night journey to Salamis from Aegina (viii. 81). Once his ship was under the coast of Salamis, it would be invisible to the enemy, who would be silhouetted afar against the rising moon. The Aeginetan deep-sea squadron, under the light cliffs of Aegina, would also be invisible from the eastward. The Egyptian squadron does not appear in the narrative, except in contemptuous references to its failure by Artemisia (viii. 68) and Mardonius (viii. 100); and as the Corinthian squadron did not encounter it in the bay of Eleusis, it was probably caught abeam

---

[1] Diodorus (xi. 17. 3) sets the Phoenicians on the right, but this is their position before they left their anchorage at Phalerum.

[2] Aeschylus (*Ag.* 307) uses *porthmos* and Strabo (335–69) *poros* of the whole Saronic Gulf, which was believed in antiquity to be much narrower than it really is: Myres, *Greece and Rome*, xii (1943), 33 ff., diagram, p. 37.

in the open and driven ashore on Salamis by the Aeginetans (viii. 86), who were then free to attack the eastern squadrons (viii. 91) in rear.

The Corinthian manœuvre (viii. 94)

Further light is thrown on this Egyptian–Aeginetan affair by the story about the Corinthians. It may be presumed that, as in the retreat from Artemisium, they were posted nearest to their own country; that is, at the west end of the gulf of Salamis, and nearest therefore to the channel into Eleusis Bay. At a signal from their own flagship, and setting sail on the inshore breeze of morning for utmost speed, the Corinthian ships left their station and disappeared into Eleusis Bay. This manœuvre was naturally misunderstood by Athenians, who (as their place in the order of battle shows) were the nearest large squadron along the beaches. But it was prompt and obvious provision for the defence of the back-way, on the news brought by Aristides that the Persians were sailing round the island. Midway, however, across Eleusis Bay an unexplained row-boat (*keles*) encountered them, and informed them—what they did not know—that the Greeks were winning. Whereupon the Corinthian admiral put about, and returned to his place in the fleet, and (by general opinion) fought very well.

Now the crew of a row-boat in the middle of Eleusis Bay could see nothing that was happening either east of Georgio Channel or outside the western entrance. They were, however, well placed for receiving and transmitting signals from a watcher on the skyline of Salamis, and *he* would see what was going on, not only round Psyttaleia, but also in the open gulf between Aegina and Megara. As the only other witnesses of the manœuvre were Corinthians, Herodotus' disparaging version must have come from the Athenians; and he admits that there was another which was generally accepted. All is explained if the row-boat was a signal-unit, deliberately and privily posted by Greek headquarters, to keep touch with the Corinthians and transmit messages in the event of any change of plan; and the only news which could directly change their plan was news that there was no longer any danger at the back-way.

The discrepancy between Herodotus' detailed information—which must have been Athenian—about the Corinthian squadron, and the general opinion that the Corinthians had fought well, suggests that he may have been at the mercy of his informants in another aspect of the same matter, the destruction of the Egyptian squadron. Though the Egyptians are twice mentioned as present at the battle (viii. 68, 100) and as behaving badly, they have no place in Herodotus' description of the Persian advance, and it is only from Diodorus (xi. 17. 2) that their special and separate task is revealed. We have seen already that the only detached force on the Greek side available to oppose them was the home squadron of Aegina. Now the Aeginetans were awarded the first prize for their contribution to the victory, and fought very well, intercepting enemy ships escaping from the narrows. They were therefore themselves outside.[1] An anecdote about the encounter of Themistocles with the Aeginetan Polycritus is more precise (viii. 92). Here again, then, there is discrepancy between the general Greek opinion and the almost complete silence of Herodotus about the Aeginetans. There is no reason to attribute this to prejudice, for he knew that there was an Aeginetan squadron in home waters, and that someone (not the Corinthians) had dealt with the danger from the back-way. But Athenian informants were the least likely to do justice to Aeginetan achievements.

As the thirty Aeginetan ships in the line of battle (46) were within the channels, this tale must refer to the detached 'home fleet' of Aegina, which we have already detected engaging the Egyptian squadron; after which it had time to turn eastward and take the disordered Persians in rear. It was from such ships destroyed outside the straits that the copious wreckage came, with which the west wind strewed the coast of Attica around Cape Colias (86). It can hardly have drifted out through the narrows. It thus becomes clear how Themistocles' flagship, leading the

---

[1] viii. 91 ὑποστάντες ἐν τῷ πορθμῷ; cf. viii. 76.

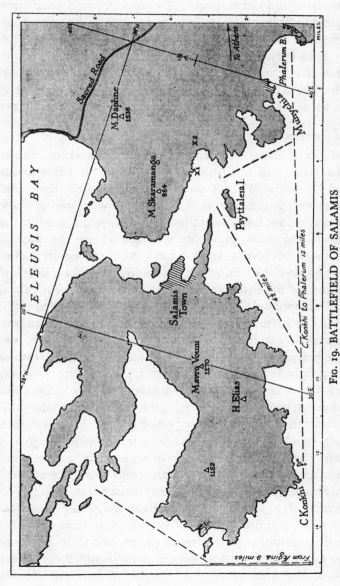

FIG. 19. BATTLEFIELD OF SALAMIS. X1, X2, alternative sites for 'Xerxes' Seat'.

To show movements between the Straits and Aegina. X1, X2, alternative sites for 'Xerxes' Seat'.

Based on British Admiralty Chart No. 1513, with the permission of the Controller of H.M. Stationery Office and of the Hydrographer of the Navy.

Athenian squadron out through the channels, could encounter
the Aeginetan ship of Polycritus, and provoke his gibe (92)
about 'medism'; for Themistocles' ship was on the same course
as the retreating enemy.

Ships which escaped this Aeginetan squadron made their way
to the long beach of Phalerum, and thence along the Attic coast to
Sunium, for at night they mistook inshore islands for Greek ships.

Ceos and Cynosura (viii. 76)

Herodotus describes that eastern squadron which kept contact
with Munychia and the Attic shore as 'those stationed about
Ceos and Cynosura'. The phrase has caused trouble to those who
have been unwilling to refer it to the well-known island of Ceos,
off Sunium—about forty-five miles from Munychia—and to the
well-known Cynosura promontory which closes the bay of
Marathon—about seventy miles—and have consequently had to
apply the name Cynosura, which is a common one for a long low
promontory, to the eastern point of Salamis opposite Psyttaleia,
and to invent a second Ceos somewhere hereabouts. But there is no
difficulty. The Persian fleet had suffered heavily at Artemisium.
The obvious way to repair its losses was to call up reserves; and
the pause between the occupation of Attica and the preparations
for the sea-fight at Salamis is explained if the fleet was not ready
to attack till it was so reinforced. Moreover, the Persian fleet, like
the land army, was recruiting contingents from the districts which
it now controlled, such as Paros (viii. 67) and Tenos (viii. 82).
The open beach at Phalerum was none too large for so great a
force, and there is no other beach or wide anchorage between
Phalerum and Marathon. It is true that ships from Marathon, if
they only started at midnight, could not reach Salamis till late on
the following day; but by signals overland they could be started
the day before; and the phrase describes in general terms the
rearward squadrons as they came up the Saronic Gulf. It may be
an echo of mainland witness, for this wing included the Ionian
squadrons, and Herodotus was brought up in Halicarnassus.
Artemisia's crews best knew where they had been posted.

The Persian squadrons, then, put to sea at midnight—which was also moonrise—in the order in which they lay along the Attic coast. The leading squadron, the Egyptian, was directed as above to the furthermost objective, the Megarian back-way; the Phoenicians escorted it till they had to wheel up the east coast of Salamis. It is in contrast to them—the 'western wing' of those who were to enter the eastern straits—that Ionians, Carians, and other rearward ships from 'about Ceos and Cynosura' followed the Attic shore, and swung northward round Munychia Point. With the Phoenicians of the western wing now on converging courses the gulf (*porthmos*) outside the straits seemed indeed 'filled with ships'.

The Main Action (viii. 83–90)

The battle itself has been reconstructed in various ways. Older views, that the Greeks came out and fought south of the channels, are obsolete. Grundy[1] placed the Greek line blocking Georgio Channel, thence advancing about half-way along the bay, then pressed back especially on the left and in danger of encirclement. Sir Reginald Custance,[2] with exceptional naval experience, and the first estimate of the sizes of ships and the sea-room they required, marshals the Greeks in an oblong mass filling about half the bay, with a front of fifteen ships resting on the long Point and a depth of twenty-five thence westward. He allows the Persians a front of nine ships in line in the eastern channel, and of six in the western; and, like Grundy, allows both Persian squadrons to pass right into the bay before they make contact with the Greeks. But such a mass formation of the Greek ships makes minimum use even of their inferior numbers and is inconsistent with the narratives.

Herodotus' story (viii. 63–83) is brief but quite clear so far as it goes, and within its frame there is room for all the known episodes. The Greeks put out from their shore-stations into the gulf. When the enemy attacked, some of them went astern till

[1] *The Great Persian War* (1901), 392–400.
[2] *War at Sea* (1919), p. 18, pl. iii.

they touched the shore. Ameinias' ship left the line, rammed, and could not disengage; so the rest attacked. Aeginetans, however, believed that first contact was made by their own dispatch-vessel, newly arrived from home, and perhaps also not fully instructed. Immediately above the encounter was Xerxes' Seat: the traditional knoll, a little inland, may well be the site, as it commands a view down the Atalanti channel as well as the main entrance to the bay. But there is a rock, almost on the shore, farther west, from which individuals on shipboard could be recognizable, as Herodotus describes.

The narrative of Aeschylus (*Persae* 339–465). To Herodotus' account Aeschylus, who was present, adds graphic details, in the messenger's speech in the *Persae* (339–465), describing all this dramatically from the Persian point of view. The Greeks have 300 ships with a special squadron of 10, the Persians 1,000 with 207 'swift' ships, perhaps the open-water squadron destined to close the backway: on both sides these are round numbers. Persian orders are (l. 364) to block the 'exits' and 'passes' (both plural), and accordingly to cut off retreat (369–71) by the back-way; there is an all-night voyage (382–7) round Salamis. The Greeks remain at their stations (385), but at dawn (388) the Greek war-cry warns the Persians that their plan has been anticipated. The Greeks, that is, were heard before they were seen; the island promontory being both long and low, and the Persians still outside the narrows. Then the advancing Greeks come suddenly in sight (396–8) from behind the island point, with the right wing leading and heading across the channels—for the Spartans eventually confronted the Ionians inshore—and the rest emerge after it in column.[1] After orders and battle-cries, in which we may include the signal-cry of Hdt. viii. 84, ship rams ship, and a Phoenician ship is sunk first (410–11). This is the work of Ameinias in Herodotus; his ship was therefore abreast of Cynosura Point and close to it, and took no part in the movement astern. For a while the 'torrent' of Persian vessels presses on through the channels (412–13); then there is crowding and con-

---

[1] ἐπεξεχώρει, 401.

fusion (413), and the Greek ships 'begin to strike in a circle around' (418), i.e. not themselves surrounded but converging on the enemy's front and flanks. The Persians row hard to escape (422), but are caught like tunnies in a net (434) until nightfall (428). The simile confirms the statement that it was the Greeks who outflanked the narrow front of the Persians entering the narrows, not conversely. Then follows the episode of Psyttaleia, occupied by Persians (447) but stormed by Greek infantry from the ships (457); the 'stones and arrows' (460–1) came from the Persians on the island. At length Xerxes orders a general retreat (465) and (summarily) the land army suffers disaster while crossing the Strymon on the ice (495–507). This last incident—not in Herodotus—is an epilogue, for the battle of Salamis was in September.

The evidence of Diodorus (xi. 17–19). This later account, derived from Ephorus, has different sources, but confirms and supplements the earlier. It is the only authority for the movement of the Egyptian squadron (17. 2). Its Phoenicians are on the right wing (17. 3), as they must have been while anchored, since they had farthest (after the Egyptians) to go, and this explains why Herodotus makes them 'wheel towards Salamis' to their place on the left of the battle-line. The Ionians, following inshore, started on their left along the beaches but crossed their rear, keeping close to the Attic shore. The Samians intended to desert during the battle (17. 4), and Themistocles was delighted to learn this; but they failed to do so. The Athenians and Spartans are placed on the left (18. 1), as indeed the Athenians were, while at anchor; and the Aeginetans and Megarians on the right (18. 2), and this would bring them into action against the Ionians, as will appear. The Spartan admiral must have been on the original right, if he was to lead into action; he was, however, on the left in the battle-line, and Diodorus has wrongly linked him with the Athenians, who faced the Phoenicians in the fighting, and were therefore now on the right.

The Greeks 'sailed out' (18. 2) and occupied the 'strait' between Salamis and a shrine of Heracles which has not been identified; it should be sought opposite the promontory, between

'Xerxes' Seat' and the entrance to Peiraeus. The King sat 'opposite Salamis' to order the attack and watch the fighting (Fig. 20. x).

When the Persian fleet entered the narrows, it had to 'change its formation' (18. 4), and there was some disorder. This may reflect the deployment which brought the Ionians into action on the Persian right. The admiral, leading, was killed (18. 5); there was panic, with contradictory orders: leading ships went astern into the open sea (18. 5), and when the Athenians rammed and disabled many (18. 6), others ceased to row, and set sail to escape. The Cilician and Pamphylian squadrons, next to those of Phoenicia and Cyprus—i.e. now on their right—fought better (19. 1), but were crowded by them under Athenian pressure (19. 2). The Greeks lost 40 ships, the Persians 200 sunk and many captured (19. 3). The Phoenicians, threatened by Xerxes, returned first to their Attic anchorage, then by night to Asia (19. 4). Themistocles sent a second message to Xerxes to warn him that the bridges were in danger (19. 5).

All this information, except as to the position of the Spartans, falls into its place, and much of it betrays Ionian (perhaps Samian) sources. The Corinthians do not appear at all among the more proficient Greek squadrons (18. 2), so they had been acting independently, as in Herodotus viii. 94; so also the Aeginetans.

The Main Action (viii. 83–90) reconstructed

Of these three independent narratives every phrase is significant. The Greeks lay along the south and west shore of the bay, from the point to Salamis town. As their prows faced north the Spartan admiral must have been on the right, nearest the channels, and as the Spartans were eventually confronted with the Ionian contingent, next to the mainland, they must have led the whole fleet into action, in column to right, and then turned individually to starboard. With the line thus facing south, the Spartans were on the left, and the Athenians and Corinthians on the eventual right, still far up the deep bay and nearest to their bases.

From this position (Fig. 20. I) Herodotus makes the Greeks move astern (II), until some of the ships went ashore. It is this detail that

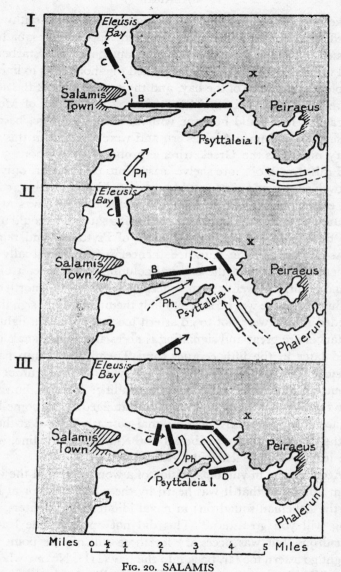

FIG. 20. SALAMIS

Movements within the straits. A. Spartans. B. Athenians. C. Corinthians.
D. Aeginetans. Ph. Phoenicians. X. Xerxes.

Based on British Admiralty Chart No. 1513 with the permission of the Controller of H.M. Stationery Office and of the Hydrographer of the Navy makes the whole manœuvre intelligible. Lest the southward-faced, leading wing should be isolated, succeeding squadrons crossed the channels, turned likewise consecutively to starboard, and went astern (III), till they touched the shore, so as to line the whole eastern shore of the bay, and the eastern part of the north shore, in front of 'Xerxes' Seat' and the steep slope of Mount Aegaleôs. This could be done without risk of damage, because these ships had no rudder astern and were beached in this way every night. As the Greek trireme probably drew about 3 feet and this stretch of shore shelves easily into clear water, only ten or twelve ships at a time would be exposed broadside in crossing the eastern strait, and these only when the enemy was at the greatest distance: the ships of the following squadrons could make the turn in succession under the lee of Psyttaleia and remain bows-on towards the entrance thenceforward. Eventually the Athenians, in rear of the original column, came abreast of the island point, and went astern, wheeling across the bay north of it.

But here there was no shore to halt them, and some signal was needed if they were not to go astern too far. In all sea fighting, distances are great and signalling is necessary. Flag signals were used later in the fifth century, and Themistocles' ship had a squadron-leader's pennant at Salamis (viii. 92). But trumpets or shouts are safer, especially for a fleet in line. There is, however, also the risk that the flagship may be damaged. With home-land adjacent, the alternative was a signal-post ashore, and at the tip of the promontory it was abreast of the middle of the line, when the leading ship reached the Attic shore.

Accordingly, in viii. 84 a 'vision of a woman' passed the word from ashore, so that it was heard by the whole fleet, or at least by the Athenian squadron: in naval idiom 'You blighters, how long will you go astern?' This did not apply to the leading squadrons, but was necessary for those still off the point who might go astern too far, back into the bay (III). No one who has heard Greek women conversing across a valley or a bay underestimates the range of their high staccato voices. Moreover, a woman's scream is quite unlike any other battle-cry. That the 'apparition' was not conspicuous was a detail of camouflage in grey limestone country.

Though the Greek ships were far fewer than the enemy—and indeed for that reason—it was the first concern of the commanders to make full use of every one of them within the limits of the bay. It may be accepted that a trireme of the early fifth century was about 100–110 feet long, about 15 feet wide amidships, and about 45 feet overall with oars outboard. For safe navigation in company, it needed at least 60 feet of clearance abeam and 100 feet between bow and stern; in line ahead, about 25 triremes to a mile; in line abeam, about 90 to a mile. At anchor, or beached, however, it would only need about 20 feet (say 7 yards). With these approximate dimensions, it can be seen what manœuvres were possible in the bay of Salamis. With its double steering oars, lateral propulsion, and slow progress— about 4 knots—a trireme had a very small turning circle and could be quickly stopped.

There were thus just enough triremes at Salamis (380) to line the beaches and to execute the proposed manœuvre. The distance from the Point to Salamis town is about 4 miles; from Salamis town to Georgio Channel about 1½ miles. The eastern shore below 'Xerxes' Seat' would accommodate about 130 ships; the north shore facing the entrances is again 1½ miles, and the long bay north of the Point is about 1½ miles wide. These three sides of the proposed trap required therefore 390 ships at most. There was therefore just sea room for the forty Corinthian ships when they rejoined from Eleusis Bay. It looks as if the manœuvre was planned with accurate knowledge of Salamis Bay.

The Persian 'torrent' of ships, in close order and deep columns, entered both straits simultaneously, intending to wheel to port and sweep up the bay, outflanking the Greek left, as at Artemisium (viii. 16). But in fact each Persian ship, as soon as it entered the bay, was exposed broadside to the bows of Greek ships at short range, and exposed still when it tried to turn up the bay, without room either to go to port or to go astern. To set sail, as Diodorus describes (xi. 19. 6), helped little, as the morning breeze is off the sea; and there had been a north wind on land the day before (p. 266). In Aeschylus' words (418) the Greeks 'began to strike in a circle around' and threw the enemy into disorder.

Aristides' commando-raid on Psyttaleia is narrated by Herodotus as an afterthought (viii. 95). It was only in the rear-most Athenian ships or in landing-craft that he could embark land-troops for a special destination, without interrupting the movement of others: he could only cross the channel after the Phoenician squadron had passed through into the bay; moreover, it was only when the action was going in favour of the Greeks that such troops were needed on the island. Probably he and his commando were posted on the tip of Cynosura. The 'phantom' signaller was therefore no irresponsible peasant-woman, but under the direct control of the most responsible of Athenian generals, the leader of the commando raid on Psyttaleia (viii. 95). There is no reason, therefore, to doubt that this operation was not 'in the confusion' (ἐν τῷ θορύβῳ) but 'according to plan'; and that the commando-craft, following the Athenian battle-squadron as far as the tip of Cynosura, passed in rear of the Phoenician column after this had entered the gulf, and before it began to retreat.

Sequel to Salamis (viii. 107–44)

This group of episodes presents no serious difficulties. The operations of the Greek fleet in the Aegean were necessary precautions against a fresh naval attack, and are instructive commentary on the 'Parian Expedition' after Marathon. Deep shadows are added to the portraits of Themistocles and Xerxes; high-lights to those of Artabazus and Alexander, anticipating their appearance at Plataea. Mardonius remains the central figure, but Artemisia is succeeded by Artabazus as his strategic rival: his campaign in Chalcidice, like the intervention of Alexander, illustrates the Persian long-term policy in Greek affairs.

PLATAEA (ix. 1–89)

The Political Situation, 479 B.C. (ix. 1–15)

Mardonius wintered in Thessaly, the most fertile region in his control. But he had been left to pacify Greece, and needed a political success to report to Xerxes. He moved south as soon as he could, but probably not till after harvest, for the second invasion of Attica was ten months after the first. The Thessalians encouraged him, and probably wished to be rid of him. The Thebans, working for dominance in northern Greece, advised him to prepare a fortified base-camp in Boeotia, and support oligarchies locally (ix. 1–3).

As before, the Athenians refused an offer of surrender, and lynched Lycidas who commended it. They withdrew again to Salamis, and were supported by Plataea and Megara in calling for Spartan help. But the Spartans were celebrating their *Hyacinthia*, moreover, in spite of pause due to an October eclipse, battlements were now being placed on the Isthmus Wall. As in the campaign of Thermopylae, however, a small force was sent forward under Pausanias, who on the death of Cleombrotus had become guardian and regent for Leonidas' son Pleistarchus. This advance was betrayed by the Argives, who were now in open though passive league with the Persians; and Mardonius withdrew into Boeotia, devastating Attica again, but making cavalry contact with the Spartan advance-guard in the Megarid. Retreating by Deceleia and Tanagra, to avoid flank attack from the west, he occupied the partly prepared position between Thebes and Plataea, flanked by wide unfortified outposts from the foot-hills of Cithaeron round Scolus and Erythrae to the upper Asopus valley. How this retreat depressed the Persians, Herodotus illustrates by the despair of a staff-officer at Thebes (ix. 15–16).

Herodotus gives no such outline of the topography as he gave of Thermopylae, and it was only with Grundy's accurate survey in 1893 that the battle of Plataea became intelligible. The recent Greek staff-map adds little to his brilliant reconnaissance; but not all his identifications are certain.

Based on the Greek Staff Map.

FIG. 21. BATTLEFIELD OF PLATAEA. I

⬛ Greek divisions on the march. ⌐I⌐II⌐ in position. Persian cavalry ▨ .

Plataea: the Battlefield

The high range of Cithaeron and Parnes, which divides Attica from Boeotia, has a straight and very steep front northward, over-looking the Asopus valley, which flows east nearly parallel with it. The city of Thebes lies in rolling country about ten miles north; nearly south of Thebes, the small independent city of Plataea, with a conspicuous temple of Hera, stands on a defensible spur of Cithaeron, among the cultivable 'shelves' or terraces which its name describes. Hysiae and Erythrae were even smaller communities, similarly perched, a few miles east; their sites are obliterated, and their boundaries uncertain, but, like Plataea, each had lands stretching northwards as far as the Asopus. About three miles east of Plataea, and nearly south of Hysiae, the head-waters of the Eleusinian Cephissus have cut back to an easy pass over the watershed, called *Dryoscephalae* from its 'oak-heads'. This was the direct road from Athens and Eleusis to Plataea (Thuc. 3. 24) and was the wagon-road, as wheel-tracks show. A little to the west a similar pass was used for traffic from Thebes and Plataea to Megara and the Isthmus. Eastward a more direct track from Eleusis to Thebes leaves the main road south of the *col*, and descends steeply on Grundy's site for Erythrae.

The Pass of the Oak Heads, Dryoscephalae (ix. 39), was identified by Grundy[1] with this more easterly road. That it is the only pass mentioned by Herodotus by name proves nothing as to its relative importance, but he distinguishes it as leading to Plataea from the pass already mentioned (ix. 19). In the cavalry raid (ix. 39) the word translated by Grundy as 'pack animals' denotes wheeled-transport,[2] and it is doubtful whether the steep descent to Erythrae was practicable for wagons, like the main road to Hysiae and to Plataea, where wheel-tracks remain. Moreover, once the Greeks were posted on the 'ridge', there was no need for their supplies to go round by Erythrae at all.

As to the name, the narrative of Thucydides iii. 24 is conclusive. Fugitives from Plataea, besieged by Thebans and Spartans, avoided the direct road to Athens, and (to elude pursuit) moved north six or seven stades till they had on their right the shrine of Androcrates (St. John: *J* on the map), then turned east through the

---

[1] *Great Persian War*, 447–75.
[2] *Zeugos: hypozygia* opposed to horses v. 16, 24 (cf. vii. 187), or to camels vii. 83 (cf. i. 31, 59, 199; iv. 46).

high ground—the 'ridge' of Herodotus—to Hysiae and Erythrae. Their pursuers followed 'the road to Citheron and *Dryoscephalae* leading to Athens'. Clearly there were two routes to Athens, either the direct road from Plataea 'by *Dryoscephalae*, or a circuitous track along the ridge to another pass above Erythrae. Hysiae, if this road passed through it, was much lower on the foot-hills of Citheron than the 'Oak Heads' pass and, like Erythrae and Plataea, it had lands down to the Asopus: compare the parishes on the Chiltern frontage.

The Ridge. The drainage of this north frontage of Cithaeron is peculiar. Long ago it was carried in parallel gullies into the Asopus, and still is so, east of the main pass, by a stream which is probably the *Moloeis* (ix. 57). West of this, and for some two miles east of Plataea, the river Oeroe, which flows into the Corinthian Gulf, has cut back parallel with the Asopus and 'captured' all the torrents from Cithaeron, in a single, wide, well-watered basin, separated from the Moloeis only by the narrow plateau, *Argopion*, above which Hysiae lay, and from the Asopus valley by a continuation of this ridge in a series of low hills (*ochthoi*) steeper towards the basin, and dissected by dry valleys which are the former beds of the Cithaeron drainage. Through the most westerly and widest of these goes the direct road from Plataea to Thebes. Landmarks on this ridge were a sanctuary of Demeter, where it curves westward, probably at the little church of St. Demetrianos, and the shrine of the hero Androcrates farther west, now a similar chapel of St. John. Along the south slope of the ridge were springs and a large fountain, Gargaphia. A little north-west of Plataea, two of the streams from Cithaeron rise close together, flow apart, and then converge, enclosing a spur which was known as the 'Island', capped by a defensible knoll.

Preliminaries

Covered by cavalry reconnaissance towards Megara (ix. 16), Mardonius withdrew his army from Attica by way of Tanagra, and built a stockaded base-camp between Thebes and the

Asopus, of which nothing remains. Here he waited for Artabazus with 40,000 men from the north.

Advancing from the Isthmus, where the wall was now finished from sea to sea, the Greek forces were joined at Eleusis by the Athenians from Salamis. The list (ix. 28) suggests a battle-order in seven regional brigades: I. Spartans and their helots, with Tegea; II. Corinth; III. Sicyon with Orchomenus; IV. Phlius, Troezen, and other Argolid cities; V. Aegina, with other contin-

The Greek Order of Battle at Plataea: Greek front to left, Persian to right

		Hoplites	*Total*	*Light-armed*
Persians	I. Spartans	5,000 ⎫	6,500	35,000
	Tegea	1,500 ⎰		
	Other Lacedae-monians		5,000	
Medes	II. Corinth	5,000 ⎫	5,300	
	Potidaea	300 ⎰		
	III. Orchomenus	600 ⎫	3,600	
	Sicyon	3,000 ⎰		
Bactrians	IV. Epidaurus	800		
	Troezen	1,000		
	Lepreum	200		
	Mycenae ⎫		3,700	
	Tiryns ⎰	400		
	Phlius	1,000		
Indians	Hermione	300		34,500
	V. Eretria–Styra	600		
	Chalcis	400		
	Ambracia	500		
	Leucas ⎫	800	3,000	
Sacae	Anactorium ⎰			
	Cephallenia	200		
	Aegina	500		
North Greeks	VI. Megara	3,000 ⎫	3,600	
50,000	VII. Plataea	600 ⎰		
	Athens	8,000	8,000	
300,000		38,700		69,500
			108,200	
	Thespians (unarmed)		1,800	
			110,000	

gents from states outside Peloponnese; VI. Megara with Plataea; VII. Athens. The Spartan commander-in-chief was on the right; the Athenians made good, against the Tegeans who had close ties with Sparta, their claim to the left wing. For it was Attica that the army was defending: compare the position of the Phocians at Thermopylae (p. 250) and of the Milesians at Lade (p. 197).

The fully armed infantry numbered 38,700 men (ix. 30); the auxiliaries 35,000 from Sparta and 34,500 from elsewhere. In his grand total Herodotus includes 1,800 Thespians, disarmed survivors from Thermopylae.

First Contact

Since the Greek army entered Boeotian territory above Erythrae, it must have used the direct easterly pass; and as it deployed westward, the Athenians (VII) must have been leading, followed by the Megarians (VI). The Spartans were therefore in rear nearest to the Persian line of retreat out of Attica.

As soon as the Greeks began to deploy, Persian cavalry attacked in successive charges, directed at the Megarian contingent, probably as it was re-forming on to the hill-side: at all events, the only available reinforcement came from the Athenians, already deployed ahead of them. In spite of a general call, no one else 'volunteered'; the Spartans themselves were far in rear, being still in route order within the pass. The Greeks were saved by the death of the Persian commander, Masistius, and consequent confusion. But when the whole Greek force was deployed it was seen that its position was ill-watered and untenable—perhaps it had not been intended to be held—and the several divisions descended in succession to their eventual positions along the ridge commanding the Asopus, with steep descent in their rear, and ample water at Gargaphia. The Athenians on the left overlooked the road from Thebes to Plataea; the Spartans commanded both the roads from Thebes to Athens. Neither, however, could prevent Persian cavalry from raiding round both flanks into the foot-hills and passes.

The Persian battle-front, resting on the stockaded camp, was

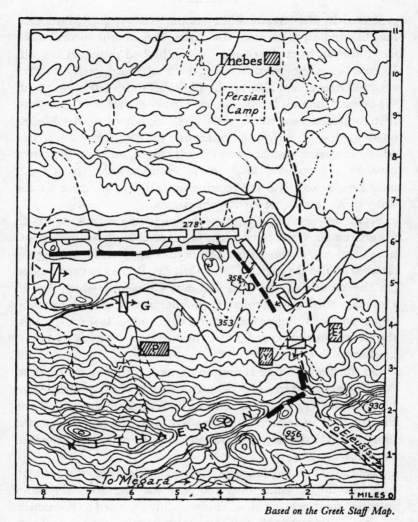

Based on the Greek Staff Map.

Fig. 22. BATTLEFIELD OF PLATAEA. II

▨ P. Plataea. Y. Hysiae. E. Erythrae. D. Demeter. G. Gargaphia.
J. Androcrates.

protected by the stream of the Asopus (ix. 31, 40). Mardonius thus blocked all roads from the passes, and commanded also the foot-hill road from the east, by which he had retreated himself. He was being reinforced from the dominated or friendly states of central Greece, and also by the Phocians to his left (ix. 17). Of the Persian forces it is only necessary to note that the largest and best contingent was from Persia itself, supported by the Medes, on the left wing facing the Spartans: on the right wing about 50,000 medizing Greeks faced the Athenians, and had their own cavalry. The reputed total array, about 300,000 (ix. 31-32), must be checked with the conclusions of Sir F. Maurice for the army of Xerxes at the Hellespont (p. 220).

From the first day's cavalry-charge to the eighth day both armies remained in position; the Greeks receiving reinforcements up to the day of the battle, Mardonius apparently waiting for Artabazus. On the night of the eighth day Persian cavalry raided 'to the mouth of the pass through Cithaeron which led to Plataea, called Dryoscephalae' (p. 285) and destroyed a convoy of 500 wagons bringing food from Peloponnese. It was clear that the Greek force could not protect its own lines of supply and must be short of food (ix. 39).

On the eleventh day Herodotus records a conference between Artabazus and Mardonius, who was also short of supplies. Artabazus wished to retire to Thebes, collect food there, and use Persian gold to seduce Greek leaders. The Thebans supported him; but Mardonius, who was in supreme command, decided to attack (ix. 41-43).

Alexander's Warning (44-45). That night Alexander of Macedon rode into the Athenian lines and gave warning that Mardonius intended to attack at dawn. This was duly reported to Pausanias.

The Counter-march (46-47). Herodotus says that Pausanias thereupon ordered the Athenians to change places with the Spartans, on the ground that they had fought Persians before and knew their tactics; he adds that Mardonius detected this counter-march, and imitated it; and that Pausanias therefore countermanded it.

It is difficult to explain this manœuvre; and even to believe that it occurred. If Pausanias had intended a general retreat, he might have wished to give the Athenians a clear road to Attica, and the Spartans the same into Megaris; but there is no other evidence for such an intention. The story looks like Athenian enhancement, or misinterpretation, of an order to reinforce the Spartans, on the ground that Athenians understood Persian tactics. So, too, later Pausanias called for Athenian archers to meet the Persian barrage (60), and again for Athenian engineers to storm the camp (70). As the order was cancelled (55), and later replaced by an unqualified call for help (60), it did not affect the course of the battle. But the story illustrates the dependence of Herodotus on his sources, and his difficulty in forming a clear account of the whole affair.

The Strategy of Pausanias. The Battle of Plataea was regarded in antiquity not only as a national victory but as a great personal achievement of Pausanias. What his manœuvre was, however, has not been clear to everyone. Herodotus, with partial and conflicting information, gives the impression of a 'soldiers' battle', in which the Greeks were forced to retreat in some disorder, but were rescued by a Spartan counter-attack when the Persians had the ridge behind them, blocking their retreat. But that the Greek retreat was an essential feature is clear from Plato (*Laches* 191 c) and from Diodorus (Ephorus) (xi. 30. 4–6). It was in accordance with the Spartan manœuvre at Thermopylae (vii. 211). It is also clear from Diodorus that the Greeks took advantage, as at Marathon, at Thermopylae, and at Salamis, of ground skilfully chosen to deprive the Persians of the advantage of numbers. This is sufficient clue to the significance of the recorded details.

The 'Asopus Ridge' with the spur connecting its eastern end with Mount Cithaeron is the only position on the whole frontier which could be held by forces such as Pausanias had (*c.* 110,000 men) against greater numbers, though at the risk of encirclement by cavalry. It was traversed by the main routes from the north, in narrow valleys through the ridge. It provided a second line of rally and defence, along the foot-hills of Cithaeron. It thus formed a trap for enemy columns after traversing the ridge.

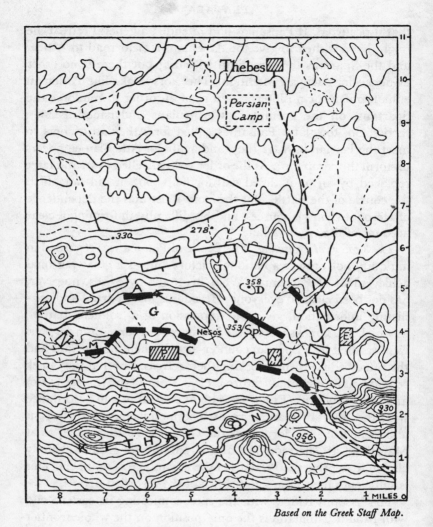

Based on the *Greek Staff Map.*

Fig. 23. BATTLEFIELD OF PLATAEA. III

J. Shrine of Androcrates. D. Demeter. M. Megarians. A. Athenians.
Sp. Spartans. C. Heraeum. G. Gargaphia.

What Pausanias did was (a) to defend this prominent bastion until most of his laggard allies had joined him and his water-supply failed; (b) to retire, when attacked, from this first position on the ridge to the second position, on the *Nesos* and the spur above Hysiae which led to the Dryoscephalae Pass, thus tempting the enemy to enter the valley roads through the ridge, dividing their forces and crowding their columns of advance; (c) to counter-attack from higher ground, and crowd them back in disorder into those valleys. The point at which the Persians were deploying for attack was marked by the erection of field-screens for their archers, and by flank attacks of their cavalry, the classical preliminaries to a Persian battle (p. 210); and these were the signal for Pausanias to counter-attack. At only three points was his plan deranged in detail.

Gargaphia and the Nesos. The Persian cavalry had already out-flanked the Greek right and cut off a convoy in the Dryoscephalae pass. Even more serious was a similar raid round the left flank, which destroyed the principal Greek water-supply at Gargaphia, and, according to Herodotus, made the whole ridge-position untenable (49). There was, however, water enough in the torrent beds which converged from Cithaeron, two of which embraced the knoll nicknamed the 'Island' (51). To this strong point of their second position the Greeks were therefore ordered to retire during the following night. It was unfortunate, but not dangerous, that many of them, in the darkness, over-passed the *Nesos*, and established themselves nearer to the deserted city of Plataea and its temple of Hera (52). This left the Athenians on the left wing unsupported, but by retiring off the ridge they evaded the notice of the enemy (59) and tried to close with the Spartans as ordered (60). Before long they were overtaken by the medizing Greeks from the Persian left.

Amompharetus. At this point Herodotus records an extra-ordinary failure of discipline (53). Amompharetus, the com-mander of the Spartan battalion from Pitane, refused to shift his ground, and Pausanias had to choose between supporting him and carrying out the movement agreed with the other commanders. The Athenians, finding that the Spartans were not moving 'according to plan', delayed their own retreat and sent for fresh orders. Their messenger was thus witness of the brawl, and returned with orders (as above) to join the Spartans and conform to their movements: all this under cover of night. The Athenians were already traversing the low ground, when Pausanias ordered his own division to leave Amompharetus, and follow the line of the ridge to the foot-hills of Cithaeron, covering thereby the right flank of the retreating centre, and retaining such hold on the passes as was still possible. Thus at dawn the Athenians and the Spartans were moving in opposite directions, but at different levels.

When Amompharetus realized that he was really deserted, he followed the rest; and found them halted near the shrine of Eleusinian Demeter, the position of which, on that knoll of the ridge which commands both the main roads, was identified by Grundy with the chapel of St. Demetrianos. The withdrawal now continued in good order, though harassed as before by Persian archers, preliminary to massed attack.

The Crisis (59–70). At dawn, after formal challenge which was ignored, Mardonius launched his Persian division against the only enemy in sight, namely the Spartans and Tegeans (59); the rest of his army, less orderly, poured through the more westerly saddles in the ridge into the low ground towards the *Nesos*. Here the medizing Greeks on the left had overtaken and halted the Athenians, so that the Spartans were left unsupported. Unfavourable omens still prevented Pausanias from counter-attacking, and gave the Persians time to erect their screens and throw forward their cavalry. Pausanias gave the Athenians freedom of action if attacked separately—as seemed imminent—but begged for the support of their archers.

The situation was saved by the Tegeans, who charged while Pausanias was at prayer (62). Hera, too, heard; new omens were favourable; the Spartans rushed the field-screens, and fell on the Persian infantry hand-to-hand. The hardest fighting was on either hand of the shrine of Demeter, but within the sacred enclosure there were no dead; it was too obvious a death-trap, but Herodotus mentions the opinion that here was divine reprisal for sacrilege at Eleusis. Hereabouts Mardonius was killed, and the rout became general, along the congested roads, as far as the stockaded camp (65).

The Greek Advance. This Spartan success was the signal for a general advance. The Corinthians rallied to the Spartans (69). The centre, incautiously traversing the low ground, was driven back into the foot-hills by Boeotian cavalry from their left. The Athenians, too, were still beset by their old enemies the Thebans, but moved forward independently and reached the stockade (70).

Artabazus, presumably in command on the Persian right, as Mardonius was on the left, was able—and, as Herodotus says, prepared—to extricate his own corps westwards.

As at Mycale (ix. 102) and Ithome (Thuc. i. 102) the stockade troubled the Athenian 'handy-men' less than the Spartans, but the first to rush the breach were shock-troops from Tegea. Within the crowded camp, only 3,000 prisoners were taken. The Spartans had lost 91 men, the Tegeans 15, the Athenians 52, all from one tribe (Plut. *Arist.* 19), but 600 fell when cavalry attacked the Greek centre (69).

Mardonius had been rightly informed that the Greeks were gaining strength; for the levies from Mantineia and from Elis arrived on the day of battle (77).

MYCALE
(ix. 90–106)

Shortly before the victory at Plataea, Leotychides, commanding the fleet at Delos, received an invitation from the Ionian commandant of Samos, and the news that the Persian fleet, though unseaworthy, had moved southward (90). He crossed therefore to Samos, and made his base on the long, reedy shore (*Calami*) between the port and the temple of Hera (Fig. 25). The Persian fleet withdrew to Mycale, flanking the strait and protected by a stockade and an Ionian garrison; the latter was soon

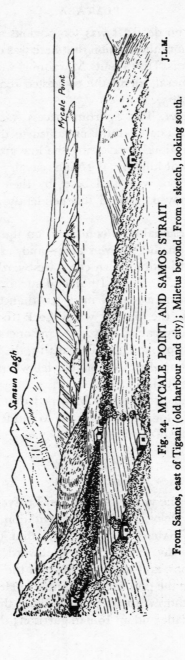

Fig. 24. MYCALE POINT AND SAMOS STRAIT

From Samos, east of Tigani (old harbour and city); Miletus beyond. From a sketch, looking south.

J.L.M.

after disarmed (99) and reinforced by Persians with archers and
field-screens (100), clearly the main available force, in battle
order.

The promontory is rocky, with several small coves, and rugged
ridges rising eastward into the interior. The only lowland with
beach is on the south side. There, with the light behind them
(101), the Greeks attacked from their ships, the Spartans on the

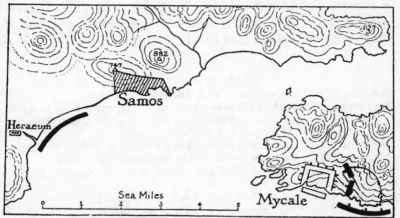

Fig. 25. MYCALE, SAMOS STRAIT, AND HERAEUM
Looking north: ■■■ Greeks. ▭ Persians.
*Based on British Admiralty Chart No. 1530 with the permission of the Controller of H.M.
Stationery Office and of the Hydrographer of the Navy.*

right towards the high ground, the Athenians on the left along
the beach, where the field-screens protected the camp. The
Ionians, though disarmed, made trouble within the Persian lines
(103–4). It was an easy but decisive victory. As both sides knew,
the prize was 'the islands and the Hellespont' (101).

A Spartan proposal to exchange the loyal Ionian population
for the medizing Greeks of north Greece, and so make the Aegean
an international frontier, was repudiated by the Athenians;
Samos, Chios, Lesbos, and other islands were enrolled in the
'alliance'; and the whole fleet moved north to the Hellespont,
unaware that the Bridges had been destroyed (106–14).

In this section there is little composition, or opportunity for embellishment: the 'lucky' name of Hegesistratus, the herald's staff washed ashore with the news of Plataea, the coincidence of date, and of another shrine of Demeter, and the usual honours list. What is memorable is the lead assumed by the Athenians, and retained in the northern campaign. With the 'second secession' of Ionia from Persia (105) a new period opens, as it had opened with the Ionian Revolt (v. 27–28). Compare the formal punctuation of the 'first conquest' by Cyrus (i. 92); and by Harpagus (i. 169); of the second under Artaphernes (vi. 32); and of the two captures of Babylon (i. 191; iii. 159).

BIBLIOGRAPHY

GRUNDY, G. B. *The Great Persian War*. London, 1901.

KROMAYER, J. (Marathon); HARMENING, LUD. F. (Thermopylae); KEIL, W. (Salamis), *Antike Schlachtfelder*, iv. Berlin, 1924; E. UFER (Plataea); J KROMAYER (Mykale), v. 1931, pp. 229–346.

GIANNELLI, G. *La spedizione di Serse da Terme a Salamina*. Milan, 1924.

MUNRO, J. A. R. *Cambridge Ancient History*, iv. Cambridge, 1926.

MAURICE, SIR FREDERICK. 'The size of the Army of Xerxes', *J.H.S.* l (1930), 210.

—— 'The Campaign of Marathon', *J.H.S.* lii (1932), 13.

MILTNER, F. 'Der taktische Aufbau der Schlacht bei Salamis', *Öst. Jahrb.* xxvi (1930), 115.

—— 'Pro Leonida', *Klio*, xxviii (1935), 225.

KÖSTER, A. 'Studien z. Gesch. d. antiken Seewesens', *Klio, Beihefte*, xxxii (1934), 54 and 81.

KIRSTEN, E. 'Athener und Spartaner in der Schlacht bei Plataiai', *Rh.M.* lxxxvi (1937), 50.

THE EPILOGUE
(ix. 107–22)

The last chapters of Book IX have been criticized as inadequate conclusion to the *Histories*, and even as being unfinished or unrevised. But in the light of other examples of Herodotus' narrative technique, their structure is significant, and their purpose clear, as a studied *Epilogue* to the whole.

As in Book III and in Books V and VI, there is a main story, and there are episodes which it enframes, illustrating an alternative theme, from different points of view. The whole composition, narrative-frame and episodes together, prepares for a final situation, the counterpart to the first introduction of Cyrus and his Persians (i. 95).

The main story follows the Greek counter-attack, from Mycale to Sestos (106, 114, 117–18, 121) and the return home at the end of the year. As it is precisely at this point that Thucydides begins his retrospect of 'events after the War' (Thuc. i. 89–118), there is no need to doubt either that the capture of Sestos was a turning-point or that Herodotus thought it so. His final detail, that the cables of Xerxes' bridges were dedicated in Greek temples, recalls the completion of the bridges (vii. 36) with which Xerxes' advance from Asia opens.

If Herodotus ever intended to carry his 'histories' farther, it was into another period, with other problems, of which he was fully conscious (vi. 92) 'when the leading states strove with each other for leadership'. It is this struggle to which Thucydides devoted himself (i. 23), 'so great a war coming upon the Greeks'.

Interpolated among the four phases of this final episode of historical narrative is a triptych of episodes illustrating Persian demoralization. The second of these, Xerxes' intrigues with the wife and daughter of his brother Masistes, and the revenge of his own wife Amestris, is on a large scale, and central. It shows the Empire rotten at its heart, in King and Court.

The first episode shows the same decay in the 'high command' of the army; the third, in the provincial government. Masistes was a Persian general of the first rank (vii. 82, 121). When he came to blows with his colleague Artayntes, they were separated by a Halicarnassian; so Herodotus may have had the story at first hand. Masistes was also the brother of Xerxes, and the victim of his outrage in the central scene.

The third incident, a pendant to the first, displays the cowardice of Oeobazus and the brutality and sacrilege of Artayctes, both civil governors in the Chersonese, and involved in the Greek operations of the main story: for it was Oeobazus who was in charge of the cables (113). Artayctes is also the link with the final scene: for it was his ancestor who propounded to Cyrus a project of world-conquest, and received from him that warning against its temptations which had preserved Persian morale so long.

So the *History* ends on the same note on which the Persian section of it began (i. 125–6), the great memory of Cyrus serving the same literary and didactic purpose as the Ghost of Darius in the *Persae*.

This Epilogue, then, is no unfinished or slipshod writing, but an unusually intricate composition, deliberate intercalation of main story and illustrative episodes, which is fundamental in the method of Herodotus; a typical example of pedimental composition, and a back-reference which spans almost the whole extent of his book, with its answer to the question:

Why they fought with one another.

TEXT-REFERENCES TO HERODOTUS

INDEX